国家语委语言文字科研项目优秀成果后期资助计划（HQ135-20）、国家自然科学基金项目"面向汉译英口语测试中自动评测方法的研究"（61877013）资助

中国学习者花园幽径句的量化研究

杜家利　于屏方　李明琳　著

中国社会科学出版社

图书在版编目（CIP）数据

中国学习者花园幽径句的量化研究 / 杜家利，于屏方，李明琳著.
—北京：中国社会科学出版社，2018.12
ISBN 978-7-5203-3856-1

Ⅰ.①中… Ⅱ.①杜…②于…③李… Ⅲ.①英语—翻译—教学研究—高等学校 Ⅳ.①H315.9

中国版本图书馆 CIP 数据核字（2018）第 292226 号

出 版 人	赵剑英
责任编辑	刘志兵
特约编辑	张翠萍等
责任校对	李　斌
责任印制	李寡寡

出　　版	中国社会科学出版社
社　　址	北京鼓楼西大街甲 158 号
邮　　编	100720
网　　址	http://www.csspw.cn
发 行 部	010-84083685
门 市 部	010-84029450
经　　销	新华书店及其他书店

印　　刷	北京明恒达印务有限公司
装　　订	廊坊市广阳区广增装订厂
版　　次	2018 年 12 月第 1 版
印　　次	2018 年 12 月第 1 次印刷

开　　本	710×1000　1/16
印　　张	20.5
字　　数	295 千字
定　　价	89.00 元

凡购买中国社会科学出版社图书，如有质量问题请与本社营销中心联系调换
电话：010-84083683
版权所有　侵权必究

序

魏向清

  2018年3月28日，杜家利博士发来电邮，嘱我为其团队的新作《中国学习者花园幽径句的量化研究》写个序言。对此，我一开始比较犹豫，主要是因为这本学术著作标题中的三个关键词，除了"中国学习者"外，"花园幽径句"和"量化研究"于我而言都是较为陌生的研究对象或学术领域。按理我应婉言谢辞，以免贻笑大方。然而，恰恰又是这两个相对小众的研究关键词勾起了我的阅读兴趣，因为它们与我较为熟悉的"中国学习者"研究关联。从题目来看，这应该是一个与中国英语学习者有关的计算语言学应用研究课题，它所涉及的具体研究对象是花园幽径句的认知问题，采用了计算语言学的新视角和新方法。这让我回想起杜家利博士在南京大学外国语学院外国语言学与应用语言学博士后流动站驻研期间所做的一项非常有意义的教学工作。当时，杜家利博士给南大外院的硕博士生集中讲授了"计算语言学"课程，他的讲解深入浅出而且生动活泼，很快就打消了大家的"畏难"情绪，大家学习热情很高，收获很大。作为那次扫盲课程的受益者之一，虽然我对计算语言学的了解至今仍止步于入门水平，但杜家利博士的讲解加深了我对不同语言研究路径的认识，也引发了我诸多后续的思考，视野得以开阔。这次杜家利博士的团队将计算语言学的理论研究与二语学习的实践问题结合起来，应该是我作为应用语言学研究者进一步拓展学习的好机会。加之杜家利博士盛情邀请，我想，作为一个外行读者，我的阅读反馈或许会给他的这项开拓性研究提供些后续深化的另类参考。于是便有了以下这些感悟式"絮言"。

　　作为语言处理过程中的一种局部歧义的复杂结构，"花园幽径句"（garden path sentences）的研究自20世纪70年代起，至今已有近半个世纪的历史。从"花园幽径句"研究的源流来看，西方学者最早开始探索，而且一直在持续开展相关研究，形成了较为丰富的理论成果。就早期研究而言，研究者关注的焦点大多在于"花园幽径效应"产生背后的理论机制，他们从各自熟悉的理论视域去解释和讨论，理论研究的跨学科性很突显。进入21世纪以来，有关"花园幽径句"的实证研究成为新的研究趋势与热点。相比之下，根据中国知网（CNKI）的数据统计与分析结果，我国的同类研究起步较晚且研究较少。具体来看，以"花园幽径句"为主题的研究文献，自2003年起至今仅26条记录，而且以计算语言学领域的理论研究为主。如果添加"（中国）学习者"这一新的研究主题检索条件，则仅有4篇文献符合条件，而其中最新的研究也是杜家利博士团队的成果。不过，值得注意的是，这4篇结合中国学习者英语学习的"花园幽径句"研究都是实证类型论文，说明中国学者的研究在这方面已经有国际化的前沿意识。而从研究的系统性和深度来看，作者团队的这部专著无疑具有代表性。这种基于中国学习者语言学习特殊性展开的应用研究可谓对长期以来西方学者理论导向为中心的研究现状的积极反映，有很好的互补价值，值得肯定。

　　通读《中国学习者花园幽径句的量化研究》一书的书稿，我有三个方面的主要感受，现与大家分享。

　　首先，该研究的问题取向和实证路径结合紧密。众所周知，实证研究的难点首先在于研究问题的提出，其次则是面向理论或应用问题的实证研究设计。对此，作者们在该书的引言部分开门见山，鲜明地提出了他们的研究问题。更为重要的是，他们提问的方式并非纯粹自上而下的理论追问，而是结合了自下而上的问题思考。这样一种独特的提问方式，我想是与杜家利博士作为一个英语学习者、教师和研究者的三重角色以及长期较为丰富的经验积累分不开的。事实上，在国内为数不多的"花园幽径句"研究者中，杜家利博士是持续研究且成果颇丰的一位。正如他在该书引言中提出的几个问题，无一例外都是从学习者的视角（"我们"）来思考"花园幽径句"解读的实际过程中的困难或障碍，并积极尝试借助语言统计和语言计算的方法来开展有针对性的实证探究。其研究目标也非常明确，即"从计算语言学视角为中国英语学习者解读复杂结构句提供理论支撑，并为英语教学提供具有统计学意义的数据"。显然，这项研究是非常接地气的，有应用研究的现实意义与实用价值。从该书全篇的实证分析与研究思路设计来看，作者们所展开的三大块主体研究内容，即"被试成绩的偏度与相关系数研究（第四章）、花园幽径句阅读时间与效果的非独立t值研究（第五章）以及时间与能力因素与花园幽径句阅读效果的方差分析（第六章）"，较好地对接了其在引言中所提出的有关中国学习者解读花园幽径句的现实问题。

其次，该研究的规范意识与创新意识融合紧密。该书的实证研究设计，从具体研究问题的提出，到三个既相互关联又彼此完整独立的研究内容设置，充分体现出作者实证研究的良好素养和扎实基础。具体到第四章到第六章的内容设计，作者首先对被试具有英语学习综合水平代表性的三类成绩（高考总成绩、高考英语成绩以及英语专业四级成绩）进行了偏度分析，研究了其正态分布情况。这一"被试成绩的偏度与相关系数研究"为后续两章涉及中国英语学习者具体的"花园幽径句"解读相关实证分析与计算研究提供了可靠的数据支撑，做好了逻辑铺垫。这一研究步骤，一方面体现了作者的实证规范意识，确保了该研究的信度和效度，增强了研究的说服力；另一方面，也体现出作者的创新意识。对于中国英语学习者相关的实证研究而言，通常研究者对于被试的二语语言能力的考量是比较单一的，而且大多会选择常规单一标准作为评价基础。而本研究中，作者从中国英语学习者二语学习水平考量的特殊复杂性出发，基于学习者高考总成绩、高考英语成绩和英语专业四级成绩的数据，充分思考了这三类数据之间的关联性及其对于后续计算研究的影响，预先做了数据分析与计算研究，这是本土化问题意识所带来的研究方法创新，提升了研究的原创适用性，值得借鉴。

最后，该研究的专业学术性与读者友好性互补紧密。就该书的专业学术性而言，全文所涉及的专业内容与表述规范，文献回顾翔实全面，条分缕析，重点突出，易于理解。对于"花园幽径现象"的理论分析层次分明，逻辑缜密，为后续的实证研究做好了理论准备。与此同时，难能可贵的是，该书作者在全文阐述的学术性基础上，还有着很好的读者意识，行文论述的可读性较其他计算语言学研究著述或许更平实易懂。我作为计算语言学研究的外行读者，通读全书的过程体验，远没有之前预想的艰涩难懂（当然，那些计算公式仍是有难度的，但大多并不太影响理解）。这在很大程度上与作者深入浅出的写作风格密不可分。比如，该书开篇引言的写法，从实例切入，直奔主题，然后引出作者和读者共同关切的问题与思考，使读者有比较好的代入感，促进了作者与读者之间的有效互动，有助于加深读者的理解与认同。再比如，第三章有关"花园幽径现象的理论分析"内容，前四小节都是理论分析的内容，相对专业性更强，对于外行读者可能有一定难度，但第五小节，作者安排了"基于实例的理论分析"内容，有效地降低了读者理解专业内容的认知负荷，增强了可理解性。这种学术写作风格方面的读者友好性对于普及专业理论知识和应用研究推广大有裨益。当然，能够深入浅出地介绍专业性较强的研究内容，这对作者本身也是比较高的要求，是其研究水平及深度外化的一种体现。

上述读后感式的三点阅读体验分享，从理论深度方面显然是不够的，但或许可以给其他读者提供一些阅读理解的参考，尤其是给不少跟我一样有外行"顾虑"的读者增添积极探索新知的勇气，从而使更多的学习者和研究者从这本书中获益。我相信这本书的价值是多方面的，除了对计算语言学本体及应用研究是重要拓展和补充外，还会给国内外关注中国英语学习者语言学习的相关研究带来启发和思考，开阔视野抑或借鉴方法。正如我读此书一般，受益良多。

　　当然，对于这部新作，我作为读者有一点期待。具体一点说，这部著作主要是从计算语言学研究的视角对中国英语学习者解读"花园幽径句"的认知机制进行了实证分析和研究，数据分析和计算研究见长，取得了积极的成果。但在此基础上，一方面，今后可否再对影响中国学习者解读"花园幽径句"的相关认知因素做数据基础上的深度探讨，可否结合二语习得研究的相关理论资源与研究成果进一步拓展其应用研究价值？另一方面，今后可否尝试以汉语的语言事实为研究素材，探究汉语"花园幽径句"的特殊性与复杂性，或许这方面的英汉对比研究会有更多有趣且有价值的发现？或许将该研究的被试调换为非母语的汉语学习者会产生新的理论增长点，提出中国学者独到的新发现和新见解？等等。我的这些想法，不揣浅陋，主要是希望不久的将来，能够看到作者在这个领域更多、更新、更好的研究成果。如此，即便我的上述想法不切实际或明显外行，想必作者也不会见怪吧。

　　杜家利博士师从我国计算语言学大家冯志伟先生，学术训练和积累丰厚，他本人非常谦逊低调，勤奋刻苦且勇于创新，值得我学习的地方很多。很感谢他邀我先睹其团队的新作为快，也正好借此一番"絮言"，表达我对作者们的祝贺和寄望。

　　是为序。

2018 年 6 月 25 日于南京大学

目　录

第一章　引言 …………………………………………………………（1）

第二章　花园幽径现象研究综述 ……………………………………（8）
　第一节　国外研究回顾 …………………………………………（10）
　　一　启动机制研究 ……………………………………………（10）
　　二　诱发条件研究 ……………………………………………（17）
　　三　检测方法研究 ……………………………………………（22）
　第二节　国内研究回顾 …………………………………………（25）
　　一　句法研究 …………………………………………………（25）
　　二　语境研究 …………………………………………………（27）
　　三　心理研究 …………………………………………………（27）
　本章小结 …………………………………………………………（29）

第三章　花园幽径现象的理论分析 …………………………………（31）
　第一节　花园幽径现象认知的先后性 …………………………（36）
　第二节　花园幽径现象认知的条件性 …………………………（38）
　第三节　花园幽径现象认知的螺旋性 …………………………（41）
　第四节　花园幽径现象理解折返与顿悟的认知基础 …………（43）
　　一　认知顿悟的前提——语义触发 …………………………（44）
　　二　认知顿悟的结果——认知折返 …………………………（44）

  三 认知顿悟的效应——跨越解码 ……………………… (44)
 第五节 基于实例的理论分析 ……………………………… (45)
 本章小结 ……………………………………………………… (52)

第四章 被试成绩的偏度与相关系数研究 ……………… (54)
 第一节 偏度 ………………………………………………… (54)
  一 被试高考总成绩偏度分析 ……………………… (58)
  二 被试高考英语成绩偏度分析 …………………… (59)
  三 被试英语专业四级成绩偏度分析 ……………… (59)
 第二节 相关系数 …………………………………………… (60)
  一 简单皮尔逊积矩相关系数公式 ………………… (61)
  二 相关系数的 EXCEL 函数计算 ………………… (63)
  三 相关系数的临界值 ……………………………… (64)
 第三节 被试高考总成绩与英语专业四级成绩的相关
     系数研究 …………………………………………… (66)
 第四节 被试高考英语成绩与英语专业四级成绩的相关
     系数研究 …………………………………………… (69)
 本章小结 ……………………………………………………… (74)

第五章 花园幽径句阅读时间与效果的非独立 t 值研究 ……… (76)
 第一节 测试前准备 ………………………………………… (76)
 第二节 非独立 t 检验 ……………………………………… (78)
  一 非独立 t 检验的公式测定法 …………………… (79)
  二 非独立 t 检验的 EXCEL 函数测定法 ………… (85)
 第三节 非独立 t 值研究 …………………………………… (94)
  一 非独立 t 检验下显著性差异测试句分析 ……… (98)
  二 非独立 t 检验下非显著性差异测试句分析 …… (105)
 本章小结 ……………………………………………………… (109)

第六章　时间和能力因素与花园幽径句阅读效果的方差分析 (112)

第一节　方差分析公式法 (112)

第二节　时间因素与花园幽径句阅读效果的方差分析 (120)

第三节　英语能力与花园幽径句阅读效果的方差分析 (124)

  一　英语专业四级成绩分组的卡方检验 (125)

  二　英语能力与阅读效果的方差分析 (129)

本章小结 (196)

结语 (199)

参考文献 (203)

附录一　花园幽径句和对照句测试样例 (254)

附录二　阅读时间与效果的非独立 t 值测试 (260)

附录三　时间因素与测试结果的方差分析 (264)

附录四（一）　高考英语成绩与英语专业四级成绩相关系数统计 (268)

附录四（二）　高考英语成绩与英语专业四级成绩相关系数分析 (273)

附录五（一）　高考总成绩与英语专业四级成绩相关系数统计 (274)

附录五（二）　高考总成绩与英语专业四级成绩相关系数分析 (279)

附录六(一)　英语专业四级成绩分组的卡方检验 ……………（280）

附录六(二)　英语专业四级不同成绩组测试结果的方差
　　　　　　分析 ……………………………………………（281）

附录七　The Penn Treebank 词类标记集 …………………………（285）

附录八　Stanford parser 的依存关系代码与解析 ………………（290）

附录九　中英文姓名对照表 …………………………………………（299）

后记 ……………………………………………………………………（305）

图 目 录

图 3-1　Kempen(1996)的句法分析器框架模型 …………（34）
图 3-2　Vtr + NP 节点模式 …………………………………（35）
图 3-3　Vtr + NP + PP 节点模式 …………………………（35）
图 3-4　普通句认知解码的顺序流程图 ……………………（36）
图 3-5　花园幽径句认知解码的顺序流程图 ………………（37）
图 3-6　花园幽径句认知解码的选择流程图 ………………（38）
图 3-7　普通句解码流程图 …………………………………（39）
图 3-8　花园幽径句解码流程图 ……………………………（40）
图 3-9　花园幽径句系统解码完整程序 ……………………（41）
图 3-10　WHILE 型循环结构 ………………………………（42）
图 3-11　UNTIL 型循环结构 ………………………………（42）
图 5-1　正态分布曲线中的数值分布图 ……………………（86）
图 6-1　句补关系错位的花园幽径句依存图 ………………（138）

表 目 录

表1-1 普通句—复杂句—对照句的剖析对照表 ……………（5）
表4-1 均值、中位数和偏度关系列表 ……………………（55）
表4-2 平均数的 EXCEL 函数计算列表 ……………………（55）
表4-3 奇数中位数的 EXCEL 函数计算列表 ………………（56）
表4-4 偶数中位数的 EXCEL 函数计算列表 ………………（56）
表4-5 奇偶数组的偏度对比 …………………………………（57）
表4-6 奇偶数组标准差的 EXCEL 函数计算列表 …………（57）
表4-7 高考总成绩偏度表 ……………………………………（58）
表4-8 高考英语成绩偏度表 …………………………………（59）
表4-9 英语专业四级成绩偏度表 ……………………………（60）
表4-10 高考英语成绩 X 与英语专业四级成绩 Y 的取样相关
系数计算表 …………………………………………（62）
表4-11 高考英语成绩 X 与英语专业四级成绩 Y 的取样相关
系数函数计算表 ……………………………………（63）
表4-12 自由度(df=8)的相关系数临界值量表 ……………（65）
表4-13 高考总成绩和英语专业四级成绩数据列表 ………（66）
表4-14 高考总成绩和英语专业四级成绩的相关系数
计算与分析 …………………………………………（68）
表4-15 高考英语成绩和换算成绩与英语专业四级成绩
数据列表 ……………………………………………（69）

表　目　录

表 4 – 16　换算后高考英语成绩与英语专业四级低分成绩
　　　　　　对比表 ……………………………………………（70）
表 4 – 17　高考英语成绩和英语专业四级成绩的相关系数
　　　　　　计算与分析 ………………………………………（73）
表 5 – 1　测试句 S1 的 5 秒和 10 秒反应时的评分及
　　　　　差异值 ……………………………………………（79）
表 5 – 2　测试句 S1 的 5 秒和 10 秒反应时的非独立 t
　　　　　检验值 ……………………………………………（84）
表 5 – 3　取样测算值的标准差计算表 ………………………（87）
表 5 – 4　测试句 S1 在 5 秒和 10 秒反应时的 TTEST 函数
　　　　　概率 ………………………………………………（91）
表 5 – 5　测试句 5 秒和 10 秒反应时的 t 值和 sig 值列表 ………（94）
表 5 – 6　反应时延长差异性影响阅读效果的测试句列表 ………（99）
表 5 – 7　反应时延长对阅读效果不明显的测试句列表 ………（105）
表 6 – 1　反应时 5 秒—7 秒—10 秒的 S1 阅读效果评分及
　　　　　平方表 ……………………………………………（115）
表 6 – 2　反应时分组与阅读效果的 ANOVA 分析列表 …………（121）
表 6 – 3　反应时分组与阅读效果 $p < .05$ 的 ANOVA 列表 ……（123）
表 6 – 4　被试的英语专业四级成绩列表 ………………………（126）
表 6 – 5　英语专业四级成绩分组的卡方检验 …………………（128）
表 6 – 6　英语能力组与阅读效果评分及平方列表 ……………（129）
表 6 – 7　能力分组和阅读效果的方差分析列表 ………………（131）
表 6 – 8　能力分组与效果评分的 100 个测试句 F 值列表 ……（132）
表 6 – 9　能力分组与效果评分的显著性差异项 F 值列表 ……（134）
表 6 – 10　频数观察中的 plan 和 plan to 差异性列表 …………（147）
表 6 – 11　在 BNC 语料库中 plan 和 plan to 的频数卡方检验 …（147）
表 6 – 12　四个对照句的结构对比与显著性差异对比 …………（166）
表 6 – 13　嵌套结构引导词 that 对花园幽径句 S3 的系统
　　　　　　剖析对照 …………………………………………（176）

第一章

引　言

　　花园幽径句是局部歧义的复杂结构。其认知解码是"单车道单向通行"的独立排他模式。这种复杂结构存在语义流中途折返、另路通过的特殊语义短路现象。

　　例1-1　The boy walked towards the door. 男孩朝门走过去。

　　该句是简单句，读者没有任何阅读障碍。利用系统进行自动剖析其结果也很正确。请见斯坦福解析器（Stanford parser）对该句的剖析结果（具体代码请见附录）：

Your query

The boy walked towards the door.

Tagging

The/DT

boy/NN

walked/VBD

towards/IN

the/DT

door/NN

./.

Parse

(ROOT

　(S

（NP（DT The）（NN boy）)
　　（VP（VBD walked）
　　　（PP（IN towards）
　　　　（NP（DT the）（NN door））))
　　（..)))

Universal dependencies
det（boy-2, The-1）
nsubj（walked-3, boy-2）
root（ROOT-0, walked-3）
case（door-6, towards-4）
det（door-6, the-5）
nmod（walked-3, door-6）

　　例1-2　The boy walked towards the door cried. 被推搡至门口的男孩哭了。

　　该句是复杂结构句。在动词 cried 出现前，读者的解码模式与例1-1是一样的。但是随着对 towards the door 的解码完成，如果读者没有任何的模式更迭，后续的动词 cried 将无法得到解读。如果将该动词纳入前期已经构建的阅读模式中，必将带来原模式的破旧立新。这种模式更迭会引发顿悟和回溯，并直接导致系统自动剖析的崩溃。请见受到行进式错位影响而出现失败的系统剖析结果：

Your query
The boy walked towards the door cried.
Tagging
The/DT
boy/NN
walked/VBD
towards/IN
the/DT
door/NN

cried/NN

./.

Parse

（ROOT

　（S

　　（NP（DT The）（NN boy））

　　（VP（VBD walked）

　　　（PP（IN towards）

　　　　（NP（DT the）（NN door）（NN cried））））

　　（..）））

Universal dependencies

det（boy－2，The－1）

nsubj（walked－3，boy－2）

root（ROOT－0，walked－3）

case（cried－7，towards－4）

det（cried－7，the－5）

compound（cried－7，door－6）

nmod（walked－3，cried－7）

从上面的剖析中我们可以看出，句法结构和依存关系都发生了塌陷性崩溃，系统完全不具有纠偏功能。究其原因，我们发现其根本在于动词walked的歧义上。系统根据出现的概率将该动词认定为不及物主动态动词。这种根据系统惯性而采用的解码模式导致了后期解码的错误。由于整个句子是正确的，而出现歧义的部分仅仅是解码过程中的局部状态，所以，我们称此类复杂结构为局部歧义结构，亦称为花园幽径模式。如果消除局部状态中的歧义点，整个句子潜在的局部歧义也将消失。请见walked被无歧义的taken取代后的系统正确剖析结果：

例1－3　The boy taken towards the door cried. 被带到门口的男孩哭了。

Your query

The boy taken towards the door cried.

Tagging

The/DT

boy/NN

taken/VBN

towards/IN

the/DT

door/NN

cried/VBD

./.

Parse

(ROOT
　(S
　　(NP
　　　(NP (DT The) (NN boy))
　　　(VP (VBN taken)
　　　　(PP (IN towards)
　　　　　(NP (DT the) (NN door)))))
　　(VP (VBD cried))
　　(. .)))

Universal dependencies

det (boy-2, The-1)

nsubj (cried-7, boy-2)

acl (boy-2, taken-3)

case (door-6, towards-4)

det (door-6, the-5)

nmod (taken-3, door-6)

root (ROOT-0, cried-7)

从上面的剖析可以看出，在消除了局部歧义点 walked 之后，整个系统剖析也变得顺畅正确了。那么，在普通句例 1-1、复杂句例 1-2、对照句例 1-3 之间到底出现了怎样的系统性偏差，以及系统又是如何在局部歧义消解后回归到正常状态的？请见我们对三个句子进行的标注—句法—依存关系的对照分析（表 1-1）。

表 1-1　　普通句—复杂句—对照句的剖析对照表

分类	例 1-1	例 1-2	例 1-3
Tagging	The/DT boy/NN walked/VBD towards/IN the/DT door/NN	The/DT boy/NN walked/VBD towards/IN the/DT door/NN cried/NN	The/DT boy/NN taken/VBN towards/IN the/DT door/NN cried/VBD
Parse	NP（DT The）（NN boy） VP（VBD walked） PP（IN towards） （NP（DT the） （NN door））	NP（DT The）（NN boy） VP（VBD walked） PP（IN towards） （NP（DT the）（NN door） （NN cried））	NP（DT The） （NN boy） VP（VBN taken） PP（IN towards） （NP（DT the） （NN door）） VP（VBD cried）
Universal dependencies	det(boy-2, The-1) nsubj(walked-3, boy-2) root(ROOT-0, walked-3) case(door-6, towards-4) det(door-6, the-5) nmod(walked-3, door-6)	det(boy-2, The-1) nsubj(walked-3, boy-2) root(ROOT-0, walked-3) case(cried-7, towards-4) det(cried-7, the-5) compound(cried-7, door-6) nmod(walked-3, cried-7)	det(boy-2, The-1) nsubj(cried-7, boy-2) acl(boy-2, taken-3) case(door-6, towards-4) det(door-6, the-5) nmod(taken-3, door-6) root(ROOT-0, cried-7)

· 5 ·

首先从标注上分析，复杂句例1-2中的错误在于对walked和后续出现的cried的标注。由于沿用前期已经构建的认知模式，系统无法将cried加入该既定模式中，只能将cried分析成名词，这是导致错误的根源。相反，如果系统在动词cried出现后能将原来的模式推倒重建，那么得到的就会是例1-3的正确模式。可惜系统无法跨越这种认知障碍。

其次从句法结构上分析，复杂句例1-2由于对原句法结构的依赖，主体结构并没有随着cried的出现而更改，形成的仍然是类似于例1-1的NP+VP+PP结构。这种对原句法结构的眷恋导致了系统的结构错误。相反，如果系统具有智能特征并勇于重建结构，其正确的句法结构就应该类似于例1-3的NP（NP+VP+PP）+VP结构。

最后从依存关系上分析，复杂句例1-2仍然认定动词cried出现后，boy和walked的语义关系符合nsubj（walked-3，boy-2）的主谓关系特征。这种语义上的惯性是对简单句例1-1语义关系的延续。系统在动词cried这个节点出现了严重的语义短路现象并导致无法回归到正常的语义关系剖析状态。这种瞬时短路的语义崩溃在例1-3中可以得到恢复，如系统成功将主谓关系认定为nsubj（cried-7，boy-2）。

通过对比三个句子的标注—句法—依存关系，我们可以清楚地看出系统经历了怎样的行进式错位，并直观地了解了系统如何在局部歧义点消解后回归到常规状态。

作为英语学习者，我们面对这些具有局部歧义的花园幽径句时，有如下几个问题需要深入思考。

（1）具有认知智能的我们是否会像机器一样受到局部歧义的干扰？

（2）受到干扰之后我们是否会像机器一样发生认知系统的崩溃？

（3）如果崩溃了，我们如何恢复，节点在哪里？如果没有崩溃，我们该如何借助自身优势为系统改良提供理论支撑？

（4）当受到局部歧义干扰的时候，延长反应时间是否可以提高阅读效果？

（5）能力高低不等的中国英语学习者是否在解读此类复杂结构句时呈现了一致性的阅读效果？各自特征是什么？

　　针对如上问题，我们将采用语言统计和语言计算的方法进行有针对性研究，并借助斯坦福解析器进行剖析对照，以期从计算语言学的视角为中国英语学习者解读复杂结构句提供理论支撑，并为英语教学提供具有统计学意义的数据。

第二章

花园幽径现象研究综述

纵观花园幽径现象的学术研究，国内外学者均具有较为深入的讨论。由于国外学者和国内学者的语言背景不同，其切入点多从自身最为熟悉的部分展开。对于国外学者来说，英语本身有着侧重语言结构组成的特点，这利于他们从句法结构变化导致的花园幽径现象开始讨论。而对国内学者来说，汉语重意合而轻形合的语言特性让他们认为认知语义使然的花园幽径现象更适合汉语范畴。不管是源于句法形态变化还是源于认知语义调整，花园幽径的局部歧义现象在神经语言学等认知科学的发展中均得到了印证。

在国外学者的讨论中，有三个讨论方向值得关注。由于在语言加工中，句子加工心理机制的分析是在实时状态下展开的，并可能与其他系统进行交互反应，甚至在不同语言体系中也存在让人困惑的花园幽径现象，因此，如何交互以及如何生成语义，根据路径和作用效果的不同，国外学者形成了虽有关联但有侧重的句子加工理解的三个方向：模块、交互及并合。

由于语言的生成与语义的理解属于黑箱状态，这就为模块、交互及并合之争埋下了伏笔。到底语言加工处理模式是串行还是并行，至今难有定论（Frazier and Fodor，1978；Crain and Steedman，1985；Kurtzman，1985；Ferreira and Clifton，1986；Gorrell，1987；Gibson，1991）。串行通常以模块说为基础，并行则一般以并合说为条件。

秉承模块串行的学者福多尔（Fodor，1983）强调句法的优先特性，多结构可供选择时，语言处理是有先后的，其原则多以概率为基准，并形成序列特征。在与语义竞争时，句法在前，语义在后。句法和语义只有在完成各自的处理之后才会进入整合模式。由于花园幽径的处理模式与模块串行很类似，所以，很多学者均将该局部歧义现象归为模块说的典型模型，即通过潜在的出现概率决定潜在优选序列，并在后期出现局部歧义时进行折返性优选序列的调整，直至解码完成。

这种串行的优选序列假设为早期花园幽径现象的解释提供了理论支撑。随着研究深入，库兹曼（Kurtzman，1985）和吉布森（Gibson，1991）提出了反例：从结构变化视角来说，源于结构频现概率不同的测试，并不必然导致花园幽径现象。从语境的补足效果来看，提供的辅助信息越多，对局部歧义的消解越有利，而这种对冲有时候并不是串行而是并行存在的（Crain and Steedman，1985；Altmann and Steedman，1988）。

鉴于有很多现象是串行模块无法合理解释的，互动并行观点得以催生。其中，最有代表性的是制约满足模型（constraint satisfaction model）（Tanenhaus, Carlson and Truswell，1989）。特鲁斯威尔（Trueswell，1996）认为语言加工不是静态的排他性加工，而是受到多因素制约的兼容性加工。达到激活阈值的因素均可以在解码中占有一席之地，其对语言加工的影响不是先后序列的，而是多头并进的。戈雷尔（Gorrell，1987）为此特定构建了句法启动范式，用实验证明了多句法模式可同时启动的并行倾向。

虽然串并行双方都列举了各自的实验以验证自己观点的正确性，但实际上，这些实验都具有一定的选向性，即各方均采用可以佐证自己的语言材料进行讨论，形成了典型的各自为政现象。兼容两者的中庸观点得以派生而出。并合观点强调串并行的共存，即侧重语言加工阶段的多元性，各阶段不是排他的串行或并行，而是两者相辅而行的。博兰（Boland，1997）在其跨模态的整合范式中利用并合观点解释了句法和语义的阶段串行和阶段并行的学术观点。他举例认为，动词论元结构的潜在性是串行的基石,并能在歧义结构中占据先机;但是,多句法结构仍可在歧义点出现时为并行提供多点访问的便利,这种线性自动模式和强弱互动模式可以在一定程度上共存,形成并合,直到语言加工动态调整后筛选出最优结构为止。

从学术研究的规模和深度来看,模块并行的讨论远远领先于后两者。并合观由于其学术思想不够鲜明,所以其学术影响相对来说要弱很多。任何一种理论都有其无法辩驳的优势,同时也具有其自身无法回避的不足。所以,在后面的讨论中我们不刻意指出研究属于哪种类型,仅着重回顾学者们对局部歧义消解的理论贡献。

第一节 国外研究回顾

国外学者对花园幽径现象的研究主要分三个视角:(1)侧重内在深层认知的启动机制研究,包括句法启动、认知容量以及运行策略等。(2)侧重外在激活因素的诱发条件研究,如外元信息、外生经验、词汇激励、语境诱发等。(3)侧重获取途径的检测方法研究,如眼动、ERP、EEG、fMRI等。

一 启动机制研究

在启动机制研究中,国外学者多关注句法调整所导致的结构启动、共享与专享容量之辩的认知容量,以及语言即时处理的运行策略。

句法启动可用于解释困惑句。阿拉里等(Arai, et al., 2015)认为句法是独立的自循环系统,外在因素难以影响到句子处理。费雷拉和克利夫顿(Ferreira and Clifton, 1986)提供的实验结果表明:预先提供的句法外信息不足以影响被试的句法解读,甚至不能阻止被试陷入花园幽径的误读陷阱。这与博克(Bock, 1986)提出的"结构启动"观点有些类似,都强调了语言应用机制中的自激活效应。句子处理有时是惯性的,与激活前的存在频率和模式新旧有关,通常敏感于句法形式特征。相似的句法结构更容易引起共鸣，增大激活启动的概率，这种观点为花园幽径句加工中优先模式的惯性选择提供了理论支撑。

多选择结构在解码中具有不同的优先级别。帕特森和沃伦（Patson and Warren, 2014）认为具有较大启动概率的相似结构在句子处理中具有显著性差异。费雷拉和亨德森（Ferreira and Henderson, 1993、1998）特别关注了都具有头名词位置效应的从属结构和并列结构。他们的实验结果说明：从属歧义结构中的动词通常要同时具备一价和二价特征，即需要具有及物和不及物语法特征，这样才能达到从属结构的要求。并列结构的要求则相对简单，其位置效应也相对弱了许多。贝利和费雷拉（Bailey and Ferreira, 2003）由此认为位置效应强烈程度决定了花园幽径效应的困惑程度，并且成正比例特征。相似句法结构具有启动的便利性，但多个潜在结构之间不是混成一体的，而是具有句法处理的差异性，这种差异性使歧义结构的消解成为可能。总体而言，歧义结构呈现多元化特征时，位置效应较明显，先于或后于歧义名词出现的修饰成分具有不同的结构启动效果。

威策尔和福斯特（Witzel and Forster, 2014）研究了词汇和句法启动的关系。诺维克、金和特鲁斯威尔（Novick, Kim and Trueswell, 2003）利用实时技术控制词汇启动因素，研究了复合句的语言加工，以及主题角色和句法偏好对启动的影响。实验说明：部分名词能够启动潜存的句法信息，这个特性可服务于动词论元结构歧义。此外，词汇叠加与分布规律也对句法解歧具有一定功能。论元的存在不仅影响可接受度的判断性，同时也影响即时性的实时构建，不同的论元结构有着不同的支撑强度。花园幽径现象发生时词汇与句法的关联性可得到证实（Pozzan and Trueswell, 2015）。

除了认知词汇对启动有影响外，被试的语言经验也影响到启动效果。耶格和斯奈德（Jaeger and Snider, 2013）认为，在对话的语境中，双方有启动相似句法结构的配合性，并实现有效的沟通。这种观点在实验中得以验证：相关预期错误对实验中前期和最近的经历很敏感。

在冯冈普尔等（Gompel, et al., 2006）的结构启动实验中，及物动词后续名词时，大概率情况会将两者进行即时结构处理，尽管事后发现这种即时处理是不正确的，但被试语言经验却仍会激活这种不当模式，直到最后出现折返和回溯。这或许与认知的记忆存留，或与被试解歧中句法分析的非完整性相关。

在口语中，句法启动具有一些特征。索萨瑞里和斯内德克（Thothathiri and Snedeker, 2008）认为，词汇在某种程度上不能影响叙述者的启动结构和目标结构，但理解者却更多地依赖于词汇知识。通过双宾语（有灵生物做双宾语中的接受者）和介词宾语（无灵生物做介词宾语）的眼动实验证明：有灵生物的双宾语结构更容易启动，这说明抽象结构信息在语言生成和理解的结构启动中扮演一定角色。此外，荣格等（Jung, et al., 2015）认为语言发音的韵律和音乐有某种关联性，而且语言和音乐在解码中有共享结构的可能（Perruchet and Poulin-Charronnat, 2013）。

认知留存对歧义消解有预先性影响。诺维克等（Novick, et al., 2014）认为通过对认知控制的训练，歧义消解的能力能够得到提升。在介词短语与其他成分附着度关系测试实验中，布兰尼根等（Branigan, et al., 2005）发现：具有动词高附着性的介词短语比低附着性的介词短语结构在认知中更容易让被试具有解读的预先性，即被试惯性倾向选择留存结构，并以先期动词为主预先构建一个缺省模式。

离线状态下的工作记忆影响歧义关系从句的解读。斯威茨等（Swets, et al., 2007）发现：记忆跨度大的被试在新旧策略方面具有优势，他们能有效储存在认知系统中刚使用过的解码模式，而且在遇到相似结构时出现最大的记忆共振。工作记忆的一般性和特定性对该效果具有解释力。相反，记忆跨度较小的读者受限于记忆容量的不足，容易将信息碎片化，直接导致对歧义关系从句产生误读。

母语转移效应对二语句法处理敏感。聂赤克等（Nitschke, et al., 2010）的句法启动实验证明：母语转移效应虽然对句法启动的强度不敏感，但对二语句子处理有影响。如果没有新的启动因子激发，被试的原启动结构可以实现母语和二语的互通，即二语学习者的母语认知对语言学习有正向性，旧的"形式—意义"匹配模式可以正迁移到二语习得中。

实验中发现：先期认知模式往往先入为主地左右新模式的结构启动。新结构通常与既定模式核验后才进入启动状态。实验语境中的幼儿会无意识地利用动词构建抽象的启动结构。

经验是影响解码的不可忽视的因素。耶格和斯奈德（Jaeger and Snider，2013）基于经验效应的实验表明：宾语从句比主语从句解歧更困难。韦尔斯等（Wells，et al.，2009）认为，在同等经验情况下，歧义宾语从句比歧义主语从句更复杂。但在获得足够经验后，歧义宾语从句的难度极大地降低，甚至比没有经验支撑的歧义主语从句更容易理解。这种差异具有统计学的显著意义，即歧义消解的速度和精度受到经验效应影响。

语境促使句法预期快速转换。法默等（Farmer，et al.，2011）认为概率线索有助于被试有效处理信息。动词词汇具有权重倾向，有效地感知输入能促使词汇线索快速转变为句法结构，语境概率对这一过程起到关键作用。

词汇激活模式可用于跨语言句法启动。萨勒穆拉和威廉斯（Salamoura and Williams，2006）借助介词宾语和双宾语格的研究，认为语言间的句法启动不是相互依赖的过程，而是具有独立意义的话语结构重复。如果从共享角度来说，跨语言的句法启动是一种等效结构模型。

ERP和眼动的高时间分辨率对启动效应敏感。图利等（Tooley，et al.，2009）通过对歧义启动句和目标句动词进行实验后发现：同一动词或意义相近动词重复出现时，启动效应会加强。如果目标句和启动句中的核心动词相同或相近，被试ERP的P600句法违例效应会衰减，眼动注视时间会缩短，理解难度会降低。相反，如果目标句主要动词与启动动词不一致，理解难度加大。句法结构的重复性提取会强化认知系统，并有序转变为缺省模式。动词论元结构的交叉使用有效诱发了启动效应。

句法启动对词头位置敏感度不高。通过对词头在尾语言的研究，阿拉里（Arai, 2012）认为句法启动通常会有先期感知，并能在后续理解中发挥先锋效应。词头位置的变化与句法启动变化相关度不高，这说明跨语言系统可能有统一的启动机制。

词汇和韵律效应有助于失语症的语言研究。戴德（DeDe, 2012）对照了失语症患者组和健康组，他分析了词汇和韵律这两个变量。失语症患者在词汇和韵律线索不一致时花费在歧义句上的听力理解时间要长很多，但正确解读的可能性还是存在的，时间代价较大。

语法预期受结构启动效率影响。法恩和耶格（Fine and Jaeger, 2013）讨论了基于错误结构启动的隐式学习，并认为结构启动效率需要关注认知基础临时增量以及隐含统计和功能动机问题。

非语言功能的改善有助于语言能力的提升。诺维克等（Novick, et al., 2003）强调了语言理解中认知的灵活性，即对固有结构的多元加工能力。实验表明：非句法的认知训练和 N 元加工模式训练能够提高被试的实时修正能力，训练组和对照组在测试中呈现较为明显的差异性，这说明语言技能对一般域认知控制培训敏感。

单论元结构具有解码的优先性。论元结构的多寡影响语言生成效率。相关事件的参与实体数量能左右延迟实验中的反应时间。实验中，单论元事件比两个或三个论元事件具有解码的优先性，但各多论元间的延迟时间没有显著差异。这意味着简单结构比复杂结构更容易在认知中凸显，而复杂结构一旦超出认知范围，理解将受到阻碍。当困惑发生时，重新分析必不可少，复评成为一种显著特征（Zervakis and Mazuka, 2013）。

失语症患者在论元违例实验中与普通被试具有差异。基拉等（Kielar, et al., 2012）认为论元结构与动词息息相关。论元数量和类型影响被试的理解。论元结构的动词生成对失语症者的脑损伤敏感。在论元结构违例实验中，健康组先出现负成分再出现正成分，与此相反，患者组在实时解码时对动词论元结构高度敏感，且只出现 P600 不出现 N400。

记忆容量影响语言加工效果。工作记忆容量的有限性决定了认知负载程度（Baddeley and Hitch，1986；Engle，et al.，1992；Just and Carpenter，1992）。当加工容量高于负载，理解是顺畅的、有序的。当加工容量低于负载，理解往往受到阻碍。工作记忆容量的大小对理解效率有影响。实验证明：（1）过于复杂的句法结构将占用更多的记忆容量，给认知带来更繁重的负担；（2）语言成分留存时间过长将导致语言加工困难；（3）个体的阅读差异可能源于记忆容量的差异，年长被试语言加工和理解能力的弱化可能与记忆力衰退有关，而不是语言知识流失的结果（Miyake，et al.，1994）。

记忆容量的相互竞争影响理解效果。贾斯特和卡彭特（Just and Carpenter，1992；Just，et al.，1996）认为，句法处理中工作记忆容量不是专享而是共享的。对于包含关系从句的句子解码来说，高记忆容量被试创建了与低记忆容量被试完全不同的解码模式，这是基于储存加工信息容量不同而形成的。工作记忆与语言知识表达密不可分。工作记忆按计划储存和信息处理。句法和主题角色是分别运行的，记忆容量大小可以通过阅读跨度的变化来衡量（McElree and Griffith，1995）。

工作记忆是语言理解的敏感因素。奥伯罗尔等（Oberauer，et al.，2013）认为，高记忆容量被试拥有充分的工作记忆，能快速理解简单句，也能整合多种歧义结构，被试通常采用简单自适应的方法对多种结构消歧。贾斯特和卡彭特（Just and Carpenter，1992）发现，从时间因素来说，多歧义结构耗费时间较多，但对非歧义句解码迅速。通常关系成分间距离越长，解码错误率越高，整合时间越长。钱格（Chang，1980）认为，高记忆容量被试在解码中能整合更多信息，增大短时记忆容量，提升效率和准确率。埃里克森和金特斯（Ericsson and Kintsch，1995）认为，与此相反，低记忆容量被试因记忆容量所限，难以同时处理多种歧义句法结构，他们会被迫放弃非优选结构而只保留缺省结构，以此减轻工作记忆容量的压力。这使得他们处理歧义结构和非歧结构时，阅读时间的显著性差异不大。

多歧义结构的消解是平行和竞争模型在特定环境下共同作用的。克利夫顿和斯托布（Clifton and Staub，2008）认为，语言加工中平行模型和竞争模型在句法歧义的语料处理中具有关联性。伊斯特威克和菲利普斯（Eastwick and Phillips，1999）竞争模型关注更多的不是句法信息或非句法信息的单独作用，而是关注在共享容量的情况下它们之间的竞争胜出机制。统计学数据说明阅读跨度大的被试和阅读跨度小的被试在语言理解中具有显著差异。在主语更迭实验中，阅读跨度小的被试无法辨别有灵主语/无灵主语所蕴含的语义线索，但阅读跨度大的被试却能借助语义消解歧义。如果语义信息出现隐晦性歧义，阅读跨度大的被试受到的影响更大，这说明阅读跨度大的被试对语义感知程度更敏感。

在共享容量理论中，阅读跨度大的被试拥有工作记忆的大能量，这成为其消解歧义的有力保证之一。但很多学者提出了反对意见（Caplan and Waters，1995；Waters and Caplan，1996；Waters and Caplan，1997；Caplan and Waters，2002；Waters and Caplan，2002）。他们利用实验证明：语言处理和工作记忆是分开进行的，既包含实时的无意识加工，也包含受控的有意识的活动。没有证据说明阅读跨度小的被试采纳的解码模式劣于阅读跨度大的被试，容量不应该作为判定被试能力大小的标准。这种观点后来成为专享容量的理论来源。

在尚好策略研究方面，学者们认为语言加工不是理想化结构，而是具有高效的能满足基本条件的"尚好"（good enough，GE）模式。克里斯琴森等（Christianson，et al.，2001）在花园幽径句动词语法实验中看出：被试在解码过程中可通过推理逐步修复错误模式并回归到正确的解码途径上来。在花园幽径句和被动句的对照实验中，费雷拉等（Ferreira，et al.，2002）发现形式有时不是意义的真实表现，语言处理有时只是局部的加工，语义陈述甚至不是完整的，中间模式并不一定完全奉行语法规则，只要能够达到交流的"尚好"条件就可以实现解码。帕特森等（Patson, et al., 2009）认为，花园幽径模式解码存在不具有完美性但又不与先期模式一致的中间模式。原有错误模式在被迫退出后，仍在认知中留有残存（Ferreira, et al, 2002; Ferreira and Patson, 2007）。相关事件电位实时研究证明了句子理解是简单的启发式而不是既定的程序式；语言理解系统的瑕疵性是产生解码模式非完美性的根本原因。费雷拉和帕特森（Ferreira and Patson, 2007）通过在花园幽径句语言实验中添加或者删减代词"it"来激活被试感受语法变化的敏感性，克里斯琴森（Christianson, 2008）获得了非完全性句法复议数据，进一步说明了语言加工中尚好策略的存在。语言处理是沿着差异化形态句法和语义路线展开的，最终胜出的并不一定是最完美的解码模式，而是在竞争中具有较低活化点的模式。为此，克里斯琴森等（Christianson, et al., 2010）对主题角色分配的非典型顺序的被动句和宾语裂变句进行了实验。

费雷拉（Ferreira, 2003）认为语言加工往往是浅处理，是算法式和启发式的交融，较低活化点启发的模式有时并不是对话语意义的详尽表达。这种现象在儿童阅读过程中也被证明存在（Wonnacott, et al., 2015）。

随着研究逐步从本体的句法结构向以经验控制为主的本体外因素转移，诱发条件开始成为热点。

二　诱发条件研究

随着句法研究的深入，越来越多的研究人员发现，非语法因素的影响在复杂句解码中不容忽视。例如，被试经验的丰富与否，实验材料的难易，是否有充足的语义或语境信息，等等。

在经验控制研究方面，麦克唐纳和克里斯蒂安森（MacDonald and Christiansen, 2002）秉承经验有效的观点。他们认为工作记忆容量虽然有效，但认知容量不是排他的，容量是内在语言理解系统的一部分，但不是单独作用单元。阅读经验对占用工作记忆容量的大小有影响。语言经验不同是被试解码策略不同的潜在原因，语言使用技巧和语言表现能力与经验有着较强的关联性。被试在自我训练中可取得解码复杂结构的经验，并以此提高解码效率。麦克唐纳等（MacDonald, et al., 1992）认为，对于阅读经验不足的被试来说，复杂结构需要他们延长阅读时间作为弥补。帕尔玛特和麦克唐纳（Pearlmutter and MacDonald, 1995）认为，经验丰富的被试对细微的约束具有感知能力，零散的解码成分可以在认知中保持较长时间的存留以便匹配，即使在低频用法中（例如，在代词和先行词两者跨度超长的情况下）仍可以实现有效解码。戈登等（Gordon, et al., 1993）认为，在基于频率的词汇解码中，经验丰富的被试无论是对高频词还是低频词都具有较好的认知。而对经验缺乏的被试来说，理解高频词没有障碍；当他们面对低频词时，由于认知经验不足，需要更长的阅读时间。在比主语关系从句更复杂的宾语关系从句的解码中，经验丰富的被试体现了较好的解码优越性（Bever, 1970; Holmes and O'Reagan, 1981; King and Just, 1991）。从句子可接受性复评效应和重复曝光效应实验来看，解码受到先前语言经验制约，如果该经验正映射后面的解码，效率将得到提升，否则解码流畅性将受到影响（Zervakis and Mazuka, 2012）。

　　法默等（Farmer, et al., 2005）认为，被试对语言材料的熟悉程度决定解码的效率。被试对材料越熟悉，阅读时间越短，经验正效应越强烈。否则，经验负效应将导致解码障碍。脑记忆容量并不是影响解码效率的主要因素。在实验中，经验不足的被试对语言中的额外信息敏感度不高，受到的干扰较少。而经验丰富的被试更容易在附加信息中筛选对解码有利的提示，在实验中也更容易被引入歧途。经验丰富的被试善于利用语境信息，如果产生正效应，会提高解码效率；如果被伪语境诱导，反而降低解码效率。句法难到认知无法解读时，经验与语境都不起作用。

　　在词汇期待研究方面，词汇不同，隐藏的期待不同。达菲（Duffy, 2014）认为，从句倾向动词比名词短语倾向动词更容易导致解码障碍。霍尔摩斯等（Holmes, et al., 1989）发现，附着较长成分的名词词组句子比附着较短成分的句子更容易引发花园幽径效应，词汇对句法结构解码具有较大影响力。霍尔摩斯等（Holmes, et al., 1987）还认为，句子倾向的动词结构在解歧时需要比名词倾向结构耗费更多的解码时间，这或许是因为认知要打破现有模式重新构建一个新句子结构，远远比重新构建一个新短语成分费力得多。

通过错误平均率分析可知：从句倾向动词（clausal-bias verbs）根据歧义字符串的长度来匹配，长度较短的成分更容易被认知优先接纳。有引导词 that 的补语（that complements）比从属补语（reduced complements）具有标志性，所以降低了解码难度。汤普森和穆拉克（Thompson and Mulac, 1991）利用语料库语料对 that 的功能进行了验证。实验发现：在英语表达中省略 that 的情况是常态，通过对语料库（University of Pennsylvania's Wall Street Journal corpus）5000 句子的统计来看，that 被省略的句子占到从属句总额的 33%。所以，部分读者会因为引导词的省略感受到解码的困难（Garnsey, et al., 1997）。

名词短语如果具有多重性，在既能作为前引动词的宾语也可以作为后续从句的主语时，解码难度要比词汇单一属性更大。霍尔摩斯等（Holmes, et al., 1987）在动词分析中认为，论元结构的使用频率差异也会导致解码障碍，次范畴特征能反映句子结构特征，具有不同倾向的动词在解码时表现了不同的解码特征，每个动词有选择不同成分的自由，即分类选择。麦克唐纳（MacDonald, 1994）认为多后续结构的动词更容易产生解码困惑。霍尔摩斯和福斯特（Holmes and Forster, 1972）认为，动词结构多样性在提取中通常依据使用的可能性进行激活排序（Fodor, 1978; Ford, et al., 1982; Holmes, 1984）。动词本身对亚范畴框架的偏好容易形成花园幽径效应（Clifton, et al., 1984; Holmes, et al., 1989; Trueswell, et al., 1993）。而且，非句法因素对解码有关联性（Keller and Zechner, 1995）。

在语义条件研究方面，格罗德内尔等（Grodner, et al., 2002）认为语义可以提升解码的效率。随着不同句法的变化，结构中隐含的语义线索不断得到凸显，但语义启动晚于结构启动，只有当读者基于句法无法处理时，语义才启动生效。有时候，句读的有无甚至让句意大相径庭。语义线索也不是持续有效的，它们会随着句法信息的不断涌入而出现功能衰退。此外，词汇语义韵律也会影响解码效率，而且句法结构调整通常会导致韵律调整，这种再调整对应的是更多的耗时（Just and Carpenter, 1992; Breen and Clifton, 2013; Niikuni and Muramoto, 2014）。

语义存在影响句子中的词汇解码。特拉克斯勒等（Traxler, et al., 2005）在实验中发现，当句子成分被部分抽取并形成关系从句时，被试的解码受到较大影响，没有语义线索的情况下，抽取宾语的从句要比抽取主语的从句更难理解。在抽取宾语的从句中，宾语空位需要填充（a filler）才能完善句法结构并赋予格和主题角色，较长的字符串阻碍了这种空位搜寻，暂存在工作记忆的认知负载延长了解码时间并导致难度加大（Gordon, et al., 2001; Mak, et al., 2002）。但在语义线索的提示下，句法复杂效应则相应衰减或消解。非句法因素的语义条件在句法结构之外为认知系统提供了解歧线索（Trueswell, et al., 1993; Spivey-Knowlton and Sedivy, 1995; Gibson and Pearlmutter, 1998），例如，经验丰富的被试更能理解句法的话外之音，充分利用主语的语义线索来推动相关成分匹配论元位置（King and Just, 1991; Pearlmutter and MacDonald, 1995）。

在语境限定研究方面，实验表明：语境在解码名词短语的句子性补语（sentential complement, SC）和关系从句（relative clause, RC）中起到重要作用。阅读时间的延宕会导致认知落差并产生花园幽径效应（MacDonald, et al., 1992; Kemtes and Kemper, 1997）。在阅读跨度（reading span）的辨析中，斯皮维和塔嫩豪斯（Spivey and Tanenhaus, 1994）发现：当"told"引领 SC/RC 结构歧义时，作为名词短语句子性补语的语境出现频率要远远高于作为对照组的关系从句语境。频率分布的不平衡是语言经验和语境复杂作用的结果。在实验中，高跨度的被试（high span reader）比低跨度的被试对具有句子性补语 SC 的构式有更强的倾向性，一旦这种预先存在的 SC 构式被非原型的 RC 构式所取代，高阅读跨度被试则会受到更多的认知困扰。在联结策略（a connectionist strategy）的分析中，帕尔玛特等（Pearlmutter, et al., 1994）借助华尔街日报（*Wall Street Journal*）语料库讨论了 MV（main verb）/RR（reduced relative）歧义模式的语境效应。在语境敏感的词汇化模型中，如果主语是有灵生物，那么 <施事，主题> 构式要比 <原因，主题> 构式更容易被接受。也就是说被试更容易接受"有灵主语 + MV"的解码模式，后期语境出现，原模式被否定，非原型的 RR 模式可以胜出。从 MV 向 RR 的转变必然会加重困惑的程度。换句话说，语境可以引领解码的方向。

具有意义倾向的语境（sense-biasing context）对阅读时间有影响。黑尔等（Hare, et al., 2003）认为动词多概率次范畴化结构是存在的，且概率受到潜在的非随机因素影响。动词次范畴信息在解码时会被激活，基于语境的概率辨别可以提升解码的效率。在语境对论元影响的研究中，特拉克斯勒和图利（Traxler and Tooley, 2007）讨论了语境效应（contextual effects）。一般情况下，语境研究是非模块化研究，语境的渗透常左右句子构成。基于眼动的实验证实了不管是句内还是句间出现的快速短时语境（short-term context），抑或延时出现的长时语境（long-term context），都影响到论元关系的加工。

语境对阅读时间和终结模式有影响。克里斯琴森和卢克（Christianson and Luke, 2011）在实验中发现：前期命题内容（propositional content of incoming text）与语境命题内容（propositional content of the context）具有时合时离的特点。两命题内容一致时，阅读效果得到加强。不一致时，阅读效果受到阻碍。语境的语义内容和句法形式深刻影响着认知后期解码模式的整合。在宾语合理性（object plausibility）效应研究中，塔嫩豪斯等（Tanenhaus, et al., 1985）指出，及物和不及物双属性的动词在宾语合理性效应作用下，及物动词属性是原型状态。在实际解码中，双属性动词的倾向性选择受语境信息影响。无语境支持，原型模式首先得到激活。有语境支持，原型或非原型模式的激活则需要分别进行讨论。新语境与过往语境一致，则先构建的模式得到加强。相反，则推翻原模式并重新构建新的备选模式。也就是说，如果解码时没有新语境的加入，认知系统将默认上次模式有效，直至足以证明默认模式无效的新语境出现。这种语言外因素对花园幽径现象的潜在影响在其他语言中（例如在波兰语中）也存在（Clifton, et al., 1984; Solska and Rojczyk, 2015）。

词频和语境具有交互性。凯勒和泽克内尔（Keller and Zechner, 1995）对宾州树库 UP（the University of Pennsylvania Treebank corpus）进行了定量分析。他们选择了 9 个随机动词（admit, assert, imply, deny, maintain, recognize, reveal, confirm, observe）作为训练集，并把语法与语义特征标注在前动词和后动词语境上，同时划分了偏句子类、偏名词短语类和无偏好三个类（S-biased, NP-biased, Equi-biased）。动词的分类完全按照频率进行，并采用就近原则无遗漏划分进入三个类别。结果发现：语境效应影响词汇分布，不同动词的论元结构频率与受到句法和语义语境限制的优选模式相关。

三 检测方法研究

随着科技发展，越来越多的检测方法推动了花园幽径研究。从早期的眼动仪到后来的事件相关电位（event-related potential, ERP）、脑电图（electroencephalograph, EEG），再到更为先进的功能性磁共振成像（functional magnetic resonance imaging, fMRI）。

眼动实时研究近 40 年取得了迅猛发展。眼动仪可用于研究词间结构关系和词距，并用于分析认知相悖的局部因素和语义整合的关系（Patson and Warren, 2010; Clifton, et al., 2016）。局部结构因素不影响新词语义整合的速度，整体事件表达决定了认知相悖因素的处理进程。在默读状态下，眼动研究取得了令人瞩目的成绩。实验中，不同使用频率的"名 + 名"复合词具有不同的头词效应。在整体语义合理的情况下，头词由首先出现的单个名词担当。如果该名词充当头词后出现语义困惑，被试将出现较长时间的阅读延宕并形成注视效应。根据眼动轨迹来进行解码分析为定量进入语言提供了捷径（Mc-

Curdy, et al., 2013; Kwon and Sturt, 2014; Muto, 2015)。

帕特森和费雷拉（Patson and Ferreira, 2009）在眼动实验中分析了引起歧义的概念复数。实验发现：（1）语言加工对复数成分的概念表达敏感；（2）先行词与后续名词形成连体名词短语时，解码没有困惑；（3）先行词与后续名词形成限定描述的复数名词时，解码困惑产生。

在 ERP 研究方面，哈古尔特等（Hagoort, et al., 1993）认为句法加工的电生理反应与语义处理的 ERP 响应具有质的不同。违例状态下的句法处理 ERP 数据表明句法正成分转移（syntactic positive shift）出现在认知系统开始解码之前，优选结构是句法处理中动态的选择，而不是一成不变的固定结构。这种特殊性可以在大脑左额下回（LIFG）区域找到注脚。实验中，该区域完好的被试能利用后续语义信息调整先前不适合的句法模式，这种语义再分析是自动而不是受控的。但如果该区域受损，语义调整将从自动转为受控。此外，与语义影响类似，语境的作用也不容忽视。ERP 实验验证了两种语境对正负成分的区别性影响：正成分对话语语境敏感；负成分对局域性词汇语境敏感（Vuong, 2010; Yurchenko, et al., 2012）。

事件动词的时间参数可激活 P600 效应，时态变化的动词屈折则无此功能。博斯等（Bos, et al., 2012）的实验讨论了时间变化量，如过去时、现在时、将来时等。虽然动词屈折变化可以在一定程度上表示时间参考，但在英语中也可以用现在完成时来表示过去时间参考，事情已经结束了，但是用的却是表示现在的 has 而不是表示过去的 had。这种时间参考的矛盾性降低了借助动词屈折变化分析时间语境的敏感度。

语言和音乐诱发的前负成分不同。语言诱发的成分多出现在脑左侧，音乐诱发部分多出现在脑右侧。两者的句法违例都可以引发前负成分 AN（an anterior negativity）。语言和音乐激活区域的不同，音乐训练提升了皮质功能的重组并可能由此提升语言解码能力。

文化差异也可以反映在基于 ERP 的语言分析中。汉语和印欧语在时间处理一致性方面有异同。与通过时态来辨别时间参考的印欧语不同，汉语时间参考不仅依赖形态句法还依赖词汇语义。胡等（Hu, et al. , 2012）在汉语超音段语调和音段元音的 ERP 研究中，讨论了成语中语调或元音误差的原因。实验说明，汉语在处理超音段语调和音段元音时会激发不同脑皮质区域。汉语的语义解读具有不同于其他语种的模式。王等（Wang, et al. , 2012）则在汉语阅读句法和语义的时间过程分析中认为汉语的句法处理不一定早于语义处理。布劳威尔等（Brouwer, et al. , 2012）认为语义整合可能不是与前期研究认定的 N400 相关，而是与 P600 相关，这些功能性解释有利于分析产生语义错觉的语言数据。

其他的 ERP 研究还包括黄和费德米尔（Huang and Federmeier, 2012）的非优选形容词顺序性研究，利用 ERP 技术分析了二语习得过程中的复杂句解码特点，支持了二语习得模型中关于"二语语法学习可以在神经基板引起质的变化"这一论证。

除了 ERP 研究，EEG 和 fMRI 等医学手段都在语言研究中得到应用。某些区域神经元的激活与否影响到解码效果。例如，从 EEG 实验中得出音乐语言和句法语言有颞叶网络重叠，并推断两者之间可能存在关联；发现句子解码是相互关联的过程而不是某个部位的单独行为，后颞、额下回和腹内侧区均在解码中得到激活等（Brennan and Pylkkänen, 2012；Vuong and Martin, 2015；Mayerhofer, et al. , 2015）。

克里斯滕森等（Christensen, et al. , 2012）利用功能性磁共振对比了 WH 从句诱发的皮质效应，最后得出结论：句法结构决定脑活动的复杂程度；关键词的位置效应影响脑活动活跃程度。艾伦等（Allen, et al. , 2012）在脑实验神经影像学中发现语言与格和双宾语句子激活模式迥异，激活的脑区域和强度明显不同。与格和双宾语句子诱发的皮质活化区域和强度是不同的。脑机制对语言迁移有正效应；外语学习者在语言条件符合一定标准的情况下可以有效利用母语的脑机制以提升外语学习水平。

由于花园幽径模式是基于英语提出来的，所以国外对此的研究广泛而深入，不仅从启动、容量、策略等角度进行了探讨，还从语言之外的经验、语境等外元信息展开分析。随着脑科学的发展，国外学者开始从定性转为定量。花园幽径的神经认知研究也获得学者们进一步关注。

将医学仪器用于语言实验，极大地推动了花园幽径模式研究。我国对此现象的研究起步相对较晚，但仍取得了可圈可点的成绩，尤其从汉语角度出发进行的讨论受到国外学术界关注。

第二节 国内研究回顾

国内的花园幽径现象研究近年由粗放型转向集约型。译介式讨论逐渐被结合心理描写和语义描述的研究所取代。从学者深入研究的视角来看，国内研究大体可分为句法研究、语境研究和心理研究。

一 句法研究

花园幽径模式本质上来说是语言结构歧义的一种。句子歧义是句子所固有的抽象句式（朱德熙，1980）。自然语言的歧义性和非歧义性是对立统一的，歧义问题总是成为某个新的语言学派崛起时向传统阵地进击的突破口。计算语言学中的 Earley 算法对解决此类回溯性歧义具有借鉴性（冯志伟，1995）。在花园幽径模式解码过程中思维图式将被激活，既可以产生滑稽幽默的表达效果，也可能加大理解难度并阻碍交流进行（石锡书，2005；刘国辉、石锡书，2005）。但如果常规语言知识图式和世界知识图式遭遇语义短路，新的图式可被激活（李瑞萍、康慧，2009）。这种现象将使语义流中途折返，并颠覆认知解码的顺序性，最终边缘模式取代优选模式并完成认知的破旧立新（杜家利、于屏方，2011、2015）。究其根本，这个过程符合最简化原则（孙肇春，2006），并源于语言处理机制中最初优选结构的错误分析和被迫中止（吴红岩，2006）。

花园幽径句可丰富英语学习的句式分析（张殿恩，2006）。这种模式如同在花园中曲折寻路，不同的歧义结果在触发性因素的启发下得到优胜劣汰（姜德杰、尹洪山，2006）。原型范畴理论和竞争模型理论在此类解读中具有可行性（王云、郭智颖，2008）。虽然动词范畴信息等语言因素、母语思维和学习水平等非语言因素使花园幽径歧义消解十分复杂（晏小琴，2008；徐艳红，2010），但巧妙运用花园幽径句，可为语言创造更广阔的理解空间（吴先少、王利琳，2007）。例如，在相声小品等语言艺术形式中使用花园幽径现象可以带来特殊的艺术效果（王璠，2009）。

　　花园幽径句可依处理长度分类，如小句花园幽径句、跨小句花园幽径句和跨句花园幽径句（陈满华，2009）。虽然语言表达多数不是明示而是隐含的，但通过有效的实验仍能系统有效地研究花园幽径现象的语言机制。句法因素能主导简单歧义句的解码，但在句法因素失效的情况下，语义和语境将适时启动（黄怀飞、李荣宝，2008）。语法分析器后续模式与前期模式不一致时，初始分析会被放弃，然后进行再分析，直至句子理解得到重构（韩迎春、莫雷，2008；黄洁、秦恺，2010）。

　　花园幽径句理解是消歧与曲解残留并存的现象（顾琦一、程秀苹，2010）。实验表明：工作记忆容量和语言水平虽然与解歧相关，但达不到显著性程度。元语言意识的培养符合"尚好"理论条件，能提升句法结构辨识能力。如果被试能力不足，其语言能力、感知能力、记忆能力和思维能力在解歧中无法得到有效配合，无法完成对花园幽径句的理解（程燕华、吴本虎，2011）。相反，如果被试对解歧线索类型、动词特征、语词加工倾向性等具有敏感性，将增大解歧效果和修复程度（黄洁，2012）。例如介词、限定词、关系代词、连词以及补语成分在花园幽径句中具有提示新节点的功能（杜家利，2015）。

　　句法研究是本体研究，结构本身蕴含的行进式错位将导致花园幽径现象的产生。如果在句法系统内无法分辨哪种结构更适合句意，句法外的语境信息将必不可少。

二 语境研究

语境的存在可从语言之外提供辅助解码信息。话语参照语境在句子加工早期就得以激活，实验说明话语参照语境可通过概念期望而非参照前提起作用（张亚旭等，2002）。花园幽径现象的理解过程则是关联期待的结果（徐章宏，2004）。这种关联在于关键句中的新假设与原有语境中的假设之间所存在的矛盾，不仅可以解释言语会话，也可以解释独白形式的花园幽径类电子幽默（陈海叶，2005）。在最佳关联原则中，话语命题、语境假设和语境效果等因素相互作用，并可以实现两个阶段最大关联的转化（黄碧蓉，2007）。从格赖斯理论角度来说，这是对质量准则的有意违反以求得特殊会话含义。语境的存在降低了歧义效应，提升了解码效率（田正玲，2007）。

上下文语境在词头居尾关系子句研究中也能降低歧义效应（Lin and Bever，2011），汉语和日语的核心词通常放在句子尾部，这种不同于英语的语言序列具有独特的语境参照方法，例如分类名词错误匹配法就可以避免出现花园幽径现象。在不同的媒介中，例如手机短信（王亚非、高越，2008）和图文广告（曾萌芽，2012）中，上下文语境也为语言的新奇性和娱乐性提供了条件。

句法研究是语言本体研究，语境研究是语言外的附加信息研究。两者在被试的解码中都起到了一定作用。国内的心理学专家将这种蕴含行进错位的折返性研究归为顿悟研究之列。

三 心理研究

花园幽径效应是一种潜意识的心理活动。这种活动能激活意识不易察觉的潜在有关信息，并在语言接收、检索、筛选和加工方面起到作用。虽然语言的输入呈现线性特征，但离线处理过程却是互动性的，语言加工机制在模块性和互动性之间切换加工（马明，2004）。

顿悟是花园幽径现象的显性特征。"问题—思考—思考的中断—顿悟"这一模式表达了顿悟的整个流程。顿悟可以弥补问题缺口，重新组合或归类后联想出可行的解决方案并在不受主体意志支配的情况下完成解读（刘儒德，1996）。对于不具备明确解决路径的问题，合适的心理表征就难以构建。这就要求思维主体能打破并超越事物之间固有的常规联系并寻求突破（钱文、刘明，2001）。这个过程不是源于个别刺激物的孤立反应，而是对情境、目的和方法的整体体验（刘菊华，2005）。顿悟前伴有失败和挫折感，但认知的灵光一闪会激发出新奇反应并能迅速对问题进行重释，从酝酿阶段进入豁然开朗阶段（师保国、张庆林，2004）。顿悟不是简单的量能积累，而是新质的飞跃（刘彦生、吕剑，2005）。在问题处于朦胧状态时，认知是紧张无序而且是不平衡的，当认知超越了问题表征且能深入内在的时候，"啊哈"体验的情感释放将形成。顿悟主要取决于在搜索问题空间中获得关键性启发信息的质量（曹贵康等，2006）。顿悟是一种认知重构，新旧模式的更迭存在较大的认知冲突，后期在关键性启发信息的帮助下突破思维定式（邱江等，2006）。一系列的脑成像技术推动了这种问题黑箱透明化的进程（罗劲，2004；罗劲、张秀玲，2006；聂其阳、罗劲，2012；朱海雪等，2012）。大脑的特定准备状态（额中回/扣带前回的激活）对顿悟的产生有积极的促进作用（邱江、张庆林，2011）。

顿悟会损耗认知资源并增加记忆负荷，降低解码的有效性。在对问题解决具有启发效果的关键信息出现前，存在一个无意识的加工过程，顿悟的创造性思维处于休眠状态，不断累加的认知负荷加重了解码负担。思维僵局不仅是顿悟问题有别于常规问题的重要因素，而且是顿悟赖以实现的基础（沈汪兵等，2012）。随着关键启发信息的出现，负荷得以瞬间释放，形成顺畅的"啊哈"体验（邢强等，2006；邢强、黄伟东，2008）。机能固着、心理成规和心理定式影响到顿悟式花园幽径效应的产生（杜家利、于屏方，2011）。认知灵活性高低与顿悟问题解决快慢成正相关，脑损伤会导致认知灵活性受损进而影响到顿悟的激活（姚海娟等，2008）。原型事件的激活更倾向于平行加工而不是序列加工，这种平行加工更贴近现实中的无意识思维（吴真真等，2009；沈汪兵等，2011）。对于场独立的被试来说，他们具有比场依赖被试更多的解码优势，但这种优势不具有显著性差异（刘汉德、朱国前，2012）。

随着医学技术的发展，脑研究得到深入探讨。虽然有所突破，但人脑是复杂多层系统，前沿技术仍未达到能够完全解释顿悟发生时脑内时空机制如何转化的灵敏度（罗跃嘉，2004）。

本章小结

国内外学者对花园幽径模式的研究各有侧重。国外主要从启动机制、诱发条件和检测方法展开讨论，国内则更多地关注句法研究、语境研究和心理研究。

在启动机制研究中，学者们认为源于结构启动的句法调整可以解释这种行进错位的幽径模式，而在启动过程中记忆容量的大小影响到认知过载的程度。容量越大的被试解码速度越快，但受到附加信息影响的可能性越大。解码过程并不是寻求毫无偏差的"精致"启动，而是秉承速成的"尚好"策略。

在诱发条件研究中，经验是重要因素。一定难度范围内，语言经验的多寡与解码效率呈现正相关，经验越丰富语言技巧则越高，解码效果越好。但是，当材料难度超过经验可控的范畴，经验因素将失去作用，两对照组解码效率差异不大。另外，在有意设定的引导性错误提示中，经验丰富的被试最先得到错误提示，并最先误入歧途直至折返性启发信息出现。这说明对经验丰富的被试来说，虽然在解码常规非歧义句时占有优势，但在解码花园幽径类的歧义句时，他们更容易受到歧义影响而产生解码效率波动。词汇期待是另一个影响性因素，主要指词汇使用频率会影响句式的变化。低频词对高频词的颠覆是产生行进式错位回溯的主要原因。由于词频在认知中的存留，当特定词汇出现，词频高的词汇模式将比词频低的词汇模式先启动，并促进系统开始解码。当逐步推进的系统解码发现首先输入的高频词汇模式无法正确解读时,备选的低频词汇模式将进入系统。这种源于先前词汇使用频率的筛选原则就受到词汇期待的影响。此外,语义因素也是不可忽视的影响性因素。花园幽径模式在语义多元性整合过程中常出现常规语义属性被边缘语义属性所取代的现象,这种语义控制的观点也逐渐被学者们所接受。

检测方法研究主要包括高时间分辨率的实时研究和高空间分辨率的定位研究,前者以眼动实时研究和事件相关电位 ERP 为主,后者以功能性磁共振成像 fMRI 为主。这些新的源于医学研究的仪器和方法正在脑研究领域攻城略地,将花园幽径的定性研究推向更高的定量研究。

国内学者花园幽径现象的研究渐由屈折的英语模式向孤立语的汉语模式转变,越来越多的学者从译介过渡到本土化研究,在被试的选择和讨论的范围方面,无论是句法方面的讨论,还是语境方面的分析,抑或是心理层面的探讨,都体现了国内研究本土化趋势。我们的研究正是迎合了这种转变和趋势,将以中国大学生为研究被试分析英语学习中的花园幽径现象。

第三章

花园幽径现象的理论分析

　　花园幽径现象是在花园幽径句分析过程中发现的,是对解码习惯和认知原型的反叛。尽管这种反叛不易被接受,但由其产生的解读模式是唯一可行的理解方式。花园幽径句语言解码困难的形成原因在于句法结构顺序的变化,与结构活性具有关联性,具有使人误入幽径、径绝路封、峰回路转、转至畅路、路通意达的特性。

　　认知算法图式的可行性研究来源于对花园幽径现象的共性分析:(1)属于语义流折返的心理现象;(2)理解初期均有多向性;(3)提取具有顺序性;(4)对缺省模式的破旧立新;(5)语义纠错由自动到受控。这些描述可归纳为具有区别性的花园幽径现象三大认知特征:先后性、条件性和螺旋性。

　　花园幽径现象得名于认知解码中的迷途知返,就好像在花园中走入了一条不能通达的幽径,径尽路绝,顿而后返。与理解折返特性相伴而生的是花园幽径现象的顿悟性。当解码初期顺畅解读时,认知负荷较小,遵循原型的省力原则,启动的是认知系统默认的模式。解码中期,后续关键成分的出现提示原模式无法继续推进,认知系统解码速度由快变慢,直至停滞。随着系统对后续关键成分的快速分析比对,在系统知识库中试图找寻到与之匹配一致的新模式。当匹配成功瞬时,否定原模式的顿悟得到激发,同时产生爆发式能力推动系统重启,并由慢到快,转轨到新模式的运行。解码后期,新模式在无其他关键信息出现的情况下,完成系统剖析。其中,让系统逐步停滞的后续关键成分就是"顿悟点",新模式确立瞬间产生的蕴含巨大推进能力的心理感知能力就是"顿悟"。

花园幽径现象理解折返性和顿悟性所组成的认知过程非常类似现实生活中蕴含"否定之否定"的"变更车道"。

解码初期,系统之车面前有两条道路:一条主道宽阔平坦,另一条辅道窄小不平。按照对道路的默认选择,驾车者选择宽阔平坦的道路行驶,并将速度由慢到快提升至正常速度。这个过程中对主道的选择就是对辅道的否定,第一次否定出现。

解码中期,驾车者发现远处道路中间疑似有路障,随着车辆驶近并放慢速度,驾车者发现路障上写着"此道封闭,请转换车道"(顿悟点出现)。环顾左右(系统重新分析比对,找寻新出路),驾车者发现养路部门把道路封闭的同时,在旁边开了一个临时通道(辅道)。于是,停滞的车辆缓慢调整方向并驶上临时通道(新模式得到尝试)。驾车者往往产生"早知如此还不如一开始就开上辅道"的抱怨感。"加速—减速—再加速"的调整过程耗费了驾车者宝贵的时间和体力,同时加大了车辆的磨损。这个选择辅道的过程就是对前期主道选择的否定,第二次否定出现。

解码后期,临时通道开始变得顺畅,驾车者加快提升速度,重新享受驾驭的快感(新模式得到确认),或许心里想着"要是不再有路障就好了,我就不用这么麻烦转换挡位并能尽快到达目的地了"。行驶逐渐归于正常。

整个道路选择的过程是否定之否定的螺旋推进:"辅道选择—否定辅道选择(选择主道)—否定之否定辅道选择(路障出现后放弃主道,选择辅道)"。经过否定之否定,车辆实现了正常行驶。这个过程不是简单的重复,而是螺旋的推进。与一开始就选择辅道行驶的驾车者不同,经过否定之否定选择的司机更珍惜受挫后得到的顺畅。所以,尽管都是在后期辅道上行驶,受挫后的司机认知上付出更多。

歧义不具有理解折返性和顿悟性,解码过程不出现路障和提示。仍以行车为例,驾车者前期选择的是宽阔主道还是窄小辅道不对后期产生停车效应。行车过程中，无论主道还是辅道都是顺畅的，既没有要求变更车道的路障出现，也没有对目的地提示的交通路牌。驾车者凭借自己对道路的熟知程度推进驾驶。通常情况下，主道和辅道通往不同的目的地。但从司机驾车角度说，两种选择都不影响驾驭的顺畅。

由以上"行车理论"分析可知，花园幽径现象不是歧义。[①]

花园幽径现象是喻指认知在曲径通幽的花园中先期迷失、后期折返的语义短路现象，其理解初期产生行进式错位并带来认知模式的否定之否定。具有使人误入幽径、径绝路封、峰回路转、转至畅路、路通意达的特性。花园幽径现象在语素、词、短语、句、文本层面均能发生。层级存在引发认知顿悟，其加重的解码负担终将引发对原认知期待的反叛。

1996年，莱顿大学实验和理论心理学部的肯彭（Kempen）发表了《人类语言理解中句法处理的计算机模型》（*Computational models of syntactic processing in human language comprehension*）。文中讨论了句法分析器的基本构架，并利用扩充转移网络分析了歧义句和花园幽径句。

肯彭认为，句法分析器的基本构架至少包括五部分：输入缓冲区（input buffer），句法处理器和工作记忆（syntactic processor and working memory），词汇和语法（lexicon and grammar），概念知识（conceptual knowledge）和句法结构（syntactic structure），如图3-1所示。

词串从输入缓冲区进入处理器，各种与其相关的词汇、形态、句法和概念知识得到整合，形成完整或零碎的句法树。虚线部分表示可选的语义（或语用）成分与词汇（或语法）信息共同平行作用于句法处理过程。肯彭指出，处理过程中的细节阐述随模型不同而有所变化，不是固定不变的，这就形成了互动模型。在人类语言句法分析语

[①] 从严式定义来说，花园幽径现象与歧义有着严格区分。但从宽式定义来说，前者也是歧义的一种。本研究秉承"对文则别，混文则同"的原则对待花园幽径现象和歧义这两个概念。

境中，语法、词汇和大部分概念知识是存储在长时记忆中的。这就为具有既定模式的扩充转移网络在语言中的应用奠定了基础。

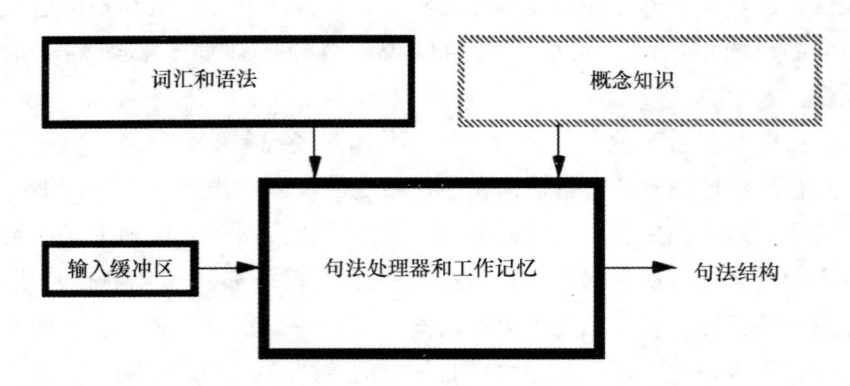

图 3-1　Kempen（1996）的句法分析器框架模型

扩充转移网络最早由卡普兰（Kaplan，1972）提出，主要用于将语言处理过程状态化。语言处理的不同状态通常用标记节点（labeled nodes）表示，两个节点之间的状态转移过程用具有方向的指示标记弧（directed labeled arcs）表示，弧上标注有特定的句法规则，转移方向由指示线条表示。这样，不同句子的解码过程就可以清晰地得到展示。肯彭借助扩充转移网络解释了歧义句和花园幽径句的不同。

例 3-1：The student read the letter to Chrysanne.（学生给 Chrysanne 读信／学生读了给 Chrysanne 的信）

例 3-2：The student read the letter to Chrysanne fainted.（那个听了给 Chrysanne 信的学生昏了过去）

例 3-3：The student who was read the letter to Chrysanne fainted.（那个听了给 Chrysanne 信的学生昏了过去）

上面三例，各有不同。例 3-1 可翻译成"学生给 Chrysanne 读信"，即 to Chrysanne 修饰动词 read，因为这样的结构节点最少。如果从句法结构分析，"学生读了给 Chrysanne 的信"（to Chrysanne 修饰名词 letter）虽然不符合最小附着原则，但仍符合句法结构。在句法结构视角下，例3-1是歧义句，例3-2是花园幽径句。

在fainted出现前，符合解码模型的句法模式［［The student］NP［［read］Vtransitive［the letter］NP［to Chrysanne］PP］VP］S已经形成，后续部分的加入将此模式变更为［［［The student］NP［［read］Vpassive［［the letter］NP［to Chrysanne］PP］NP］RRC］NP［fainted］VP］S，这种既定模式的后续变化和更迭导致顿悟的产生，并引发花园幽径现象出现。

例3-3是普通句。短时记忆在解码to Chrysanne时受词语长度影响较大，符合右连接的就近原则，所以采用［［read］Vtransitive［［the letter］NP［to Chrysanne］PP］NP］VP（Vtr+NP节点）模式（图3-2），而不采用［［read］Vtransitive［the letter］NP［to Chrysanne］PP］VP（Vtr+NP+PP节点）模式（图3-3）。该句不产生歧义或花园幽径现象。

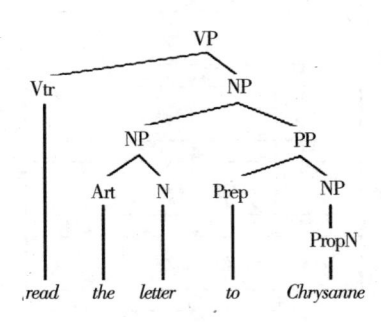

图3-2　Vtr+NP节点模式

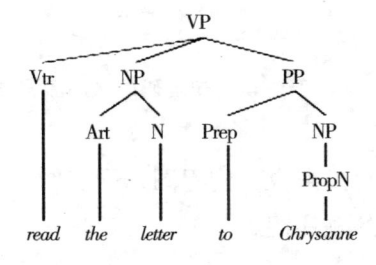

图3-3　Vtr+NP+PP节点模式

第一节　花园幽径现象认知的先后性

花园幽径现象的认知先后性是指解码初期，系统流程阶段性的顺次展开，包括字符串输入、语音解码、词汇解码、句法解码、认知语义解码。这个先后过程可以用直观易懂的流程图进行表示。

按照自然语言解码流程，普通句流程图是一个完整而不是阶段性的顺序状态图式。

例3-4：Time flies like an arrow. 时间像箭一样流逝。

该句是一个典型的呈现线性解码的普通句，系统从开始到结束顺次解读，没有任何障碍和回溯，流程图表现为完整的顺序图（图3-4）。

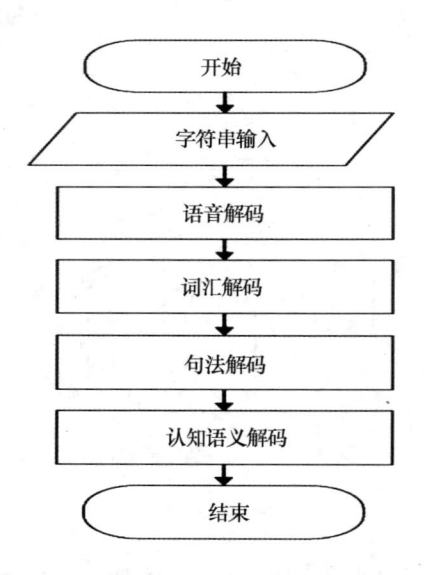

图3-4　普通句认知解码的顺序流程图

对于花园幽径句解读来说，流程图不同于图3-4。它呈现阶段性的先后性而不是完整的顺序图式。

例3-5：Time flies like an arrow; fruit flies like a banana. 时间像箭一样流逝；果蝇喜欢香蕉。

上例中，两个句子都符合句法解码的要求，也就是说从开始到认知语义匹配前，属于普通句流程状态。但第二个分句受到第一个分句句式影响，认知语义匹配模式被模式化，导致第二个分句解码失败，被迫重新理解，产生花园幽径现象。第二个分句阶段性的先后性替代了完整的顺序性。like 在两个分句中充当不同的语法成分，第一分句中作为介词使用而在后一分句中作为动词使用，解码模式引发认知的行进式错位（图3-5）。

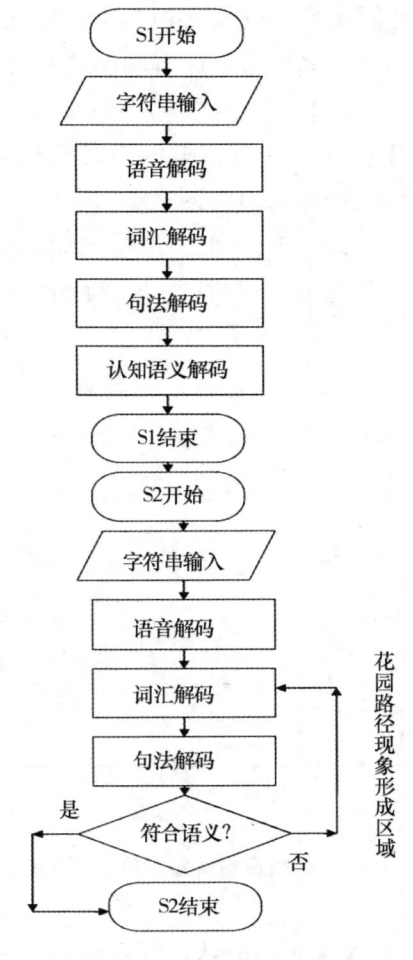

图3-5 花园幽径句认知解码的顺序流程图

花园幽径现象认知的先后性在于符合认知习惯和认知原型的理解模式优先进入解码程序,其流程图式是阶段性而不是完整的顺次结构,该阶段的流程图对应于程序算法中的顺序结构。

第二节 花园幽径现象认知的条件性

花园幽径现象认知的条件性是指语义纠错由自动到受控,首先对原模式"破",再对新模式"立"。此破旧立新必然有顿悟点:符合条件,直接解码;否则,系统打破原解码模式并返回到上一层重新进行模式匹配。

在图3-5流程图符号中,菱形框的作用是对给定条件进行判定,并根据是否符合条件来选择后面的系统操作。由于花园幽径现象存在对既定条件的选择,所以,可以利用程序算法的选择结构来解释花园幽径现象的条件性。花园幽径句认知解码的选择流程图如图3-6所示。

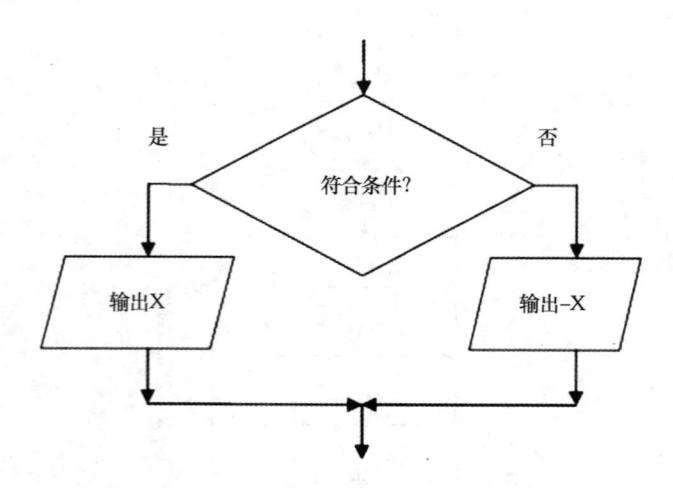

图3-6 花园幽径句认知解码的选择流程图

图3-6中,设定X为正确的认知解码模式,-X为非正确模式。这样,花园幽径现象认知的条件性决定了解码的选择性。

例 3-6：The building blocks the sun. 建筑物遮挡了阳光。

上例是普通句，其正确的解码模式 [［the building］NP + [［blocks］V + ［the sun］NP］VP］S 符合句法和语义条件，系统完成解码，输出的是 X。具体解码程序如图 3-7 所示。

```
开始
字符串输入         1. The building blocks the sun
语音解码           2. Det building blocks the sun
词汇解码           3. Det N blocks the sun
                  4. NP blocks the sun
句法解码           5. NP V the sun
认知语义解码       6. NP V Det sun
结束              7. NP V Det N
                  8. NP V NP
                  9. NP VP
                  10. S
```

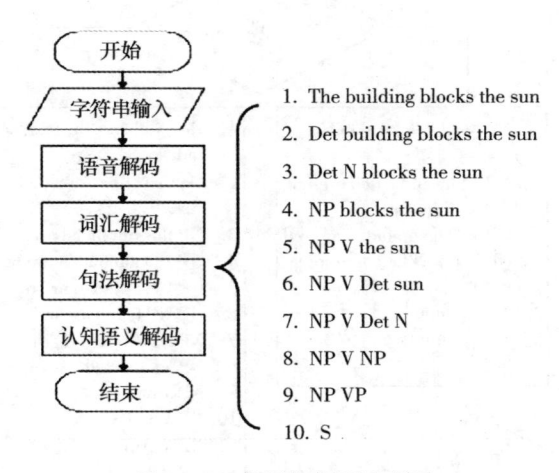

图 3-7　普通句解码流程图

与此不同，花园幽径句的认知过程则比较复杂，稍加调整则可形成回溯。

例 3-7：The building blocks the sun faded are red. 阳光（照射）褪色的积木是红色的。

花园幽径句理解过程中，blocks 的词性是名词还是动词面临选择。如果按照认知原型选择 blocks 为动词，与普通句相同的解码模式得到构建，后续的 faded are red 无法被识别，解码失败，系统输出的是 -X，即非正确模式。系统返回到 blocks 的词性选择上进行补偿性解码，名词词性得到选择，新的解码模式得到构建，符合系统识别条件，解码成功（图 3-8）。

```
┌─────────────────────────────────────────┐
│  The building blocks the sun faded are red. │
└─────────────────────────────────────────┘
              ↓
┌─────────────────────────────────────────┐
│  Det building blocks the sun faded are red │
└─────────────────────────────────────────┘
              ↓
┌─────────────────────────────────────────┐
│  Det N blocks the sun faded are red      │
└─────────────────────────────────────────┘
              ↓
         ◇ V→{blocks}? ◇
        Yes ↙       ↘ No
```

Yes 分支：
1. NP blocks the sun faded are red
2. NP V the sun faded are red（V→{blocks}）
3. NP V Det sun faded are red
4. NP V Det N faded are red
5. NP V NP faded are red
6. NP VP faded are red
7. S faded are red
8. Fail

No 分支：
1. Det N blocks the sun faded are red
2. Det N N the sun faded are red（N→{blocks}）
3. NP the sun faded are red
4. NP Det sun faded are red
5. NP Det N faded are red
6. NP NP faded are red
7. NP NP V are red
8. NP CL are red
9. NP are red
10. NP V red
11. NP V Adj
12. NP VP
13. S
14. SUCCESS

◇ Return? ◇ Yes / No

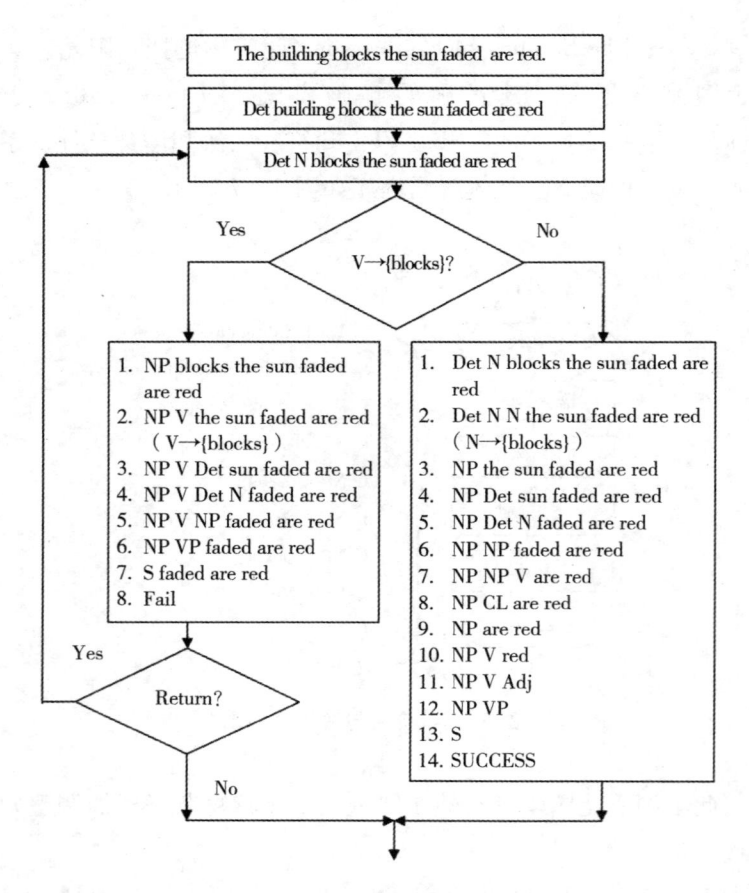

图 3-8 花园幽径句解码流程图

图 3-8 解码面临两次选择。第一次是在对 blocks 词性的选择上，第二次是在解码失败后返回与否的选择上。花园幽径句系统解码完整程序可见图 3-9。

花园幽径现象认知的条件性是指系统解码存在一个选择性：符合条件则直接成功输出；不符合条件则系统输出为无法识别。后者需要系统回溯到选择条件处重新进行选择，或者说进行第二次条件判定。这个有条件的选择在程序算法中对应于系统的选择结构。

1. The building blocks the sun faded are red
2. Det building blocks the sun faded are red
3. Det N blocks the sun faded are red
4. NP blocks the sun faded are red
5. NP V the sun faded are red（V→{blocks}）
6. NP V Det sun faded are red
7. NP V Det N faded are red
8. NP V NP faded are red
9. NP VP faded are red
10. S faded are red
11. Fail
12. Return to Step 3
13. Det N blocks the sun faded are red
14. Det N N the sun faded are red（N→{blocks}）
15. NP the sun faded are red
16. NP Det sun faded are red
17. NP Det N faded are red
18. NP NP faded are red
19. NP NP V are red
20. NP CL are red
21. NP are red
22. NP V red
23. NP V Adj
24. NP VP
25. S
26. SUCCESS

图3-9 花园幽径句系统解码完整程序

第三节 花园幽径现象认知的螺旋性

花园幽径现象认知的螺旋性是指先期解码遇阻后，折返调整，重新解读并再次通过的过程。表面上是认知的重复，实际上是对前认知模式的否定之否定，呈现螺旋上升的非思维平面的立体解读。其对应于算法的循环结构。

在计算机程序中有两类循环结构：当型（WHILE）循环结构和直到型（UNTIL）循环结构。

在WHILE型中，当给定的条件C得到满足（YES）时，执行A操作，执行完A后，再判断条件C是否成立，当条件不再成立（NO）时，系统解码成功（图3-10）。

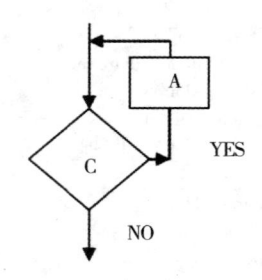

图 3 – 10　WHILE 型循环结构

UNTIL 型循环结构则是先执行 B，然后判断条件 C′，当不满足条件（NO）时，系统返回重新执行，直到系统满足条件（YES），顺利完成解码（图 3 – 11）。

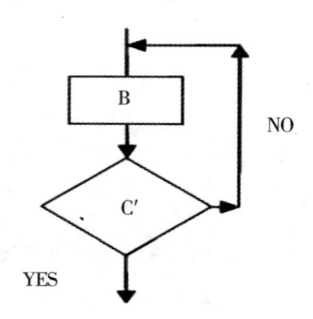

图 3 – 11　UNTIL 型循环结构

这两种循环结构都可以用于花园幽径现象螺旋性的解读。当型循环结构是先判定条件再决定是否运行。直到型循环结构则是先运行再判断。两个结构的主要区别在于提供条件的先后和不同上。以上面花园幽径句解码为例。

在当型循环结构中，系统首先判定 blocks 的词性，并尝试对照系统知识库中预存的信息。如果选择的 blocks 词性与提供的条件 C = V→{blocks} 符合时（处于 YES 的状态，即 blocks 被视为动词时），系统进入解码程序并产生回溯。当条件不再符合 C 时（处于 NO 的状态，即 blocks 被视为名词时），循环结构中止。这就是当型循环结构的简单描述。

在直到型循环结构中，系统首先按照缺省模式对该句进行解码。当系统选择的词性与条件 C′=！V→{blocks} 不一致时（处于 NO 的状态，即 blocks 的词性为动词时），系统进入循环状态，对原来的解码模式进行调整，然后再进入条件判定式，直到符合给定条件。C′=！V→{blocks} 时（处于 YES 的状态），即 blocks 的词性为名词时，系统结束解码，循环结构中止。

第四节 花园幽径现象理解折返与顿悟的认知基础

近年心理学对顿悟的研究在三个方面取得了较快发展：对大脑机制的探寻、对原型模式的阐释和认知负荷对顿悟的影响。

罗劲（2004）基于功能性磁共振成像数据总结后认为：顿悟源自新异有效模式的形成、问题表征方式的有效转换和思维定式的打破与转移，这些依赖于大脑不同部位的协同作用。

张庆林等（2004）认为心理学原型是指能对目前的创造性思维起到启发作用的认知事件。顿悟源自搜索过程中突然获得关键性的启发信息；在问题解决的过程中存在不同水平的顿悟，它主要取决于在搜索问题空间中获得的启发信息的质量。如果个体能从已有知识经验中搜索到与当前问题解决相关的知识（图式），并从中获取关键的启发信息（原型激活），那么个体就能尽早获得顿悟。

邢强和黄伟东（2008）认为顿悟问题解决有许多影响因素，其中认知资源的耗费会影响到工作记忆的容量及加工效果，进而影响顿悟问题解决的效果，认知资源耗费越多，关键启发信息越难激活。

认知顿悟点提供关键性的启发信息并带来语义触发，这是认知顿悟的前提。认知顿悟的感知过程就是问题表征方式的有效转换过程，计算科学的循环算法可重现顿悟回溯的认知过程。解码者通过原型激活获取到解决问题的相关图式和关键启发信息，顿悟产生并带来迫使认知返回到分叉节点进行重新选择的结果。在耗费了超常规的认知资源后，顿悟效应得到凸显：认知解码能力得到跨越式提升。

一 认知顿悟的前提——语义触发

语义触发是指顿悟必须有一个提供关键性启发信息的点，凭借这个触发点，原来的认知语义链出现断裂，新的语义链得以重构。在花园幽径现象中语义触发点是具有转折性的认知点。它们是原认知模式的禁止前行符号，也是加大认知负荷的关键，强行跨越该点将导致解码失败。语义触发的隐性存在成为花园幽径现象显性顿悟的前提，也是与歧义相左的区别性特征之一。请见下例：

例 3-8：Mike hit the cat with a bone. 麦克用骨头打猫/麦克打叼骨头的猫。

该句有两种解码途径，无论认知倾向哪种途径都能够解码成功，原认知链条不会断裂，新链条也不会重新生成，也就是说，本句解码不存在语义触发。这是歧义句与花园幽径句的根本区别。

二 认知顿悟的结果——认知折返

顿悟形成后，原认知模式打破，新的模式等待重新塑立，此时认知有两种倾向：没有语义触发点的认知被系统直接解码为"无法解读"（非解码错误），而对具有关键启发信息的认知则在顿悟后重新返回到原来的认知分叉点，这个顺原路折回的过程就是顿悟产生的直接结果（对解码错误否定之否定的重新纠正）。

认知折返是花园幽径现象所具有的特性之一，也是隐性顿悟特性的外在表现。其过程类似由根向节点进行扩展，失败后的解码模式被迫顺原路返回到根，再顺着下一个节点进行解读。而返回后重新扩展的依据则是格式塔知觉场理论中的完形原则。

三 认知顿悟的效应——跨越解码

折返后的认知必须在语义触发点提供的启发信息支持下重塑新的

认知模式，这便产生了不同于原认知模式的解码渠道。由于错误解码模式是对正确解读模式的否定，而回到正确解码渠道的再次解码又是对错误模式的否定之否定，所以说，认知顿悟带来的效应必然是跨越式解码。

如果被试由于内在或其他环境因素影响，在解码过程中没有遵守机能固着、心理成规和心理定式理论，则会形成特有的花园幽径效应。具体形成的否定之否定的解码如下：（1）假设句子模式的正确解读的代码为 A。（2）因概率和认知原型等因素影响，默认形成的高概率和原型模式的代码为 B。（3）最后形成的具有低概率和非原型特征的解码模式的代码为 C。解码时，被试具有潜在的原型模式 B，在最终完成解码前，被试并不知道该模式是不合时宜的。待语法监控机制启动产生顿悟并迫使错误模式折返来重新选择时，重新生成的模式表面看是 C，但实际上却是模式 A 的螺旋形式，或者说是对 A 否定模式 B 的再次否定，即认知折返后生成的模式是 A 模式的否定之否定，是认知的跨越式解码。

花园幽径现象是具有顿悟性的认知现象。机能固着、心理成规和心理定式理论阻碍错误认知模式的破解，但格式塔知觉场理论加速新异认知模式的重塑，两者拉锯式认知博弈带来顿悟的产生。在花园幽径现象的认知中，语义触发所提供的关键性启发信息是认知顿悟的前提，其感知的复杂程序可借助循环算法进行描述。花园幽径现象顿而后悟的特性带来认知折返这一结果，并通过对原正确解读模式的否定之否定实现花园幽径现象的跨越式解读。

第五节 基于实例的理论分析

句法花园幽径现象在国内外探讨得很充分，主要从句法学角度进行阐释。早期研究中，贝弗就是在分析花园幽径句时提出"花园幽径现象"的。我们下面采用金博尔（Kimball，1973）提出的"尽早闭合策略"（principle of early closure）来分析。

例3-9：Because he always jogs a mile seems a short distance to him. 他经常慢跑，一英里对他来说距离不长。

例3-10：Because he always jogs, a mile seems a short distance to him. 他经常慢跑，一英里对他来说距离不长。

根据尽早闭合策略，Because he always jogs a mile 符合成句条件，认知系统在初期接受该从句的解码模式。后续顿悟点 seems 出现后，要求系统重新解读并中止了原模式的前行。jogs 由最初的 Vt 转变为后期的 Vi，句法表层结构发生了变化，深层语义也随之进行了调整。解码过程较普通句加重了认知负荷。

通过 http://nlp.stanford.edu:8080/parser/index.jsp 在线查询，我们可以分析一下斯坦福大学 parser 对上面两例的剖析情况。剖析结果如下[①]：

Tagging
Because/IN   he/PRP   always/RB   jogs/VBZ   a/DT
mile/NN   seems/VBZ   a/DT   short/JJ   distance/NN
to/TO   him/PRP   ./.

Parse
(ROOT
　(S
　　(SBAR (IN Because)
　　　(S
　　　　(NP (PRP he))
　　　　(ADVP (RB always))
　　　　(VP (VBZ jogs))))
　　(NP (DT a) (NN mile))
　　(VP (VBZ seems)

---

① 斯坦福 parser 采用圆括号 parentheses 进行成分分析，在引用剖析结果时，我们也采用 parentheses。但是，我们自己讨论句法结构时，为区分不同，采用方括号 brackets 进行解释。

```
           ( NP ( DT a) ( JJ short) ( NN distance)))
         ( PP ( TO to)
           ( NP ( PRP him))))
      (..)))
```

在有标点符号切词的情况下，斯坦福 parser 剖析结果如下：
Tagging
Because/IN   he/PRP   always/RB   jogs/VBZ   ,/,
a/DT   mile/NN   seems/VBZ   a/DT
short/JJ   distance/NN to/TO   him/PRP   ./.
Parse
```
( ROOT
   ( S
( SBAR ( IN Because)
     ( S
       ( NP ( PRP he))
       ( ADVP ( RB always))
       ( VP ( VBZ jogs))))
(,,)
( NP ( DT a) ( NN mile))
( VP ( VBZ seems)
       ( NP ( DT a) ( JJ short) ( NN distance)))
     ( PP ( TO to)
       ( NP ( PRP him))))
    (..)))
```

由上面分析可知，斯坦福 parser 具有较强的鲁棒性，即使在没有切词的情况下系统对该花园幽径句也能够取得满意的剖析结果。但是，该 parser 在处理其他花园幽径句时有一定的偏差。

例 3－11：The business tycoon sold the oil tracts for a lot of money and wanted to kill the kidnapper. 财阀卖掉油田得到了一大笔钱，他想

杀死绑架者。

上例是普通句，陈述了两个分列左右的事实，中间由连词 and 进行连接。该例作为花园幽径句的对照组出现（为了解读方便，我们把 kill 的宾语由原引作者的 JR 改为 the kidnapper，其他部分略有调整）。斯坦福 parser 具体剖析如下：

Tagging

The/DT　business/NN　tycoon/NN　sold/VBD
the/DT　oil/NN　　　tracts/NNS　for/IN
a/DT　　lot/NN　　　of/IN　　　money/NN
and/CC　wanted/VBD　to/TO　　　kill/VB
the/DT　kidnapper/NN　./.

Parse
（ROOT
　（S
　　（NP（DT The）（NN business）（NN tycoon））
　　（VP
　　　（VP（VBD sold）
　　　　（NP（DT the）（NN oil）（NNS tracts））
　　　　（PP（IN for）
　　　　　（NP
　　　　　　（NP（DT a）（NN lot））
　　　　　　（PP（IN of）
　　　　　　　（NP（NN money））））））
　　　（CC and）
　　　（VP（VBD wanted）
　　　　（S
　　　　　（VP（TO to）
　　　　　　（VP（VB kill）
　　　　　　　（NP（DT the）（NN kidnapper）))))))

（..）））

上面的剖析结构清晰，The business tycoon 作为 NP 出现，是由连词连接的两个并列动词的主语。其中包括三个成分（NP（DT The）（NN business）（NN tycoon））。后续的 VP＋CC＋VP 构成谓语结构。

第一个主动词部分是 sold the oil tracts for a lot of money。整体结构是 VP＋NP＋PP，VP 由过去式（VBD sold）承担。NP 由次一级 NP（DT the）（NN oil）(NNS tracts）构成。PP 部分由"介词＋名词短语"构成，介词为（IN for）。更次一级 NP 由 NP＋PP 构成，即［NP（DT a）（NN lot）］NP＋［PP（IN of）（NP（NN money））］PP。

第二个主动词部分是 wanted to kill the kidnapper。整体结构是 VP＋S 结构①，过去式 VP（VBD wanted）充当 VP，不定式 to 引导成分共同充当 S，即［［VP（VB kill）］VP＋［NP（DT the）（NN kidnapper）］NP］S。

两个主动词由（CC and）连接后并列出现，最后的剖析结果符合语法。

斯坦福 parser 具有鲁棒性，但我们还应该看到它在解读花园幽径句时可能出现偏差。为比较方便，我们把形式略微调整了一下，形成"The business tycoon sold the oil tracts for a lot of money wanted to kill the kidnapper."也就是说，比较而言，新形成的句子只是缺少了连词 and。句子结构和语义随着调整发生变化并产生花园幽径现象。剖析如下：

Tagging

The/DT	business/NN	tycoon/NN	sold/VBD
the/DT	oil/NN	tracts/NNS	for/IN
a/DT	lot/NN	of/IN	money/NN
wanted/VBD	to/TO	kill/VB	kidnapper/NN
		./.	

---

① 斯坦福 parser 把不定式 to 引导部分作为特殊分句 S 对待。

Parse
(ROOT
  (S
    (NP (DT The) (NN business) (NN tycoon))
    (VP (VBD sold)
      (SBAR
        (S
          (NP
            (NP (DT the) (NN oil) (NNS tracts))
            (PP (IN for)
              (NP
                (NP (DT a) (NN lot))
                (PP (IN of)
                  (NP (NN money))))))
          (VP (VBD wanted)
            (S
              (VP (TO to)
                (VP (VB kill)
                  (NP (DT the) (NN kidnapper)))))))))
    (. .)))

由结果可知,斯坦福 parser 在对照组剖析中无法生成正确的句法生成式。剖析中整体结构是 NP + VP + S,NP 由(NP(DT The)(NN business)(NN tycoon))充当,VP 由(VBD sold)充当,S 由其余成分[the oil tracts for a lot of money wanted to kill the kidnapper]S 充当。剖析系统默认(VBD sold)可以由宾语从句来修饰,而且[(DT the)(NN oil)(NNS tracts)]NP 可以作为该从句的主语。从表层结构来看,这种剖析符合语法规范,但是从深层语义来看却是行不通的。主要的关键点有两个:(1)sold 不能由宾语从句作为直接宾语;(2)the oil tracts 通常情况下不能做 kill 的主语,应该由有灵生物充当。如果我们把 sold 改由 said 充当，tracts 改由 owner 充当，就可以实现正确剖析。请见下例：

例 3-12：The business tycoon said the oil owner with a lot of money wanted to kill the kidnapper. 财阀说有钱的油田主想杀死绑架者。

Tagging

The/DT　　business/NN　　tycoon/NN　　said/VBD
the/DT　　oil/NN　　　　owner/NN　　 with/IN
a/DT　　　lot/NN　　　　of/IN　　　　money/NN
wanted/VBD　to/TO　　　 kill/VB
the/DT　　kidnapper/NN　 ./.

Parse
（ROOT
　（S
　　（NP（DT The）（NN business）（NN tycoon））
　　（VP（VBD said）
　　　（SBAR
　　　　（S
　　　　　（NP
　　　　　　（NP（DT the）（NN oil）（NN owner））
　　　　　　（PP（IN with）
　　　　　　　（NP
　　　　　　　　（NP（DT a）（NN lot））
　　　　　　　　（PP（IN of）
　　　　　　　　　（NP（NN money））))))
　　　　　（VP（VBD wanted）
　　　　　　（S
　　　　　　　（VP（TO to）
　　　　　　　　（VP（VB kill）
　　　　　　　　　（NP（DT the）（NN kidnapper)))))))))

(..)))

上例剖析结构与对照组是完全一样的，虽然语法上是符合规则的，但是对照组剖析在语义上不能成立，也就是说斯坦福 parser 在剖析花园幽径句对照组时出现了语义上的失败，剖析结果没有意义。

斯坦福 parser 是计算语言学领域取得的令人瞩目的成就，解决了很多句法学方面的问题。由对照组剖析的语义失败来看，该 parser 既有成功的一面，也有需要改进的地方。

本章小结

本章是以语言本体模块论为基础展开讨论的。花园幽径现象具有层级存在性、理解折返性、认知顺序性和纠错控制性，其反映在认知中的先后性、条件性和螺旋性对应于程序算法的顺序、选择和循环结构。通过对花园幽径句程序化分析的认知解读，验证了其所具有的对先期理解行进式错位和对原有认知模式否定之否定的认知回溯特点。基于程序算法剖析和上下文无关语法（CFG）展开的认知解读，使程序性在花园幽径现象诸多特性中得到凸显。基于算法的认知图式还证明歧义是能带来图式固化的对先期认知的错解，而花园幽径现象是能产生顿悟并导致图式重新调整的纠错性折返。基于算法的认知图式验证了花园幽径现象产生的非歧义性。程序算法为语言研究者提供了程序化解读自然语言的良好途径，并为深化理解语言的折返性和顿悟性提供了条件。

顿悟发生时的瞬时感悟具有认知共性，不需要特殊的认知技能；顿悟发生间的单向认知具有跨越障碍的认知能力，认知线性化使障碍凸显时不能采用多向迂回的方法而只能迎面直击以获取解码出口，并在成功破解后伴随情感释放"啊哈"体验。顿悟发生后的结果习得使认知对此类障碍具有抗体，再次遇到不会产生顿悟。

通过对基于程序运行的花园幽径句法关系分析，我们实现了如下几个目标：（1）拓展了句法研究的领域；（2）验证了心理学有关顿悟的论断，即具有跨越式解读特点的花园幽径现象占用系统资源较多、解码较复杂且蕴含"啊哈"体验；（3）证明了歧义现象具有语义宽松的多选特点和花园幽径现象具有语义触发的单选性折返机制；（4）为面向语言学实践的计算语言学的语言本体观提供了有效的思路。

  理论研究最终要回到服务于实践的轨迹上来。作为蕴含复杂结构的花园幽径句，其折返错位效应是如何影响中国学习者的外语学习的过程和结果的？这一领域值得我们深入研究和探讨。如果我们能够从语言统计和语言计算的全新视角分析该效应对中国学习者的潜在影响，便可以更好地为英语教学提供数据支撑，并为中国学习者提升英语复杂句理解能力提供可行性的建议。

第四章

被试成绩的偏度与相关系数研究

本研究中的被试均为普通高等院校大学二年级英语专业学生。为了衡量学生的综合能力和英语水平，我们首先对被试的高考总成绩、高考英语成绩以及英语专业四级考试成绩进行偏度分析，研究其正态分布情况。然后，分别测算高考总成绩和英语成绩与英语专业四级考试成绩的相关系数，以便为后期的计算研究提供数据支撑。

第一节　偏度

偏度是对引用数据的对称性分析，通常分为三种情况：正偏度、无偏度和负偏度。用来衡量偏度的数值包括集中趋势量数（measures of central tendency）中的两个：中位数（median）与均值（mean）。

一般情况下，集中趋势量数包括众数（mode）、中位数与均值。三者都称为平均数。

众数指出现次数最多的数值。

中位数指整个数组的中心点，即上下各占50%的平衡点。奇数组的中心点是独立存在的某个数值，而偶数组的中心点则为中间两个数值的算数平均数。

均值也就是我们接触最多的算数平均数，即数组之和除以个数所得。

上述平均数中，众数用于分类的属性，便于区分不同类别。中位数和均值用于量化属性，用于定量分析。其中，中位数侧重的是个体，极值对其影响甚微。均值强调的是数值的中间点而非个体的中间点，所以对极值很敏感。

通过对中位数和均值的大小比较，我们可以获得偏度的概念。具体关系请见表4-1。

表4-1　　　　　　均值、中位数和偏度关系列表

分类	正偏度	无偏度	负偏度
均值	大	中	小
中位数	小	中	大
偏度（均值-中位数）	正数	零	负数
特征	左偏	正态	右偏

均值为算数平均值，即所有数值之和除以总个数。例如，5名被试的高考总成绩分别为400，605，490，421，480，那么其均值为（400+605+490+421+480）/5=479.2。在EXCEL表格中，其计算函数为"=AVERAGE（数值1：数值n）"（表4-2）。

表4-2　　　　　　平均数的EXCEL函数计算列表

编号	A
1	400
2	605
3	490
4	421
5	480
=AVERAGE（A1：A5）	479.2

中位数的计算分为两种情况：

（1）如果参与计算的个数为奇数，作为数据中点的中位数则为排序后的［（奇数+1）/2］所在的数。例如，上例中5个数值的大小

排序分别为400，421，480，490，605，那么，中位数则是［（5＋1）/2］＝3所在的数，即480为这5个数值的中位数。在EXCEL表格中，无须排序，其计算函数为"＝MEDIAN（数值1：数值n）"（表4－3）。

表4－3　　　　　奇数中位数的EXCEL函数计算列表

编号	A
1	400
2	605
3	490
4	421
5	480
＝MEDIAN（A1：A5）	480

（2）如果参与计算的个数为偶数，中位数的选定则需要进行计算，即取位于中间的两个偶数（［偶数/2］和［偶数/2］＋1）的平均数作为整组数据的中位数。例如，上例中的5个数据再添加591，经过排序后形成如下序列：400，421，480，490，591，605。其中位数为两个偶数（［6/2］和［6/2］＋1）的平均数，即（480＋490）/2＝485。在EXCEL表格中，无须排序，其计算函数为"＝MEDIAN（数值1：数值n）"（表4－4）。

表4－4　　　　　偶数中位数的EXCEL函数计算列表

编号	A
1	400
2	605
3	490
4	421
5	480
6	591
＝MEDIAN（A1：A6）	485

第四章 被试成绩的偏度与相关系数研究

上面两组数据（400，421，480，490，605 和 400，421，480，490，591，605）可进行偏度计算（表4-5）。

表4-5　　　　　　　　　　奇偶数组的偏度对比

分类	数据1	数据2
均值	479.2	497.83
中位数	480	485
偏度	-0.8	12.83
特征	负偏度（右偏）	正偏度（左偏）

以上两个数据分别讨论了正负偏度，如果中位数与均值恰好重合，则为正态分布，即为零偏度。通常情况下，理想状态才会得到零偏度的正态分布。

此外，数据的变异性研究也将列入我们的讨论范畴。主要涉及极差、标准差和方差。极差为数据组中的最大值与最小值之差。方差为标准差的平方。标准差的计算较为复杂，即数据组中每个数值与均值的偏差的平均数。变量有每个数值、均值和数值个数。在 EXCEL 中进行计算较为便捷，其函数为"=STDEV（数值1：数值n）"（表4-6）。

表4-6　　　　　　奇偶数组标准差的 EXCEL 函数计算列表

编号	A	编号	B
1	400	1	400
2	605	2	605
3	490	3	490
4	421	4	421
5	480	5	480
=STDEV（A1：A5）	80.00	6	591
		=STDEV（B1：B6）	84.88

从上面的计算可以看出，奇数组的标准差为80，偶数组的标准差为84.88。这说明在添加了新数值591之后，偶数组每个数值与均值

的平均距离增大了 4.88，即变异性出现了较大增幅，波动幅度也随之加大。

本研究共涉及 126 名被试，我们获取了被试的三个成绩，分别为其高考总成绩、高考英语成绩和英语专业四级成绩。下面我们将结合极差、标准差、均值、中位数来讨论三个成绩的偏度（作为标准差平方的方差在此不做讨论）。

一 被试高考总成绩偏度分析

高考总成绩代表的是被试的综合能力。在附录五（一）中，我们可以清楚地看到所有被试的高考总成绩（X 列）。按照前面的讨论，我们对该数据组进行了中位数和均值的计算，并测算出具体偏度。计算结果见表 4-7。

表 4-7　　　　　　　　高考总成绩偏度表

分类	高考总成绩
均值	557.29
中位数	570
偏度	-12.71
特征	负偏度（右偏）

被试组的高考总成绩最低 322，最高 605，极差为 605-322=283。该数组与均值 557.29 的平均距离（标准差）为 54.17，偏度特征为负偏度。

该数据说明虽然被试都同为大学英语二年级学生，但学生的生源地不同导致录取分数不同，因此出现了较大的极差和标准差。负偏度特征说明，大多数生源质量较好，中位数较均值偏高 12.71。

后期实验中，高考总分代表的学生综合实力的变异性特征将在测试中得到反映。

二 被试高考英语成绩偏度分析

高考英语成绩代表的是被试的语言能力。作为高考总分中重要的一个分项，英语成绩占有很高的比重。尤其对英语专业的学生来说，高考英语成绩在某种程度上预示着被试后期的英语学习所具有的发展潜力。我们在附录四（一）中对这些被试的高考英语成绩（X 列）进行了中位数和均值的计算。计算结果见表 4-8。

表 4-8　　　　　　　　　高考英语成绩偏度表

分类	高考英语成绩
均值	123.8
中位数	126.5
偏度	-2.7
特征	负偏度（右偏）

被试组的高考英语成绩最低 81，最高 142，极差为 142-81=61。该数组标准差为 12.13，偏度特征为负偏度，幅度为 -2.7。

该数据特征说明被试英语成绩变异性较大，极差和标准差的波动也较大。尽管高分学生和低分学生决定了极差的两端，但中位数 126.5 较均值 123.8 偏高，体现了整体被试具有良好的英语学习背景。这些特点为后期的英语花园幽径句的测试打下了基础。

三 被试英语专业四级成绩偏度分析

英语专业四级成绩代表的是被试进入高校学习一年后的语言测试成绩。被试从高中阶段进入大学，教学方法的转变必然带来被试学习方法的调整。在适应性学习过程中，被试的英语能力和成绩均会发生差异性波动。这种变化可通过附录四（一）中数值的计算得到体现。计算结果见表 4-9。

表 4-9　　　　　　　　英语专业四级成绩偏度表

分类	英语专业四级成绩
均值	63.25
中位数	63
偏度	0.25
特征	正偏度（左偏）

被试组的英语专业四级成绩（Y 列）最低 46，最高 81，极差为 81－46＝35。均值为 63.25，中位数为 63，偏度幅度 0.25，正偏度特征。被试组数据与均值的标准差为 7.88。相比较被试高考英语成绩的标准差 12.13 而言，英语专业四级成绩的标准差收窄，波动幅度变小，变异性减弱。

该数据说明，经过一年的英语专业学习，被试们取得了较好的成绩。相对于高考总成绩和高考英语成绩的负偏度来说，英语专业四级成绩呈现了正偏度，而且偏度幅度相对较小，近似于正态分布。这从一个侧面反映了低分学生经过一年的大学英语训练，在本次测试中有了较好表现，提升了均值，弱化了波动率。

英语专业四级成绩是本科二年级阶段被试英语能力的集中反映，具有很强的参照性。成绩高低与能力大小在一定程度上具有相关性。后期花园幽径句的测试中，不同能力被试的不同测试结果将直接影响语言实验效果。为便于以后将实验前移至学生入校的第一学期并进行跟踪测试，以及为后期的语言实验筛选能力相近的被试，我们需要测定英语专业四级成绩和一年前的高考总成绩（或高考英语成绩）的相关系数，为被试语言能力的发展提供预见性数据。

第二节　相关系数

简单相关系数（correlation coefficient）常用于解释两个变量之间的相关性，即一个变量的改变将如何影响另一个变量的变化。通常情况下，变量间的关系是线性的，相关性的值域范围在 -1 和 1 之间。如果两个变量变化方向相同，则为正相关。否则，为负相关。计算得出的相关系数的值越大，相关性就越强（不分正负）。

概述情况下，相关系数的值在 0.8—1.0，是极强相关；0.6—0.8，强相关；0.4—0.6，中度相关；0.2—0.4，弱相关；0—0.2，弱相关或无关。相关系数的正负号只表示方向而不是程度，所以，相关度的强弱无正负区分。

精确讨论相关系数时，需要引入决定系数的概念。决定系数是相关系数的平方，常用于精准确定两个变量共享方差的程度，即一个变量的方差可以被另一个变量的方差所解释的程度。例如，极强相关 0.8—1.0 中的决定系数为 0.64—1.0（或 64%—100%），这表明两个变量中共享的方差是 64%—100%，即一个变量的 64%—100% 方差可以被另一个变量的方差所解释。强相关 0.6—0.8 中的决定系数为 0.36—0.64（或 36%—64%）；中度相关 0.4—0.6 中的决定系数为 0.16—0.36（或 16%—36%）；弱相关 0.2—0.4 中的决定系数为 0.04—0.16（或 4%—16%）；弱相关或无关 0—0.2 中的决定系数为 0—0.04（或 0—4%）。

由上可知，决定系数是以相关系数为依托而存在的。因此，我们在讨论中主要涉及的是相关系数，具体计算中采用简单皮尔逊积矩相关系数公式。

一 简单皮尔逊积矩相关系数公式

简单皮尔逊积矩相关系数公式如下：

$$P_{X,Y} = \frac{N\sum XY - \sum X \sum Y}{\sqrt{N\sum X^2 - (\sum X)^2} \sqrt{N\sum Y^2 - (\sum Y)^2}} \quad (4-1)$$

式中：$P_{X,Y}$ 为变量 X 和 Y 的相关系数；

$N(n)$ 为样本的规模或数量；

X 为第一个变量的具体数值；

Y 为第二个变量的具体数值；

XY 为两个变量数值的乘积；
$\sum XY$ 为两个变量乘积之和；
$\sum X$ 为变量一的数值之和；
$\sum Y$ 为变量二的数值之和；
X^2 为变量一数值的平方；
Y^2 为变量二数值的平方；
$\sum X^2$ 为变量一数值平方之和；
$\sum Y^2$ 为变量二数值平方之和；
$(\sum X)^2$ 为变量一数值之和的平方；
$(\sum Y)^2$ 为变量二数值之和的平方。

在分别计算了各自的数值之后，我们可以将分项值代入公式并求得两个变量的相关系数。为便于理解，我们取附录四（一）中的前10项作为实例分析，具体见表4-10。

表4-10 高考英语成绩 X 与英语专业四级成绩 Y 的取样相关系数计算表

N	X	X^2	Y	Y^2	XY
1	95	9025	46	2116	4370
2	127	16129	47	2209	5969
3	109	11881	47	2209	5123
4	81	6561	48	2304	3888
5	102	10404	49	2401	4998
6	107	11449	50	2500	5350
7	92	8464	50	2500	4600
8	130	16900	50	2500	6500
9	118	13924	51	2601	6018
10	123	15129	51	2601	6273
sum	$\sum X=1084$	$\sum X^2=119866$	$\sum Y=489$	$\sum Y^2=23941$	$\sum XY=53089$

分子变量的计算：

$n\sum XY = 10 \times 53089 = 530890$

$\sum X \sum Y = 1084 \times 489 = 530076$

$n\sum XY - \sum X \sum Y = 530890 - 530076 = 814$

分母变量的计算：

$n\sum X^2 = 10 \times 119866 = 1198660$

$(\sum X)^2 = (1084)^2 = 1175056$

$n\sum X^2 - (\sum X)^2 = 1198660 - 1175056 = 23604$

$n\sum Y^2 = 10 \times 23941 = 239410$

$(\sum Y)^2 = (489)^2 = 239121$

$n\sum Y^2 - (\sum Y)^2 = 239410 - 239121 = 289$

$[n\sum X^2 - (\sum X)^2][n\sum Y^2 - (\sum Y)^2] = 23604 \times 289 = 6821556$

代入公式后所得：

$P_{X,Y} = 814/2611.81 = 0.31$

根据上面的公式可知，如果样本的规模较大或变量数值较大，相关系数公式的计算量是比较大的。EXCEL开发了可以进行相关系数计算的函数，大大减轻了计算的压力。如果不考虑计算过程，仅希望求得最后结果的话，采用函数计算将便捷很多。

二 相关系数的EXCEL函数计算

在EXCEL中，相关系数的求解函数为"=CORREL（数组1区域，数组2区域）"。仍以上面的数据为例，我们可以构建两个数组的相关系数的计算列表。具体请见表4-11。

表4-11　高考英语成绩X与英语专业四级成绩Y的取样相关系数函数计算表

N	X	Y
1	95	46
2	127	47

续表

N	X	Y
3	109	47
4	81	48
5	102	49
6	107	50
7	92	50
8	130	50
9	118	51
10	123	51
	= CORREL（X1：X10，Y1：Y10）	=0.31

比较公式计算结果和函数计算结果，我们可以看出两者是一致的。公式计算的逻辑性和层次性比较强，而函数计算简单快捷。在分析被试高考总成绩（以及英语成绩）与英语专业四级成绩的相关系数时，我们采用数据呈现清晰的公式计算法，便于读者进行验证。

三 相关系数的临界值

具体的相关系数需要与对应的临界值进行比对以检验该值的显著性。相关系数的计算中，数值结果比方向更重要。数值的大小表示的是相关的程度，而方向仅表示变化所呈现的一致性与否，即相同或相反。因此，将数值大小和方向性两个变量同时作为临界值的参数时，我们可以得到单侧检验和双侧检验两种情况下的临界值。

单侧检验首先设定方向变化。比如在前面的讨论中，如果我们预先设定高考英语成绩（X）与英语专业四级成绩（Y）呈现正相关（或负相关），那么这种检验就是单侧检验。

双侧检验不侧重方向变化。这种检验的无方向性只是陈述变量之间的关系性，而不讨论方向的制约性。对变量之间的变化不进行方向预测。

显著性水平的设定因人而异。在设置零假设的风险水平过程中，我们一般选择.01或.05。一般情况下，风险水平的高低与研究结果的意义没有直接关系。显著性水平是推论统计的关键，通常用于单一独立的零假设检验而非多元检验。有时候，我们得到的结果是高显著性的，却没有多少意义。与此相反，有时得到的有意义的结果却是低显著性的。

自由度 df（degrees of freedom）是样本规模的近似选定。对相关系数的检验统计量来说，自由度是计算过程中的配对数量 n-2。上例中，我们选定了 10 个取样，则 n=10，自由度 df=10-2=8。

临界值可以通过量表查阅。在确定了单/双侧检验，显著性水平（.01 或 .05）和自由度（df=8）之后，我们可以查阅量表得到相关系数的临界值，具体见表 4-12。

表 4-12　　自由度（df=8）的相关系数临界值量表

单侧检验			双侧检验		
df	.05	.01	df	.05	.01
8	.5494	.7155	8	.6319	.7646

通过比对临界值和计算结果值（0.31），我们可知：无论是单侧检验还是双侧检验，也无论是 .05 还是 .01 的显著性水平，计算结果值都小于临界值。也就是说，仅通过取样的前 10 个高考英语成绩（X）与英语专业四级成绩（Y）的相关系数计算，我们无法得出两者具有相关性的结论，更不涉及变化方向的选择。

上面的讨论仅是我们用于简单化的相关系数陈述，展现给读者一个较为简洁的计算和分析流程，并不代表我们的计算结论。通常情况下，取样的规模至少是 30 项，而我们为了讨论方便，随机取样只选择了附录四（一）中的前 10 项。所以，结论也只是便于读者理解的象征性解释。

下面的讨论是我们取样 126 个被试后进行的大规模计算分析，主要测定所选被试高考总成绩与英语专业四级成绩的相关系数，以及被试高考英语成绩与英语专业四级成绩的相关系数。

第三节 被试高考总成绩与英语专业
四级成绩的相关系数研究

英语专业四级考试（Test for English Majors-Band 4，TEM - 4）是每个英语专业学生必须参加的考试。其全称为"全国高校英语专业四级考试"，其推广的初衷是考查国内英语专业学生在听、说、读、写四个方面的能力。其目的是检查学生是否达到教学大纲要求，考核其对语法结构和词语用法的掌握程度。既关注综合能力，也侧重单项技能。自 1991 年首次实施至今，进行了多次改革。在确保试卷的信度方面，多采取多项选择题形式。在效度方面，写作及听写部分为主观试题，旨在测试学生灵活运用语言的能力。总体来说，英语专业四级成绩可用于分析被试的综合英语水平。

高考总成绩是测试学生包括英语能力在内的大学科的综合能力。该成绩是否以及在多大程度上与英语专业四级成绩相关，将在这里进行讨论。

被试高考总成绩和英语专业四级成绩所提供的详细数据见表 4-13，成绩列表请见附录五（一）。

表 4-13　高考总成绩和英语专业四级成绩数据列表

分类	高考总成绩	英语专业四级成绩
最大值	605.00	81.00
最小值	322.00	46.00
极差	283.00	35.00
中位数	570.00	63.00
均值	557.29	63.25
偏度	-12.71	0.25
标准差	54.17	7.88

上表中，我们可以看到 126 个被试组成的两个成绩组的详细数据，包括最大值、最小值、极差、中位数、均值、偏度和标准差。该列表呈现了被试数组的数据分布。

被试高考总成绩（X）和英语专业四级成绩（Y）的相关系数的计算，我们可参照前面的流程进行讨论，分项计算请见附录五（二）。

$n = 126$

$\sum X = 70218.1$

$\sum X^2 = 39498428.69$

$\sum Y = 7969$

$\sum Y^2 = 511773$

$n\sum XY = 562366980$

$\sum X \sum Y = 559568038.9$

$n\sum XY - \sum X \sum Y = 2798941.1$

$n\sum Y^2 = 64483398$

$(\sum Y)^2 = 63504961$

$n\sum X^2 = 4976802015$

$(\sum X)^2 = 4930581568$

$n\sum X^2 - (\sum X)^2 = 46220447.33$

$n\sum Y^2 - (\sum Y)^2 = 978437$

$\sum XY = 4463230$

$[n\sum X^2 - (\sum X)^2][n\sum Y^2 - (\sum Y)^2] = 4.52238E+13$

将以上数值代入相关系数的求证公式，可得到相关系数的值为 .42。

由此，我们可以进行临界值的设定并与计算值进行比对，以便确认该计算值是否具有显著性差异。

显著性水平设定为 .05。

自由度 $df = 126 - 2 = 124$。

方向性设定为无预测的双侧检验。

查阅相关系数的临界值量表可知，当 $df > 100$ 时，量表默认大样本规模的自由度与 df = 100 时一致，即具有无穷大的特性。临界值可以采用 df = 100 时的值，本例为 .1946。

比对计算值 .42 与临界值 .1946 可知，计算值远大于临界值。这说明在风险水平 .05 并且双侧检验情况下，126 个被试的高考总成绩和英语专业四级成绩的相关系数具有显著性差异（p < .05）。相关程度在 0.4—0.6，属于中度相关。其决定系数为 $(0.42)^2 = 0.1764$（或 17.64%）。具体计算与分析请见表 4-14。

表 4-14　高考总成绩和英语专业四级成绩的相关系数计算与分析

n	$\sum X$	$\sum X^2$	$\sum Y$	$\sum Y^2$
126	70218.1	39498428.69	7969	511773
$n\sum XY$	$\sum X \sum Y$	$n\sum XY - \sum X \sum Y$	$n\sum Y^2$	$(\sum Y)^2$
562366980	559568038.9	2798941.1	64483398	63504961
$n\sum X^2$	$(\sum X)^2$	$n\sum X^2 - (\sum X)^2$	$n\sum Y^2 - (\sum Y)^2$	$\sum XY$
4976802015	4930581568	46220447.33	978437	4463230
$[n\sum X^2 - (\sum X)^2][n\sum Y^2 - (\sum Y)^2]$			$r_{126-2} = .42$	
4.52238E+13			p < .05	

备注：在 .05 风险水平下，自由度无穷大（df > 100）时双侧临界值为 .1946

结论：高考总成绩与英语专业四级英语成绩具有中度相关性

通过上面的相关系数和决定系数的讨论，我们可以看出：高考总成绩与一年之后的英语专业四级成绩的相关度为中度，相关系数为 .42，共享方差为 17.64%。这说明具有较高高考总成绩的学生，他们高考总成绩的方差可以预测第二年英语专业四级成绩 17.64% 的方差。

高考总成绩作为学生综合能力的反映，具有较好的评估价值，但对英语单科的评估价值相对来说有些弱化。不少学生侧重点不在英语学习上，导致其英语成绩与高考总成绩不成正比。这种不对称性对非英语专业学生来说影响不大。但是，对于英语专业的学生来说，高考中的英语单科成绩的高低却预示着该生是否掌握了坚实的英语基础知识，对进入高校后的英语专业学习将起到极其关键的作用。由此，我们推断被试高考英语成绩应该与英语专业四级成绩的相关系数更大，相关度更高，两者共享的方差也应该具有更大比例。

第四节 被试高考英语成绩与英语专业四级成绩的相关系数研究

高考英语成绩与英语专业四级成绩均为必修成绩，分别代表被试高中阶段和大学初级阶段的英语水平。两个成绩都是评估英语教学质量不可或缺的部分。被试从高中进入大学，作为教学者，我们需要了解这两个成绩之间的相关程度以便于对班中不同高考成绩的学生分别进行侧重指导，帮助低分同学通过英语专业四级考试并获得学士学位（国家有规定，专四考试通过是获得英语专业学士学位的必备条件）。同样，作为测试者和计算者，我们也需要知道高考英语成绩有多大可能预测与其关联度很高的英语专业四级成绩。

被试高考英语成绩和英语专业四级成绩所提供的详细数据见表4–15，成绩列表请见附录四（一）。

表4–15 高考英语成绩和换算成绩与英语专业四级成绩数据列表

分类	原高考英语成绩	百分制换算后英语成绩	英语专业四级成绩
最大值	142.00	94.67	81.00
最小值	81.00	54	46.00
极差	61.00	40.67	35.00
中位数	126.50	84.33	63.00
均值	123.80	82.53	63.25
偏度	-2.70	-1.80	0.25
标准差	12.13	8.09	7.88

上表中，我们可以看到高考英语成绩提供了两份列表，第一列原高考成绩是150分制，第二列是将原成绩换算成百分制后得到的结

果。这样的换算是为了满足我们与专四成绩对比的需要。

最大值方面：换算后的高考英语成绩有学生获得了 94.67 的高分。相比较而言，专四成绩的最高分仅为 81。一方面说明：专四考试更专业，难度更大，学生较难获得高分。另一方面也说明：高考是选拔性考试，被试只有背水一战才有可能获得成功并进入高校学习；而专四考试仅仅是通过性考试，只要达到及格线就可以获得学士学位资格，所以在最高分方面动力略显不足。

最小值方面：换算后的高考英语成绩最小值为 54，英语专业四级成绩最小值为 46。我们把英语专业四级成绩低于 60 分（不含）的成绩排列如下，同时提供他们的高考英语成绩以便于对照（表 4-16）。

表 4-16 换算后高考英语成绩与英语专业四级低分成绩对比表

编号	换算后高考英语成绩	英语专业四级成绩
1	63.33	46
2	84.67	47
3	72.67	47
4	54.00	48
5	68.00	49
6	71.33	50
7	61.33	50
8	86.67	50
9	78.67	51
10	82.00	51
11	70.00	51
12	66.00	52
13	80.67	52
14	63.33	52
15	62.00	53
16	85.33	54
17	56.00	54

续表

编号	换算后高考英语成绩	英语专业四级成绩
18	74.67	54
19	79.33	55
20	79.33	56
21	66.67	56
22	82.67	56
23	81.33	56
24	80.00	56
25	86.00	56
26	78.00	56
27	87.33	56
28	82.00	56
29	62.67	57
30	88.00	57
31	78.67	58
32	85.33	58
33	82.67	58
34	60.67	58

从上表中可以看出，高考的最低分54分虽然不再是最低分，但其分数仍处于底部的48分。而专四中的最低分46分却是高考中的63.33分。尤其让人唏嘘的是高考中84.67分的英语高分学生却在专四中只拿到了47分。由此可见，高考英语成绩在某种程度上并不与专四成绩绝对相关，或者说不成因果关系。

在表4－15中的极差方面：换算后的高考英语成绩极差为40.67分，大于专四的35分。这说明经过一年的大学学习，被试间的成绩差异在逐渐缩小。

中位数方面：换算后的高考英语成绩中位数为84.33分，大于专四的63分。这种情况与专四试卷专业性较强得分不易，以及专四学生只求通过的考试心理有关。

均值方面：换算后成绩为 82.53，远大于专四的 63.25。分析与中位数差异类似。

偏度方面：专四成绩与换算后高考英语成绩呈现正负偏度的相互背离局面。前者为正偏 0.25，即均值较中位数大 0.25。后者为负偏 1.80，为右偏模式，均值小于中位数。

标准差方面：虽然两个英语成绩出现了不同的波动幅度，但相差不大。换算后高考英语成绩的波动在 8.09，略大于专四成绩波动幅度的 7.88。这体现了同组被试在不同考试中具有某种程度的一致性。

以上的讨论中，高考英语成绩的百分制换算提供了数据比对的便利。但在换算中牺牲了一部分数值。为了更精准地分析高考英语成绩与英语专四成绩的相关系数，下面在测算相关系数时，我们仍以原始的被试高考英语成绩作为测试数据。

我们可参照前面的流程进行相关系数讨论，分项计算请见附录四（二）①。

$n = 126$

$\sum X = 15599$

$\sum X^2 = 1949575$

$\sum Y = 7969$

$\sum Y^2 = 511773$

$n \sum XY = 125197506$

$\sum X \sum Y = 124308431$

$n \sum XY - \sum X \sum Y = 889075$

$n \sum Y^2 = 64483398$

$(\sum Y)^2 = 63504961$

$n \sum X^2 = 245646450$

---

① 分项讨论中，我们没有区分高考总成绩的代码，以及高考英语成绩的代码，都使用（X）表示。这种情况也出现在后面的讨论中。由于各种分析一般情况下都囿于分项，鲜有交叉，所以不会引起歧义和误解。因此，我们采用较少引用变量的简洁原则进行数据分析。

$(\sum X)^2 = 243328801$

$n\sum X^2 - (\sum X)^2 = 2317649$

$n\sum Y^2 - (\sum Y)^2 = 978437$

$\sum XY = 993631$

$[n\sum X^2 - (\sum X)^2][n\sum Y^2 - (\sum Y)^2] = 2.26767E+12$

将以上数值代入相关系数的求证公式，可得到相关系数的值为.59。

相关条件的设定中，显著性水平设定为.05，自由度 df = 126 - 2 = 124，方向性设定为无预测的双侧检验。

查阅相关系数的临界值量表可知，当 df > 100 时，量表默认大样本规模的自由度与 df = 100 时一致，即具有无穷大的特性。临界值可以采用 df = 100 时的值，本例为.1946。具体计算请见表 4 - 17。

表 4 - 17　高考英语成绩和英语专业四级成绩的相关系数计算与分析

n	$\sum X$	$\sum X^2$	$\sum Y$	$\sum Y^2$
126	15599	1949575	7969	511773
$n\sum XY$	$\sum X \sum Y$	$n\sum XY - \sum X\sum Y$	$n\sum Y^2$	$(\sum Y)^2$
125197506	124308431	889075	64483398	63504961
$n\sum X^2$	$(\sum X)^2$	$n\sum X^2 - (\sum X)^2$	$n\sum Y^2 - (\sum Y)^2$	$\sum XY$
245646450	243328801	2317649	978437	993631
$[n\sum X^2 - (\sum X)^2][n\sum Y^2 - (\sum Y)^2]$			$r_{126-2} = .59$	
2.26767E+12			$p < .05$	

备注：在.05 风险水平下，自由度无穷大（df > 100）时双侧临界值为.1946

结论：高考英语成绩与英语专业四级英语成绩具有强相关性

上表中可见，相关系数的计算值.59 大于临界值.1946。符合显著性差异的条件，即在风险水平.05 并且双侧检验情况下，高考英语成绩和英语专业四级成绩的相关系数具有显著性差异（p <.05）。

在相关程度的分析中，由于相关系数计算值为.59，近似于.60，相关程度在 0.6—0.8，属于强相关。其决定系数为 $(0.59)^2 =$

0.3481（或34.81%）。这说明高考英语成绩与英语专业四级成绩为强相关，相关系数为.59，共享方差为34.81%。高考英语成绩在预测英语专业四级成绩方面具有34.81%的方差优势。

在共享方差方面，高考总成绩与英语专业四级成绩共享17.64%，而高考英语成绩与英语专业四级成绩则共享34.81%。后者比前者的解释精准度高达近一倍。这个结果与我们先期的推断相一致。数据证明：被试高考英语成绩较高考总成绩更好地预测英语专业四级成绩，两个英语成绩的相关系数更大，相关度更高，两者共享的方差具有更大比例。

相关并不代表因果。高考英语成绩与英语专业四级成绩在共享34.81%方差之外，仍有65.19%的方差无法获得解释。这说明即使是强相关的两项，在相互联动方面也不具有绝对的一致性，特例随时存在。

本章小结

本章主要对代表被试综合能力的高考总成绩、代表单项能力的高考英语成绩，以及代表被试后期发展能力的英语专业四级成绩进行了偏度和相关系数的研究。

偏度方面，被试组的高考总成绩呈现右偏特征，均值小于中位数12.71。高考英语成绩同样呈现负偏度特征，其分布较狭，峰度较高，均值小于中位数2.7。英语专业四级成绩偏度为正偏度0.25，左偏而且近似于正态分布。三个偏度对比说明，高考总成绩较均值的偏离程度最高，数据分布最广，变异性最大。高考英语成绩的数据离散度次之。英语专业四级成绩变异性最小，数据分布最为集中，中位数近似落在均值左右，符合正态分布的特征。三个数据组对比中，英语专业四级成绩更适合作为后期研究的来源数据。

相关系数方面，高考总成绩与英语专业四级成绩呈现中度相关性，相关系数为.42，两者共享方差为17.64%。高考英语成绩与英语专业四级成绩呈现强相关性，相关系数为.59，两者共享方差为34.81%。高考英语成绩较高考总成绩与英语专业四级成绩具有更好的方差拟合，两个英语成绩的关联性更高。尽管如此，我们需要注意相关并不等于因果，共享方差外仍有大比例无法解释的未知因素的存在。

在确定了三个成绩中英语专业四级成绩更适合作为语言测试分类的数据来源之后，我们需要对被试进行语言统计和数据计算。在对这些被试进行测试前，我们还需要对花园幽径句测试进行目标设定。具体的研究方向包括两大类。

（1）同一被试组在不同的时间变量下，是否会产生类似的阅读效果？如果答案是肯定的，这些类似的阅读效果呈现什么特征？如果答案是否定的，那么不同的阅读效果之间有什么系统关联和差异？

（2）不同被试组对相同条件下的测试句阅读效果是否会形成组间差异？如果组间差异大于组内差异，呈现什么组别特征？如果组间差异小于组内差异，又能够得到什么样的结果？

对这两个大类的问题，我们将分别从非独立 t 检验和方差分析角度进行统计与计算分析。

第五章

花园幽径句阅读时间与效果的非独立 t 值研究

本研究中所引入的英语花园幽径句均摘自母语是英语的作者的文章，源于 SSCI 索引的国际期刊。为便于探讨中国英语学习者在解读这些英语花园幽径句过程中的认知变化，我们对这些英语花园幽径句增加了对照组，并将对照句进行了部分句法方面的调整，具体的 100 个句子请见附录一。

上一章我们讨论了被试的语言技能的相关系数研究，并以此分析了被试呈现层级性的英语水平。本章我们将讨论相同的被试在不同的阅读时间因素中的表现。

第一节 测试前准备

被试的基本情况介绍如下：

（1）普通高等学校大二学生，身体健康，裸眼视力或矫正视力正常。

（2）学生具有良好的英语阅读能力，有至少 7 年英语教育经历，并已经通过英语专业的第一年学习，具备英语专业四级水平。

（3）实验近期均无急性感染或服用过任何药物，对英语语料等实验数据具有良好认知。

（4）听从主试安排，并愿意参加语言测试实验，能保证实验的准确性和严肃性。

实验介绍：将同一组被试在限时 5 秒情况下阅读材料所得到的实验结果，与将阅读时间延长一倍至 10 秒时的结果进行非独立 t 检验研究，以检测被试对英语花园幽径句及对照句的理解是否受到了阅读时间的影响。

在花园幽径句的研究中，如果延长阅读时间，隐含行进错位效应的花园幽径句是否就可以得到有效解码，这具有一定的争论。我们将以该实验来研究证明时间因素对花园幽径句的影响。

测试方法介绍：

在统计数据前，我们需要对被试进行简短的测试介绍和培训，涉及测试的基本情况以及如何答题等。具体的介绍均以书面形式出现在测试单的上方。同时，我们将为被试进行讲解。具体的测试介绍和答题方式如下（仅以 10 秒测试为例，5 秒测试类推即可）。

下面测试中有 100 个英语句子，每个句子都将在屏幕上保留 10 秒时间，请根据自己的理解选择：−2，−1，0，+1，+2，并将结果（限一项）勾画在方框内。为缓解视疲劳，测试中每 10 个句子为一组，每组限时 100 秒，共计 10 组。每组完成后，都会有 10 秒间隔时间以便休息和放松。10 秒休息过后，页面将会翻转至下一组测试。测试最后一组的最后一个句子之后，屏幕将显示"Thank you"，表示整个测试结束。

测试打分标准如下：

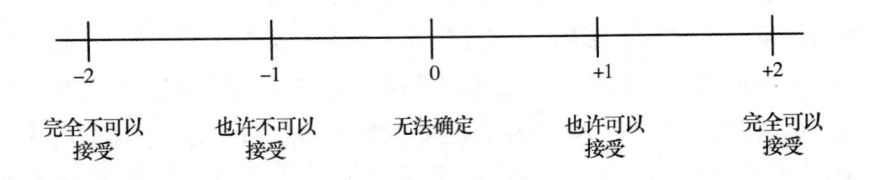

−2	−1	0	+1	+2
完全不可以接受	也许不可以接受	无法确定	也许可以接受	完全可以接受

示例如下：

例子 1：当屏幕出现句子 "The horse raced past the barn." 时，请

根据自己的理解选择 5 个选项中的一个（备注：此处是 +2），并在选中的选项前打钩。

　　S A：Result：□ -2；□ -1；□0；□ +1；√□ +2

　　例子 2：当屏幕出现句子"The horse past the barn."时，请根据自己的理解选择 5 个选项中的一个（备注：此处是 -2），并在选中的选项前打钩。

　　S B：Result：√□ -2；□ -1；□0；□ +1；□ +2

　　这两个句子使用了标度上的最高值和最低值（即 +2 和 -2），请在适当的时候使用中间的值。"0"表示你无法确定句子是否可以接受。

　　完成所有句子的限时判断需要 15—25 分钟。

　　非常感谢您对这个实验的支持与合作。

第二节　非独立 t 检验

　　非独立 t 检验，即非独立均值检验，主要用于测试相同的群体在不同的条件下所进行的相同的研究。其主要目的在于研究条件的改变是否会带来该群体的显著性变化。

　　本研究中的非独立 t 检验，将对 126 个被试进行两次测试，所有条件不变，仅改变阅读时间的长短，以期带来被试反应时 RT（reaction time）的变化。为了避免先后两次测试变量发生变化，我们将两次测试间隔控制在一个月。一般情况下，被试花园幽径句语言解读能力的调整在一个月内较难发生显著性提升或下降，所以，被试的测试能力便不会受到较大影响。

　　在测试之初，我们预测延长阅读时间会有两种情况出现：（1）随着阅读时间的延长，被试的解读能力发生显著性变化（提升或下降），其敏感值 t 将落在拒绝零假设的值域范围之外，即两次测试结果具有显著性差异。结论是时间因素将对阅读效果起到差异性的作用。（2）被试的测试数据没有随着阅读时间的加倍增加发生较明显变化，非独立 t 值小于显著性差异所需的临界值。这种小范围的 t 值波动很可能是抽样误差或者组内的某些变化所致，并非时间变量所致。结论是阅读效果不会因为阅读时间的调整发生显著性变化。

一　非独立 t 检验的公式测定法

非独立 t 检验是同一群体两次测试的均值比较，核心在于分析不同数值之间的差异。其公式如下：

$$t = \frac{\sum D}{\sqrt{\frac{n \sum D^2 - (\sum D)^2}{n-1}}} \quad (5-1)$$

式中：t 为非独立 t 检验值；

$\sum D$ 为两次测试差异的总和；

$\sum D^2$ 为两次测试差异平方的总和；

n 为参与两次测试的被试的数量。

我们在间隔一个月的情况下对 126 个被试进行了 100 个花园幽径句和对照句（样例请见附录一）的测试。每个句子都获得了 5 秒和 10 秒的测试成绩。具体的 t 检验的过程数据及结果请见附录二。为便于读者理解，我们采用第一个句子的数据进行详细分析，其他 99 个句子的分析可以此进行类推。

测试句 S1：Because he always jogs a mile seems a short distance to him.

测试句 S1 的 5 秒和 10 秒反应时的评分及差异值请见表 5-1。

表 5-1　测试句 S1 的 5 秒和 10 秒反应时的评分及差异值

Number	5S1（X）	10S1（X）	D	D²
1	0	1	-1	1
2	-2	-2	0	0
3	1	1	0	0

续表

Number	5S1（X）	10S1（X）	D	D²
4	1	-1	2	4
5	2	-2	4	16
6	2	1	1	1
7	1	0	1	1
8	2	-2	4	16
9	0	2	-2	4
10	2	2	0	0
11	1	1	0	0
12	0	-2	2	4
13	2	-2	4	16
14	1	1	0	0
15	-1	-2	1	1
16	0	-2	2	4
17	-1	0	-1	1
18	-2	-2	0	0
19	0	0	0	0
20	1	2	-1	1
21	-2	-2	0	0
22	1	-2	3	9
23	1	-1	2	4
24	1	-2	3	9
25	0	-2	2	4
26	0	1	-1	1
27	0	-2	2	4
28	0	-2	2	4
29	-1	2	-3	9
30	1	-2	3	9
31	0	0	0	0
32	0	0	0	0
33	2	2	0	0

第五章 花园幽径句阅读时间与效果的非独立 t 值研究

续表

Number	5S1（X）	10S1（X）	D	D^2
34	0	0	0	0
35	2	-2	4	16
36	0	-2	2	4
37	0	-1	1	1
38	2	2	0	0
39	2	0	2	4
40	-2	2	-4	16
41	-2	-2	0	0
42	2	1	1	1
43	0	-1	1	1
44	1	-1	2	4
45	2	-2	4	16
46	1	-2	3	9
47	-1	1	-2	4
48	0	-2	2	4
49	0	-2	2	4
50	-2	-2	0	0
51	2	-2	4	16
52	2	2	0	0
53	-1	-2	1	1
54	-1	-2	1	1
55	0	2	-2	4
56	2	1	1	1
57	2	-2	4	16
58	-2	2	-4	16
59	0	-2	2	4
60	0	-2	2	4
61	-2	1	-3	9
62	2	0	2	4
63	2	1	1	1

续表

Number	5S1（X）	10S1（X）	D	D²
64	-2	-2	0	0
65	1	1	0	0
66	-2	-2	0	0
67	0	1	-1	1
68	1	-2	3	9
69	0	-2	2	4
70	1	0	1	1
71	-2	2	-4	16
72	0	2	-2	4
73	1	1	0	0
74	0	-2	2	4
75	0	-1	1	1
76	-2	-2	0	0
77	0	-2	2	4
78	2	1	1	1
79	-2	1	-3	9
80	2	-2	4	16
81	1	-2	3	9
82	0	-2	2	4
83	1	-2	3	9
84	0	-2	2	4
85	2	2	0	0
86	0	-2	2	4
87	-2	-2	0	0
88	-1	-2	1	1
89	0	-2	2	4
90	0	-2	2	4
91	-2	-2	0	0
92	0	1	-1	1
93	0	0	0	0

第五章 花园幽径句阅读时间与效果的非独立 t 值研究

续表

Number	5S1（X）	10S1（X）	D	D²
94	-2	2	-4	16
95	1	2	-1	1
96	0	-2	2	4
97	-2	-2	0	0
98	0	0	0	0
99	-2	-2	0	0
100	-2	-2	0	0
101	0	1	-1	1
102	-1	-1	0	0
103	1	-2	3	9
104	1	2	-1	1
105	-2	-2	0	0
106	0	2	-2	4
107	0	-2	2	4
108	-2	-2	0	0
109	-1	0	-1	1
110	2	2	0	0
111	0	-2	2	4
112	-1	2	-3	9
113	1	-2	3	9
114	0	-2	2	4
115	-1	-2	1	1
116	1	-2	3	9
117	-2	-2	0	0
118	2	2	0	0
119	-2	-2	0	0
120	-2	-2	0	0
121	-2	-2	0	0
122	2	2	0	0
123	-2	2	-4	16
124	-2	-2	0	0
125	2	-2	4	16
126	-1	2	-3	9

测试句 S1 的 5 秒和 10 秒反应时的非独立 t 检验值见表 5-2。

表 5-2　测试句 S1 的 5 秒和 10 秒反应时的非独立 t 检验值

n	126
ΣD	80
ΣD^2	512
$(\Sigma D)^2$	6400
$n * \Sigma D^2$	64512
$n * \Sigma D^2 - (\Sigma D)^2$	58112
$[n * \Sigma D^2 - (\Sigma D)^2]/125$	464.90
SQRT $\{[n * \Sigma D^2 - (\Sigma D)^2]/125\}$	21.56
t	3.71

.05 风险水平下，df = 126 - 1，t 临界值分别为 1.96（双侧无向）和 1.645（单侧有向）

由以上分析可知，测试句 S1 的非独立 t 检验值为 3.71，远远大于单侧有方向或者双侧无方向的 t 临界值。

从双侧无方向角度来说，该结果证明 126 个被试在一个月的时间里，对同一个句子的理解出现了显著性差异。由于我们的测试其他所有的变量都没有发生变化，只有对提供给被试的阅读反应时间进行了系统调整，所以，我们可以得出结论：该花园幽径句"Because he always jogs a mile seems a short distance to him"的解码受到时间因素的影响而产生了系统性差异，即阅读时间的调整引发了解码效果的差异。

从单侧有方向角度来说，该结果证明了随着被试反应时间的延长（从 5 秒延长至 10 秒），被试可以产生较好的阅读效果，即长时阅读将优于短时阅读，这在某种程度上揭示了字斟句酌的重要性。因此，同样条件下，被试可以有更充足的时间考虑句式的变化，从而得出更正确的答案。

以上是我们采用公式方法进行的非独立 t 检验测定，其计算过程逻辑性强、清晰明了。其缺点在于计算量较大，变量需要多次计算，如果在计算过程中出现失误，将会导致整个计算前功尽弃。所以，对于想了解计算过程和思路的分析来说，这种方法较为合适。但当我们想尽快对两次测试进行配对均值检验，并得出两者究竟是否具有显著性差异的时候，该公式法将不具有选择优势。而且，在得出 t 值后，我们还需要对比量表的临界值进行分析，才能决定是否具有显著性差异。

是否有简化的便捷测算方法可以帮助我们快速了解 t 值并做出结果测定呢？在 EXCEL 表格中，有一个内嵌函数 TTEST，可以满足我们这个要求，实现一键测定。这种函数方法与公式法具有很大的不同。其主要体现在显著性 sig（significance）值的得到和分析上。

二　非独立 t 检验的 EXCEL 函数测定法

在 EXCEL 表格中，有一个计算 t 值的函数 TTEST，它主要用于测定单尾（或双尾）、非独立（或独立）t 值的概率值。这里我们可以看出与公式法的不同。

在公式法中，我们得到的结果是 t 值，而在函数方法中得到的却是概率值，即 sig 值。两者有着较大的不同，具体体现在以下两方面。

（1）公式 t 值只是我们计算的中间过程，最后需要与临界值对比才能知道是否具有显著性差异。

（2）函数概率值是计算的终极结果，通过该值我们可以直接得出两次非独立的检验是否具有显著性。所以说，该概率值更具有直观性。

EXCEL 函数 TTEST 的概率值默认测试前提是两组数据（独立或非独立）均值相同。如果得出的值与 .05 的概率水平相比较大，即 $p > .05$，则表示该值落在 95% 概率的区域，两组数据是没有区分度的。如果概率值与 .05 的概率水平相比较小，即 $p < .05$，则表示该值落在 5% 概率区间。由于 5% 概率在统计学中往往作为极限区间出现，如果值落在这个区间通常将被认为可能性很小。所以，当 $p < .05$ 出现时，我们就推断两组数据相等（前提设定它们均值相等）的可能性是不存在的，换句话说，两组数据是有显著性差异的。

概率水平5%在正态分布曲线中，作为统计学研究的临界值有其坚实的计算基础。请见图5-1所示的正态分布曲线中的数值分布图。

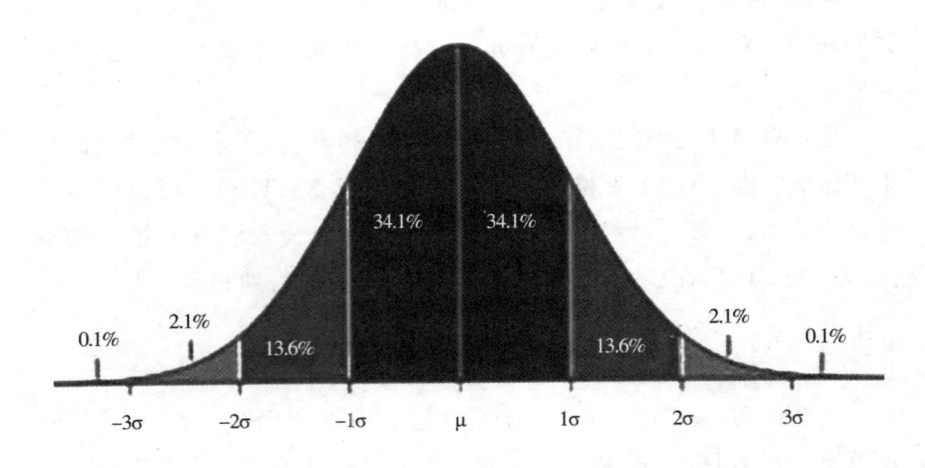

图5-1　正态分布曲线中的数值分布图

在前面的偏度分析中，我们曾经分析过无偏度定义，即均值与中位数相等的曲线。正态分布曲线的定义与此有些类似，除了均值与中位数还需要涉及众数。简单地说，正态分布曲线是三个数（众数，中位数，均值）相等合一的曲线，它们都落在整个曲线的同一点上。正态分布是无偏度分布，最高的波峰只有一个，就是三数合一的那个点，而且波峰正好处于整个图形的中间位置。以该中心线为轴，两边是呈现对称图形的，类似钟的形状，因此，正态分布的曲线也称为钟形曲线。

从正态分布曲线图可以看出，两侧线与横轴渐近但不相交。从概率角度说，两侧线的渐近性表明存在非常大和非常小的极值，而且极值出现的可能微乎其微。图形中表示的百分比是出现概率比例，笼统说就是大多数事件出现概率分布在正态分布图的中间，极端少的事件出现概率分布在图形两边。具体的概率比例涉及标准差的差异。

标准差（standard deviation，SD）是三个变异性量数（极差、标准差和方差）中重要的一个，是标准化了的与均值的偏差，表示与均值的平均距离。标准差的大小与数据点分布和均值的平均距离大小成正比。通常来说，我们研究的标准差都是无偏估计的，与其相关的平均绝对偏差和有偏估计不在讨论之列。

在偏度分析时，我们对标准差的 EXCEL 函数 STDEV 的计算有过详细分析，其函数表达式为 STDEV（number1，number2，…）。现在，我们对标准差的公式和计算过程进行解读，以便于为正态分布曲线中基于标准差的概率分析提供理论支撑。

标准差公式如下：

$$s = \sqrt{\frac{\sum (x - \bar{x})^2}{n - 1}} \quad (5-2)$$

式中：s 为标准差；

$\sum$ 为累加符号；

x 为具体的测试值；

$\bar{x}$ 为所有测试值的均值；

n 为样本规模。

标准差公式表示：每一个测试数值与均值之差的平方之后再取和，所得的值除以样本规模（减去1），最后求得的平方根即为标准差。我们以附录四（一）中前10个被试的高考英语成绩为例，进行标准差公式计算分析，见表5-3（为了表示方便，我们把表格中均值的符号改换成 X′）。

表 5-3　　　　　　取样测算值的标准差计算表

N	X	X′	X - X′	(X - X′)²
1	95	109	-14	196
2	127	109	18	324
3	109	109	0	0
4	81	109	-28	784

续表

N	X	X′	X − X′	(X − X′)²
5	102	109	−7	49
6	107	109	−2	4
7	92	109	−17	289
8	130	109	21	441
9	118	109	9	81
10	123	109	14	196
∑ (X − X′)² = 2364				n − 1 = 9
∑ (X − X′)²/(n − 1) = 262.67				s = 16.21
STDEV (X1：X10) = 16.20				

从上表的计算可以看出，公式法得到的标准差为 16.21，而通过 EXCEL 函数 STDEV 计算的标准差为 16.20，两者微小的差异来源于系统偏差，不影响我们的分析。所以，两者近似相等。公式法和函数法取得了相同的计算结果。意义分析方面：该数值表示取样的这 10 个高考英语成绩与其均值的平均距离为 16.20，即每个数值与均值的标准化了的平均距离是 16.20。此数值是一个标准差的数值。那么，两个标准差的数值则为 16.20 × 2 = 32.4，三个标准差的数值则为 16.20 × 3 = 48.6。在我们明确了标准差的计算过程之后，便可以较为便捷地分析正态分布曲线中的概率值。

标准差个数与正态分布曲线概率密切相关。在经过测算的正态分布曲线中，关于均值和标准差的一个规律是：对于任何钟形曲线上的数值来说，其分布秉承以下规律。

（1）近乎 100% 的数值均落在（均值 − 3 个标准差，均值 + 3 个标准差）的曲线范围内。我们以上面的样例为例，正态分布情况下 10 个高考成绩必然落在（109 − 48.6，109 + 48.6）的范围内，即 60.4 < Y < 157.6。以此可知，对于该例来说，两端的极值则分别为 60.4 和 157.6。

（2）近乎 34.1%（单侧）的数值落在（均值 − 1 个标准差，均

值 +1 个标准差）的曲线范围内。我们以上面的样例为例，正态分布情况下 10 个高考成绩中 68.2%（双侧）的数值必然落在（109 − 16.20，109 + 16.20）的范围内，即 92.8 < Y < 125.2。这说明，68.2% 的大部分数值被涵括在 92.8 < Y < 125.2 的范围内。

（3）近乎 13.6%（单侧）的数值落在 [（均值 − 2 个标准差）< Y <（均值 − 1 个标准差），（均值 + 1 个标准差）< Y′ <（均值 + 2 个标准差）] 的曲线范围内。我们以上面的样例为例，正态分布情况下 10 个高考成绩中 27.2%（双侧）的数值落在 [（109 − 32.4）< Y <（109 − 16.2），（109 + 16.2）< Y′ <（109 + 32.4）] 的范围内，即（76.6 < Y < 92.8，125.2 < Y′ < 141.4）。

（4）近乎 2.1%（单侧）的数值落在 [（均值 − 3 个标准差）< Y <（均值 − 2 个标准差），（均值 + 2 个标准差）< Y′ <（均值 + 3 个标准差）] 的曲线范围内。我们以上面的样例为例，正态分布情况下 10 个高考成绩中 4.2%（双侧）的数值落在 [（109 − 48.6）< Y <（109 − 32.4），（109 + 32.4）< Y′ <（109 + 48.6）] 的范围内，即（60.4 < Y < 76.6，141.4 < Y′ < 157.6）。

（5）三个标准差之外的数值占比相当低，约 0.1%（单侧）。通常情况下，我们对此忽略不计。

请注意上面规律的讨论中，关注的是均值与标准差的个数，即均值之外（或之内）的标准差的个数。这个规律是超标准差数值的，不论标准差的数值是多少，该规律均成立。

再举例来说，如果一个标准差的数值为 10，那么两个标准差的数值则为 20，三个标准差的数值则为 30。假定均值为 100。则该正态分布曲线中（双侧），大概率的分析用到的是一个标准差距离，即 90 至 100 和 100 至 110 的数值约为 68.2%。次概率的分析用到的是一个和两个标准差距离，即 80 至 90 和 110 至 120 的数值约为 27.2%。小概率的分析用到两个和三个标准差的距离，即 70 至 80 和 120 至 130 的数值约为 4.2%。极值概率在 0.3% — 0.4%，可以忽略不计。

从概率水平来看，大概率 68.2% 和次概率 27.2% 之和约是

95.4%。小概率和极值概率约为4.6%。四舍五入,前者约为95%,后者约为5%。由此我们可以推断:

(1) 如果在测算时,出现概率比5%大（$p > .05$）,则这种情况出现的可行性是落在95%之内范围的,是经常的、大众的、不显著的、没有区分度的,即无显著性差异。

(2) 如果在测算时,出现概率比5%小（$p < .05$）,则这种情况出现的可行性是落在95%之外范围的,是偶然的、鲜见的、显著的、有区分度的,即具有显著性差异。

(3) 因此,如果概率水平 $p > .05$ 则表示结果无显著性差异,没有效果或效果不明显。相反,如果得到的概率水平 $p < .05$ 则证明效果显著。该分析结果将用于非独立t检验的函数测定分析。

EXCEL中t检验的TTEST函数法可帮助我们快速测定非独立(或独立)t检验的概率水平。

在EXCEL中,TTEST函数的语法表达式为TTEST（array1, array2, tails, type）,用于判断两个样本(独立t检验)或者同一个样本的两次测试(非独立t检验)是否来自两个具有相同均值的总体,即看两者是否具有显著性差异。

参数array1和array2分别代表的是两个数据集。

参数tails用来表明分布曲线的尾数。共涉及两种情况的尾数:如果tails = 1,该函数为单尾分布,即单侧有向；如果tails = 2,该函数为双尾分布,即双侧无向。

参数type是t检验的分类。(1) 非独立t检验:如果type = 1,该t检验为非独立的,即配对t检验,同一组被试进行两次测试的检验。(2) 独立t检验:如果type = 2,该t检验为独立的等方差双样本检验,即首先是两组被试相互独立而不是同一组,而且是在经过对两组被试进行方差分析之后得出不具有显著性差异的结论时才使用。(3) 独立t检验:如果type = 3,该t检验为独立的异方差双样本检验,即两个不关联的独立组在组间方差分析结果显示为具有显著性差异时使用。

第五章　花园幽径句阅读时间与效果的非独立 t 值研究

参数 type 的分类中涉及的后两个选项与组间方差分析密切相关，我们后面的章节会有讨论。由于我们这里的分析是同一组被试两次测试的结果对比，属于非独立（配对）t 检验，所以，采用 type = 1 的参数设定。

我们仍以测试句 S1 在 5 秒和 10 秒反应时的被试评分为例，分析 TTEST 函数的概率（表 5 – 4）。

表 5 – 4　测试句 S1 在 5 秒和 10 秒反应时的 TTEST 函数概率

Number	A（5S1）	B（10S1）	Number	A（5S1）	B（10S1）
1	0	1	64	−2	−2
2	−2	−2	65	1	1
3	1	1	66	−2	−2
4	1	−1	67	0	1
5	2	−2	68	1	−2
6	2	1	69	0	−2
7	1	0	70	1	0
8	2	−2	71	−2	2
9	0	2	72	0	2
10	2	2	73	1	1
11	1	1	74	0	−2
12	0	−2	75	0	−1
13	2	−2	76	−2	−2
14	1	1	77	0	−2
15	−1	−2	78	2	1
16	0	−2	79	−2	1
17	−1	0	80	2	−2
18	−2	−2	81	1	−2
19	0	0	82	0	−2
20	1	2	83	1	−2
21	−2	−2	84	0	−2
22	1	−2	85	2	2

续表

Number	A (5S1)	B (10S1)	Number	A (5S1)	B (10S1)
23	1	-1	86	0	-2
24	1	-2	87	-2	-2
25	0	-2	88	-1	-2
26	0	1	89	0	-2
27	0	-2	90	0	-2
28	0	-2	91	-2	-2
29	-1	2	92	0	1
30	1	-2	93	0	0
31	0	0	94	-2	2
32	0	0	95	1	2
33	2	2	96	0	-2
34	0	0	97	-2	-2
35	2	-2	98	0	0
36	0	-2	99	-2	-2
37	0	-1	100	-2	-2
38	2	2	101	0	1
39	2	0	102	-1	-1
40	-2	2	103	1	-2
41	-2	-2	104	1	2
42	2	1	105	-2	-2
43	0	-1	106	0	2
44	1	-1	107	0	-2
45	2	-2	108	-2	-2
46	1	-2	109	-1	0
47	-1	1	110	2	2
48	0	-2	111	0	-2
49	0	-2	112	-1	2
50	-2	-2	113	1	-2
51	2	-2	114	0	-2
52	2	2	115	-1	-2

续表

Number	A (5S1)	B (10S1)	Number	A (5S1)	B (10S1)
53	-1	-2	116	1	-2
54	-1	-2	117	-2	-2
55	0	2	118	2	2
56	2	1	119	-2	-2
57	2	-2	120	-2	-2
58	-2	2	121	-2	-2
59	0	2	122	2	2
60	0	-2	123	-2	2
61	-2	1	124	-2	-2
62	2	0	125	2	-2
63	2	1	126	-1	2

TTEST（A1：A126，B1：B126，1，1）= 0.000155065，单侧有向 sig = 0.0001 < 0.05

TTEST（A1：A126，B1：B126，2，1）= 0.000310129，双侧无向 sig = 0.0003 < 0.05

结论：无论是单侧有向还是双侧无向，非独立 t 检验的概率均为 $p < .05$，说明反应时从 5 秒延长到 10 秒后，被试解码效果产生显著性差异

TTEST 函数得到的值直接是 sig（significance）值，其结果可以直接与概率 $p = .05$ 进行比较分析，大于则不具有显著性差异，小于则相反，较为便捷。前面我们用公式法计算得到的 t 值只是 sig 值计算的中间过程。在计算 t 值之后，我们还需要查表并与临界值进行比对才能决定是否具有显著性差异。这两种方法均可用于我们对非独立 t 检验进行分析。从上面两者的结果来看，结论是一致的：反应时从 5 秒增加到 10 秒，被试阅读效果得到极大改善，两次测试结果具有显著性差异。

以上是我们对测试句 S1 进行的示例性研究，其他句子的研究可以此类推。下面我们将根据附录二"阅读时间与效果的非独立 t 值测试"表中的 t 值结果进行系统性分析，研究是否所有的花园幽径句或对照句都会随着阅读时间的延长产生如同 S1 一样的差异性效果。

第三节　非独立 t 值研究

对测试句 S1 的研究发现，被试在不同的阅读时间下选择了不同的阅读答案，形成了不同的具有显著性差异的阅读效果。是否这种研究结果适用于所有句子？如果适用，适用比例是多少？如果不适用，差异是多少？请见我们统计的所有测试句的 t 值列表和相应的 sig 值（表 5-5）。

表 5-5　测试句 5 秒和 10 秒反应时的 t 值和 sig 值列表

Number	t	sig（1tail）	sig（2tails）	p
S1	3.71	0.0002	0.0003	A
S2	-6.82	0.0000	0.0000	A
S3	2.78	0.0031	0.0063	A
S4	-0.13	0.4477	0.8954	B
S5	1.08	0.1419	0.2837	B
S6	-4.71	0.0000	0.0000	A
S7	-2.95	0.0019	0.0038	A
S8	-2.80	0.0030	0.0060	A
S9	-0.04	0.4833	0.9665	B
S10	3.85	0.0001	0.0002	A
S11	0.19	0.4241	0.8483	B
S12	1.40	0.0821	0.1643	B
S13	5.48	0.0000	0.0000	A
S14	1.97	0.0257	0.0515	B
S15	-2.39	0.0093	0.0186	A
S16	0.24	0.4041	0.8081	B
S17	-0.59	0.2785	0.5569	B
S18	-3.11	0.0012	0.0023	A
S19	-3.66	0.0002	0.0004	A
S20	-1.69	0.0466	0.0932	B

续表

Number	t	sig（1tail）	sig（2tails）	p
S21	0.98	0.1634	0.3268	B
S22	0.40	0.3439	0.6877	B
S23	0.92	0.1803	0.3605	B
S24	−0.90	0.1844	0.3688	B
S25	−0.34	0.3679	0.7358	B
S26	2.59	0.0054	0.0108	A
S27	2.39	0.0091	0.0182	A
S28	4.39	0.0000	0.0000	A
S29	−3.38	0.0005	0.0010	A
S30	−0.28	0.3900	0.7801	B
S31	−1.78	0.0385	0.0769	B
S32	0.79	0.2164	0.4327	B
S33	3.70	0.0002	0.0003	A
S34	1.23	0.1098	0.2197	B
S35	−0.52	0.3007	0.6014	B
S36	0.31	0.3788	0.7576	B
S37	1.07	0.1435	0.2870	B
S38	−2.80	0.0029	0.0059	A
S39	−3.44	0.0004	0.0008	A
S40	−3.66	0.0002	0.0004	A
S41	−4.12	0.0000	0.0001	A
S42	−2.76	0.0033	0.0066	A
S43	−3.07	0.0013	0.0026	A
S44	−0.23	0.4098	0.8196	B
S45	−3.27	0.0007	0.0014	A
S46	−2.32	0.0109	0.0218	A
S47	−0.20	0.4222	0.8443	B
S48	−2.76	0.0033	0.0066	A
S49	1.96	0.0263	0.0526	B
S50	2.58	0.0056	0.0111	A

续表

Number	t	sig (1tail)	sig (2tails)	p
S51	-2.06	0.0206	0.0411	A
S52	-2.56	0.0058	0.0116	A
S53	-0.26	0.3991	0.7982	B
S54	0.40	0.3465	0.6930	B
S55	2.02	0.0226	0.0452	A
S56	-2.78	0.0032	0.0063	A
S57	1.27	0.1034	0.2069	B
S58	-3.69	0.0002	0.0003	A
S59	-2.41	0.0088	0.0175	A
S60	-1.09	0.1396	0.2792	B
S61	-4.12	0.0000	0.0001	A
S62	-3.57	0.0003	0.0005	A
S63	-3.28	0.0007	0.0013	A
S64	1.34	0.0908	0.1816	B
S65	-2.37	0.0097	0.0194	A
S66	1.78	0.0387	0.0775	B
S67	-3.04	0.0014	0.0029	A
S68	-1.48	0.0704	0.1407	B
S69	0.59	0.2768	0.5536	B
S70	-1.55	0.0621	0.1243	B
S71	-2.42	0.0002	0.0003	A
S72	1.58	0.0587	0.1175	B
S73	-0.68	0.2499	0.4997	B
S74	0.59	0.2768	0.5536	B
S75	-1.21	0.1148	0.2296	B
S76	-4.33	0.0000	0.0000	A
S77	0.86	0.1953	0.3906	B
S78	-4.71	0.0000	0.0000	A
S79	-0.10	0.4611	0.9222	B
S80	-3.65	0.0002	0.0004	A

第五章　花园幽径句阅读时间与效果的非独立 t 值研究

续表

Number	t	sig（1tail）	sig（2tails）	p
S81	3.49	0.0003	0.0007	A
S82	3.05	0.0014	0.0028	A
S83	-1.15	0.1265	0.2529	B
S84	-3.85	0.0001	0.0002	A
S85	-0.61	0.2718	0.5437	B
S86	-0.33	0.3728	0.7456	B
S87	-2.32	0.0111	0.0221	A
S88	5.04	0.0000	0.0000	A
S89	-2.89	0.0023	0.0046	A
S90	-3.90	0.0001	0.0002	A
S91	-0.13	0.4488	0.8976	B
S92	-1.18	0.1196	0.2393	B
S93	0.26	0.3965	0.7931	B
S94	-1.28	0.1018	0.2037	B
S95	1.77	0.0400	0.0799	B
S96	-3.10	0.0012	0.0024	A
S97	-1.25	0.1061	0.2122	B
S98	2.99	0.0017	0.0033	A
S99	-2.14	0.0171	0.0342	A
S100	0.22	0.4123	0.8246	B

备注1：.05 风险水平下，df = 126 - 1，非独立 t 临界值分别为 1.96（双侧无向）和 1.645（单侧有向）

备注2：sig < .05，p < .05，具有显著性差异；sig > .05，p > .05，不具有显著性差异

备注3：以双侧无向 sig 为标准，p < .05 标识为 A 类；p > .05 标识为 B 类

　　在上表的数值中我们可以发现，在非独立 t 检验下并不是所有的测试句都呈现显著性差异。我们将显著性差异项（p < .05）标为 A，将非显著性差异项（p > .05）标为 B。

　　为什么被试在反应时从 5 秒延长到 10 秒后，对部分测试句的理解产生了迥异的阅读效果，呈现了显著性差异变化？以及为什么对部分测试句而言，阅读效果对反应时调整并不敏感？我们将分别予以

讨论。

一 非独立 t 检验下显著性差异测试句分析

反应时延长导致的阅读效果差异性变化涉及二次解码和错位。被试在 5 秒的反应时背景下，需要对测试句进行快速阅读并给出阅读效果评分。如下的三个主要条件将影响被试的评分。

（1）测试句的难度。从提供的测试材料角度来说，如果测试句的结构较复杂，被试难以在短时间完成对句子结构的理解，势必造成被试解码效果的偏差。一般来说，越复杂的句子结构，需要的平均解码时间就越长。如果实验提供的反应时短于这个基本的解码时间，将会给阅读带来障碍。

（2）被试的阅读能力高低。从被试的阅读能力来说，如果被试的阅读量较小，对测试材料较为生疏，甚至对测试句中提供的英语单词都很生疏，那么其提供的阅读效果评分将具有随机性。通常情况下，被试阅读量越大，阅读能力越强，其整合和理解阅读材料的能力也就越突出。

（3）隐含歧义效果的有无。从语义角度来说，测试句中是否隐含歧义（整体或局部），这种歧义是否会导致二次解码的行进错位（局部歧义，即花园幽径现象），以及被试解歧策略的使用和回溯解码能力都将左右评分效果。

在这三个条件中，第一个条件是对阅读材料的分析，第二个条件是对被试的分析，第三个条件是对前两个条件的综合讨论。由于对被试的分析需要按照被试既往成绩（如我们前面讨论的高考总成绩、高考英语成绩和英语专业四级成绩）进行分组，并讨论各个组间的差异以最终评定各组之间在阅读同一测试材料时是否具有显著性差异。这部分需要涉及方差分析，我们会在下一章重点分析。对阅读材料的分析可以在获得了非独立 t 检验结果和概率的情况下进行，并最终给出 5 秒反应时和 10 秒反应时显著差异性的材料理据。请看表 5-6 中有显著性差异的测试句。

表 5 – 6　　反应时延长差异性影响阅读效果的测试句列表

Number	p	Number	p
S1	A	S51	A
S2	A	S52	A
S3	A	S55	A
S6	A	S56	A
S7	A	S58	A
S8	A	S59	A
S10	A	S61	A
S13	A	S62	A
S15	A	S63	A
S18	A	S65	A
S19	A	S67	A
S26	A	S71	A
S27	A	S76	A
S28	A	S78	A
S29	A	S80	A
S33	A	S81	A
S38	A	S82	A
S39	A	S84	A
S40	A	S87	A
S41	A	S88	A
S42	A	S89	A
S43	A	S90	A
S45	A	S96	A
S46	A	S98	A
S48	A	S99	A
S50	A		

从上表可知，在我们提供的 100 个测试句中，有 51 个测试句根据反应时变化出现了显著性效果。很多的被试在延长的时间中改变了他们的初衷，并给出了不同于第一次测试的效果评分。

在附录一中，我们对反应时延长后会产生差异性阅读效果的测试句进行了星号标记，同时，在末尾分别给出了 5 秒和 10 秒的被试组的总得分。虽然这些总分对分析组的差异略显单薄（具体的组间和组内分析将在后面的方差分析中讨论），但却可以从整体上来看被试组的理解变化。

根据得分类型，我们可以将 51 个测试句分成相反项、负数项和正数项三类，具体如下：

（1）相反项即前后得分相反的项。相反项意味着被试组发生了阅读颠覆，原来的理解与延长反应时后的理解产生了强烈偏差。这种颠覆不是程度性的，而是根本性的。前后矛盾的阅读效果因反应时变化而起。被试在给予足够阅读时间的情况下推翻了原来的结果，并产生了极强的对比错位。其中，趋正性相反项 4 个，趋负性相反项 8 个。

趋正性相反项是指被试在 5 秒和 10 秒反应时状况下，出现了由错误评分向正确评分的转化。初始的 5 秒反应时，被试认为是错误的测试句，在 10 秒反应时则给出了相反的正确评分。这样，负理解向正理解的强偏移形成了趋正性变化。其评分体现在由负值向正值的变化。具体的 4 项如下：

＊S38 – The cotton that clothing is made of grows in Mississippi. （-17；53）

＊S45 – The fat that people eat accumulates in their bodies. （-10；68）

＊S58 – The man whistling tunes pianos. （-33；56）

＊S59 – The man who hunts ducks out on weekends. （-17；36）

趋负性相反项是指被试在 5 秒反应时状况下，认为测试句是正确的，但在反应时延长一倍之后，便更改原来的正向理解为负向理解，形成了趋负性变化。其体现在评分上为由正值向负值的变化。具体的 8 项如下：

＊S1 – Because he always jogs a mile seems a short distance to him. （5；-75）

*S10 – I told the girl the cat scratched that Bill would help her. （83；-10）

*S13 – Mary gave the child that the dog bit a cake. （13；-107）

*S26 – The boat floated down the river sank. （22；-34）

*S28 – The building blocks the sun shining on the house faded are red. （80；-16）

*S55 – I told the girl the cat scratched Bill would help her. （36；-9）

*S82 – The statue stands in the park are rusty. （68；-2）

*S88 – The teacher told the children the ghost story had frightened that it wasn't true. （16；-92）

（2）负数项即前后得分都是负数（偏向错误）的项。负数项的存在表示被试组在反应时延长后，虽然没有从根本上颠覆原来的理解，却在程度上给出了具有差异性的得分，使前后两次理解出现了较大的认知落差。其中，回归性落差 2 项，离心性落差 4 项。

回归性落差项是指被试对测试句的理解从完全错误端向不完全错误端的转化。其评分体现在由负极值端向中心位置的回归，即较大绝对值负数向较小绝对值负数的回归。具体的 2 项如下：

*S56 – The man returned to his house was happy. （-64；-5）

*S71 – The prime people number few. （-129；-75）

离心性落差项与回归性落差项呈反方向趋势。具体指被试从不完全错误理解向完全错误理解的离心运动。这种离心性变化体现在评分上就是由较小绝对值负数向较大绝对值负数的变化。具体的 4 项如下：

*S27 – The building blocks the sun faded are red. （-21；-66）

*S50 – The government plans to raise taxes were defeated. （-38；-95）

*S81 – The sour drink from the ocean. （-67；-135）

*S98 – Until the police arrest the drug dealers control the street.

（-95；-151）

（3）正数项即前后得分都是正数（偏向正确）的项。正数项是指被试组不受反应时变化影响，也没有调整对测试句的正确评分，即没有根本性颠覆原认知。但是，前后两次的理解却存在较大的程度差异。其中，渐强性效果项31个，渐弱性效果项2个。

渐强性效果项是指被试在5秒和10秒反应时的阅读得分由小到大的项。这种增大性效果体现了被试认知由弱到强的理解模式。具体的31项如下：

*S2 - Because he always jogs, a mile seems a short distance to him. (77；194)

*S6 - I convinced her that children are noisy. (123；215)

*S7 - I know that the words to that song about the queen don't rhyme. (23；86)

*S8 - I know the words to that song about the queen don't rhyme. (71；130)

*S15 - Please have the students who failed the exam take the supplementary. (98；146)

*S18 - She told me that a little white lie will come back to haunt me. (97；160)

*S19 - Single and married soldiers and their families are housed in the complex. (77；143)

*S29 - The building blocks the sun shining on the house. (65；135)

*S39 - The cotton that clothing is usually made of grows in Mississippi. (27；104)

*S40 - The dog that I had as a pet really loved bones. (169；218)

*S41 - The dog that I had really loved bones. (166；229)

*S42 - The drink that was sour is from the ocean. (100；154)

*S43 - The fact that Jill is never here hurts me. (85；147)

*S46 - The girl told the story and cried. (152；187)

第五章 花园幽径句阅读时间与效果的非独立 t 值研究

* S48 – The girl who was told the story cried. （156；203）

* S51 – The government's plans to raise taxes were defeated. （129；170）

* S52 – The large pins are bright red. （177；208）

* S61 – The man who whistles all the time tunes pianos for a living. （125；190）

* S62 – The man, who hunts animals, ducks out on weekends. （149；203）

* S63 – The map pins are bright red. （133；190）

* S65 – The men run through the arches and screamed. （153；190）

* S67 – The old dog follows the footsteps of the young. （156；206）

* S76 – The shotgun pins were rusty from the rain. （121；183）

* S78 – The sniper guards the victim in the woods. （91；172）

* S80 – The sniper pins were rusty from the rain. （102；165）

* S84 – The stone rocks during the earthquake. （65；146）

* S87 – The table rocks during the earthquake. （124；166）

* S89 – The teacher told the children the ghost story that she knew would frighten them. （125；174）

* S90 – The tomcat curled itself up on the cushion and seemed friendly. （90；149）

* S96 – The tycoon, who was sold the offshore oil tracts for a lot of money, wanted to kill JR. （147；202）

* S99 – Until the police make the arrest, the drug dealers control the street. （111，152）

渐弱性效果项是指被试的阅读效果得分由大到小，即在 5 秒反应时的阅读得分大于 10 秒反应时得分。这种趋缓的阅读效果体现了被试认知由强到弱的理解模式。具体的 2 项如下：

* S3 – Fat people eat accumulates. （136；74）

* S33 – The clothing, which is made of cotton, grows in Mississippi.

(99；11)

  根据以上对 51 个测试句的分类，我们可以很好地看出，被试组反应时变化引发了显著性差异的阅读效果评分的变化。对这种差异性效果的出现，究其原因，我们总结如下：

  (1) 错位效应影响。阅读材料中隐含行进错位的花园幽径效应，被试需要假以时间进行斟酌。一旦反应时延长至可以斟酌完成的临界点，被试则修改原有的效果评分。错位效应可以看成是被试在理解过程中产生的回溯现象。5 秒反应时和 10 秒反应时的时间间隔不同，带来了被试组近乎迥异的阅读效果。被试前后两次的评分出现的颠覆性效果分歧程度加大时，这种认知理解的行进式错位效应便会愈加明显。

  (2) 字符串长短与嵌套影响。阅读材料字符串偏长，在 5 秒反应时间隔内无法较快整合并给出正确的效果评分。后期的 10 秒反应时中，被试有了较为充足的时间对原来无法完成的解码重新审视认定，有可能颠覆原有的评分选项。此外，嵌套结构的出现也会加大阅读的难度，较长的反应时便于多重嵌套结构的理解。

  (3) 生僻表达方式影响。测试句中出现了部分被试感到生僻的单词和表达方式，这将耗费被试宝贵的反应时。但是，间隔只有一个月的两次测试，又无法提升被试的阅读能力和认知，即无法改善其对生僻字段的理解效果，所以，当再次理解同一材料时，被试莫衷一是，可能导致两次测试评分偏差较大。

  (4) 干扰成分影响。为了取得较好的测试效果，我们在测试材料中放入了部分旨在干扰被试选项的对照句。有些对照句不是正确的句子而只是字段，或缺少主要成分的短语（如 S81）。在较短的反应时中，部分被试可能由于语言惯性和语言认知，会自动填补缺少的成分，从而认为这些错误的对照句是符合句法条件的。但是，在给予足够的反应时间的情况下，这些被试将重新审视这些对照句，可能会给出截然相反的答案。

  (5) 莫名因素影响。除了上面提到的几种对阅读效果的影响之外，我们认为还可能会有其他无法预期的因素影响。在下一章的方差分析中，我们将继续分析组间和组内的差异，深入讨论这些差异项存在的语言和认知背景。

二 非独立 t 检验下非显著性差异测试句分析

与前面讨论的 51 个显著性差异的测试句数量不同，非独立 t 检验下非显著性差异测试句共有 49 个。反应时的变化并没有让被试取得不同的阅读效果。具体的测试句编号见表 5-7。

表 5-7　　反应时延长对阅读效果不明显的测试句列表

Number	p	Number	p
S4	B	S54	B
S5	B	S57	B
S9	B	S60	B
S11	B	S64	B
S12	B	S66	B
S14	B	S68	B
S16	B	S69	B
S17	B	S70	B
S20	B	S72	B
S21	B	S73	B
S22	B	S74	B
S23	B	S75	B
S24	B	S77	B
S25	B	S79	B
S30	B	S83	B
S31	B	S85	B
S32	B	S86	B
S34	B	S91	B
S35	B	S92	B
S36	B	S93	B

续表

Number	p	Number	p
S37	B	S94	B
S44	B	S95	B
S47	B	S97	B
S49	B	S100	B
S53	B		

与前面讨论的反应时延长差异性影响阅读效果的测试句列表不同，这里的列表项都是阅读效果前后不明显也不显著的项。如果从量变和质变的逻辑来解释的话，前者出现的显著性差异项应该是阅读效果由量变引起质变的项。后者则相反，虽有量的变化但尚不足以引发质变。因此，前者是异质的而后者是同质的。

与显著性差异的51个测试句相比，此处的49个非显著性差异项有其自身独有的特征：5秒和10秒反应时的评分差距相对显著性差异项来说要小很多，即存在的差异不足以导致系统性偏误。这种缩小化的评分差距是两个反应时出现非显著性差异的根本。

在类型上，非显著性差异也有类似于显著性差异的分类，即相反项、负数项和正数项。

（1）非显著性差异的相反项包括2个，具体如下：

S72 – The raft floated down the river sank. （34；-4）

S85 – The stone rocks were by the seashore. （-4；10）

（2）非显著性差异的负数项包括回归性落差4项，离心性落差7项，具体如下。

回归性落差负数项（4个）：

S4 – Fat that people eat accumulates. （-31；-28）

S44 – The fat that people eat accumulates. （-54；-49）

S47 – The girl told the story cried. （-50；-46）

S68 – The old dog the footsteps of the young. （-173；-150）

第五章 花园幽径句阅读时间与效果的非独立 t 值研究

离心性落差负数项（7个）：

S14 – Mary gave the child the dog bit a cake. （-49；-92）

S34 – The complex houses married and single soldiers and their families. （-74；-101）

S54 – The man pushed through the door fell. （-10；-18）

S66 – The men run through the arches screamed. （-1；-37）

S69 – The prime number few. （-151；-161）

S95 – The tycoon sold the offshore oil tracts for a lot of money wanted to kill JR. （-25；-65）

S100 – When Fred eats food gets thrown. （-124；-128）

（3）非显著性差异的正数项共36项，其中包括渐强性效果项20个，渐弱性效果项16个，具体如下。

渐强性正数项（20个）：

S9 – I told the girl that the cat that scratched Bill would help her. （57；58）

S17 – She told me a little white lie will come back to haunt me. （5；19）

S20 – The army stands on guard. （165；193）

S24 – The biggest rocks were by the seashore. （12；31）

S25 – The boat floated down the river quietly. （204；209）

S30 – The building blocks the sun. （152；157）

S31 – The chestnut blocks are red. （156；185）

S35 – The cotton clothing is made in sunny Alabama. （190；198）

S53 – The man came back to his house and was happy. （167；171）

S60 – The man who is whistling melodies plays pianos. （165；182）

S70 – The prime number is forty. （213；228）

S73 – The raft that was floated down the river sank. （101；116）

S75 – The sentry stands on guard. （179；196）

S79 – The sniper pins the victim in the woods. （87；89）

S83 – The statue stands in the park. （196；211）

S86 – The stopper blocks the sink. （101；107）

S91 – The tomcat curled up on the cushion seemed friendly. （100；103）

S92 – The tomcat that was curled up on the cushion seemed friendly. （169；188）

S94 – The toy rocks near the child quietly. （25；55）

S97 – The whistling man tunes pianos. （126；150）

渐弱性正数项 16 个：

S5 – I convinced her children are noisy. （53；27）

S11 – I told the girl the cat that scratched Bill would help her. （117；113）

S12 – I told the girl who was scratched by the cat that Bill would help her. （143；117）

S16 – Returned to his house, the man was happy. （70；65）

S21 – The author composed the novel and was likely to be a best-seller. （111；90）

S22 – The author wrote that the novel in question was likely to be a best-seller. （71；61）

S23 – The author wrote the novel was likely to be a best-seller. （48；27）

S32 – The chestnut blocks the sink. （41；25）

S36 – The cotton clothing is made of grows in Mississippi. （32；24）

S37 – The cotton clothing is usually made of grows in Mississippi. （37；11）

S49 – The government is planning to raise taxes, which was defeated. （172；136）

S57 – The man who was returned to his house was happy. （125；96）

S64 – The map pins onto the wall. （54；24）

S74 – The sentry stands are green. （115；103）

S77 – The sign pins onto the wall. （71；50）

S93 – The toy rocks near the child are pink. （119；114）

根据对上面的 49 个具有非显著性差异特征的测试句分析可知，被试组虽然在 5 秒和 10 秒反应时变化后产生了不同的阅读效果，但是，由此引发的评分差异尚达不到系统性偏差的地步，所以，未产生显著性差异的特征。这些非显著性差异项具有如下效应特征：

（1）简单效应。本来在词汇或句式上就很容易的测试句，被试对其理解稳定而正确，不需要随着反应时变化改变他们的初衷。

（2）复杂效应。测试材料中极难的表达方式超出了被试的认知范围。这种难度较大的测试句，往往字段过于冗长或者取词范围过于生僻，导致被试根本无法理解。这样，即使延长反应时，被试也无法从根本上改变认知上的不足。两次评分可能都维持在同一认知水平，遂得出前后一致的评分效果。

（3）标记效应。测试句本身较难，但是在测试中我们提供了相应的标记性成分，如标点符号和提示词 that 等。这些标记性成分的存在，帮助被试在较短时间内划分句子结构，完成对解码的整合。标记成分降低了阅读材料的难度。

（4）纠偏泛化效应。被试理解过程中会受到认知的影响，自动对阅读材料中一些难度较大的解码模式纠偏成便于理解的低难度模式。这种纠偏泛化效应与国外学者（Ferreira, Patson, 2007；Wonnacott, et al., 2015）提出的"尚好"模式有异曲同工之效。

本章小结

本章主要进行了非独立 t 检验的研究。为了测试同一被试组在间隔一个月的情况下，其对 100 个花园幽径句或对照句的阅读效果是否会随着 5 秒和 10 秒反应时变化而发生改变，我们对 126 个被试进行了相应的语言实验，并获取了相关数据。

在非独立 t 检验的公式测定法中，我们分别计算了这 100 个测试句的 t 值，并与量表中的临界值进行了比对，最后得出每个测试句 $p<.05$（或 $p>.05$）的结论。该公式法逻辑清楚，计算流程清晰，但计算量较大，耗时较长，而且计算得出的 t 值只是一个中间量，尚需要进行二次比较才能得到是否具有显著性差异的结论。因此，从便捷性出发，我们引入 EXCEL 函数法进行验证。

EXCEL 函数法采用系统函数 TTEST（array1，array2，tails，type），其结果直接是概率 sig 值。通常情况下，如果概率 $p<.05$，则为显著性差异。否则，则为非显著性差异。函数中 array1 和 array2 表示数据集的采样。tails 有两个选项：tails = 1 表示单侧有向的单尾分布；tails = 2 表示双侧无向的双尾分布。函数中 type 有三个选项：type = 1 表示非独立的配对 t 检验；type = 2 表示独立的等方差双样本检验；type = 3 表示独立的异方差双样本检验。通过公式法和函数法的比对可知：两者都适合对非独立 t 检验进行测算；前者关注过程，后者侧重结果，其结论均具有相互验证性。

为便于理解函数法中的概率 sig 值，我们引入了标准差和正态分布的讨论，并分析了正态分布的情况下"近乎 100% 的数值均落在均值 - 3 个标准差或者均值 + 3 个标准差的曲线范围内"这一统计学结论。从概率水平来看，大概率事件的比率在 95% 左右，小概率事件在 5% 左右。如果概率比 5% 大（$p>.05$），则该事件出现的可能性将落在 95% 之内，所以不具有显著性差异。如果概率比 5% 小（$p<.05$），则这种情况出现的可能性是落在 95% 之外的，是偶然且有区分度的，即具有显著性差异。

在非独立 t 检验下的 51 个显著性差异测试句分析中，我们讨论了被试阅读效果评分的三种类型：相反项、负数项和正数项。相反项意味着被试组发生了阅读颠覆，前后理解有强烈的根本性偏差，评分呈现对立性。主要包括两类：由错误评分向正确评分转化的趋正性相反项，在评分上由正值向负值变化的趋负性相反项。负数项是指前后两次测试均为负数的项，包括从完全错误端向不完全错误端评分转化的回归性落差项，以及从不完全错误理解向完全错误理解的离心性落差项。正数项是前后评分均为正数的项，包括阅读得分由小到大的渐强性效果项，以及认知效果由强到弱的渐弱性效果项。

显著性差异测试句出现的原因大体包括五个方面：错位效应影响、字符串长短与嵌套影响、生僻表达方式影响、干扰成分影响和莫名因素影响。

在非独立 t 检验下的 49 个非显著性差异测试句分析中，我们认为这些测试句也具有与差异性测试句相同的类别，但评分差异较小尚不足以引起系统性偏差。在产生原因方面，非差异性项有其独特的效应特征：简单效应、复杂效应、标记效应和纠偏泛化效应。

显著性差异与否带来了测试句阅读效果的截然不同。这些差异性特征是否源于 126 个被试所构成的不同分类组的组间或组内差异？我们将从方差分析中寻找到答案。

第六章

时间和能力因素与花园幽径句阅读效果的方差分析

在上一章讨论非独立 t 检验时，我们采用的是 5 秒和 10 秒的反应时变量，并给出了不同的阅读效果分析。总体来说，分成显著性和非显著性差异两类。其各自具有不同的次分类和原因特点。非独立 t 检验对两个群体的分析是具有优势的。尽管我们已经得到了 5 秒和 10 秒反应时的效果分析，但仍不能据此就非常确定时间因素对花园幽径句阅读效果具有怎样的趋势变化。还需要对两个以上的反应时分类组进行方差分析。

为此，我们在 5 秒和 10 秒外引入第三个反应时变量——7 秒反应时，并通过方差分析测算这三个反应时所形成的效应组之间是否具有显著性差异。如果我们使用的方差分析（analysis of variance，ANOVA）检验假设能证明三个效应组检验统计量 F 值所代表的平均成绩得分具有（或不具有）显著性差异，那么，我们便可以得出花园幽径句阅读效果和不同反应时因素之间的内在关系。

第一节 方差分析公式法

方差分析根据不同的测试要求具有不同的形式，我们这里使用的是简单方差分析（simple analysis of variance）。在研究中，我们只分析反应时所代表的时间因素是如何影响被试的阅读效果的。

第六章 时间和能力因素与花园幽径句阅读效果的方差分析

简单方差分析只有一个分组维度,所以是一元(one-way)方差分析。不同测试组差异产生的方差可以分解为群体内个体差异产生的方差和群体间差异产生的方差(组内方差和组间方差),对这两种方差差异进行比较就可以得到相应的分析结果。

简单方差分析的逻辑在于:组内的差异往往是随机因素产生的,即被试的选择不是刻意的,而组间的差异却有可能是我们刻意分组所造成的。从统计意义来说,如果能够证明组内随机因素的差异不存在,或者差异较小可以忽略的话,所有的组间差异都是有意义的。换句话说,当组间差异远远大于组内差异的时候,这种分组所产生的效果就具有显著性差异。相反,如果组间差异还没有组内差异显著的话,就说明组间差异效果尚未达到可以忽略组内差异的程度,即分组效果不具有显著性差异。因此,简单方差分析 F 值可以用组间差异与组内差异的比值进行表示,具体分为两种情况。

(1)组间差异大于或远远大于组内差异时,比值 F 大于 1 或者远远大于 1。这说明 F 值变化主要源于组间差异,随机因素之外的因素起到了决定性效果。分组具有显著性差异。

(2)组间差异等于或小于组内差异时,比值 F 等于或小于 1。这表示相比较分组因素的组间差异来说,随机因素的组内差异起到了决定性作用。效果差异源于随机的话,分组就不具有显著性差异。简单方差分析的公式如下:

$$F = \frac{MS_{between}}{MS_{within}} \quad (6-1)$$

式中:F 为方差分析的 F 值;

$MS_{between}$ 为组间差异变化量所引起的平方和的均值(组间均方);

MS_{within} 为组内差异变化量所引起的平方和的均值(组内均方)。

由方差分析的公式可以看出,如果我们得到了组间和组内的差异变化量均方的话,F 值就能够计算得出。组间均方和组内均方的计算略有不同,其各自的公式也不同。组间均方公式如下:

$$MS_{between} = \frac{\sum[(\sum X)^2/n] - [(\sum \sum X)^2/N]}{N'_{between}} \quad (6-2)$$

式中：$MS_{between}$ 为组间均方；
n 为单组个数；
N 为总个数；
$N'_{between}$ 为组间自由度 df，即组数减去 1；
X 为个体评分；
$\sum X$ 为单组评分和；
$(\sum X)^2$ 为单组评分和的平方；
$(\sum X)^2/n$ 为单组评分和的平方与单组个数之比；
$\sum[(\sum X)^2/n]$ 为单组评分和的平方与单组个数之比，再取和；
$(\sum\sum X)^2$ 为多个单组评分总和的平方；
$(\sum\sum X)^2/N$ 为多个单组评分总和的平方与总个数之比。
组内均方公式如下：

$$MS_{within} = \frac{\sum\sum(X^2) - \sum(\sum X)^2/n}{N'_{within}} \quad (6-3)$$

式中：MS_{within} 为组内均方；
n 为单组个数；
N'_{within} 为组内自由度 df，即个数减去组数；
X 为个体评分；
X^2 为个体评分的平方；
$\sum(X^2)$ 为单组个体评分平方之和；
$\sum\sum(X^2)$ 为多个单组个体评分平方之和；
$\sum X$ 为单组评分和；
$(\sum X)^2$ 为单组评分和的平方；
$\sum(\sum X)^2$ 为多个单组评分和的平方；
$\sum(\sum X)^2/n$ 为多个单组评分和的平方与单组个数之比。

为便于分析，我们把附录三中的 S1 作为样例，使分析过程更加清晰，同时让数值代入更加友好。具体请见 126 个被试在 5 秒—7 秒—10 秒反应时过程中对 S1 的阅读效果评分（表 6-1）。

第六章 时间和能力因素与花园幽径句阅读效果的方差分析

表 6-1　反应时 5 秒—7 秒—10 秒的 S1 阅读效果评分及平方表

n	5S1（X1）	（X1）²	7S1（X2）	（X2）²	10S1（X3）	（X3）²
1	0	0	1	1	1	1
2	-2	4	-2	4	-2	4
3	1	1	-1	1	1	1
4	1	1	-1	1	-1	1
5	2	4	1	1	-2	4
6	2	4	1	1	1	1
7	1	1	-2	4	0	0
8	2	4	-2	4	-2	4
9	0	0	1	1	2	4
10	2	4	2	4	2	4
11	1	1	-1	1	1	1
12	0	0	-1	1	-2	4
13	2	4	-2	4	-2	4
14	1	1	2	4	1	1
15	-1	1	-2	4	-2	4
16	0	0	-2	4	-2	4
17	-1	1	1	1	0	0
18	-2	4	-2	4	-2	4
19	0	0	-2	4	0	0
20	1	1	2	4	2	4
21	-2	4	-2	4	-2	4
22	1	1	1	1	-2	4
23	1	1	-2	4	-1	1
24	1	1	-2	4	-2	4
25	0	0	-1	1	-2	4
26	0	0	2	4	1	1
27	0	0	-2	4	-2	4
28	0	0	2	4	-2	4
29	-1	1	1	1	2	4
30	1	1	-1	1	-2	4

续表

n	5S1（X1）	（X1）²	7S1（X2）	（X2）²	10S1（X3）	（X3）²
31	0	0	-2	4	0	0
32	0	0	-1	1	0	0
33	2	4	2	4	2	4
34	0	0	-1	1	0	0
35	2	4	-2	4	-2	4
36	0	0	-2	4	-2	4
37	0	0	-2	4	-1	1
38	2	4	2	4	2	4
39	2	4	-2	4	0	0
40	-2	4	2	4	2	4
41	-2	4	-2	4	-2	4
42	2	4	-2	4	1	1
43	0	0	-2	4	-1	1
44	1	1	2	4	-1	1
45	2	4	2	4	-2	4
46	1	1	-1	1	-2	4
47	-1	1	1	1	1	1
48	0	0	-2	4	-2	4
49	0	0	-2	4	-2	4
50	-2	4	-2	4	-2	4
51	2	4	-2	4	-2	4
52	2	4	-2	4	2	4
53	-1	1	-2	4	-2	4
54	-1	1	-1	1	-2	4
55	0	0	-2	4	2	4
56	2	4	1	1	1	1
57	2	4	-2	4	-2	4
58	-2	4	-2	4	2	4
59	0	0	-2	4	-2	4
60	0	0	-2	4	-2	4

第六章　时间和能力因素与花园幽径句阅读效果的方差分析

续表

n	5S1（X1）	（X1）²	7S1（X2）	（X2）²	10S1（X3）	（X3）²
61	-2	4	-2	4	1	1
62	2	4	-2	4	0	0
63	2	4	2	4	1	1
64	-2	4	-2	4	-2	4
65	1	1	1	1	1	1
66	-2	4	-2	4	-2	4
67	0	0	-1	1	1	1
68	1	1	-2	4	-2	4
69	0	0	-2	4	-2	4
70	1	1	2	4	0	0
71	-2	4	-2	4	2	4
72	0	0	2	4	2	4
73	1	1	-1	1	1	1
74	0	0	-1	1	-2	4
75	0	0	-1	1	-1	1
76	-2	4	-2	4	-2	4
77	0	0	-2	4	-2	4
78	2	4	-1	1	1	1
79	-2	4	-2	4	1	1
80	2	4	1	1	-2	4
81	1	1	-2	4	-2	4
82	0	0	-2	4	-2	4
83	1	1	-2	4	-2	4
84	0	0	2	4	-2	4
85	2	4	-2	4	2	4
86	0	0	-2	4	-2	4
87	-2	4	-2	4	-2	4
88	-1	1	1	1	-2	4
89	0	0	-2	4	-2	4
90	0	0	-2	4	-2	4

续表

n	5S1（X1）	(X1)²	7S1（X2）	(X2)²	10S1（X3）	(X3)²
91	-2	4	-2	4	-2	4
92	0	0	-2	4	1	1
93	0	0	-2	4	0	0
94	-2	4	2	4	2	4
95	1	1	0	0	2	4
96	0	0	1	1	-2	4
97	-2	4	-2	4	-2	4
98	0	0	-2	4	0	0
99	-2	4	-2	4	-2	4
100	-2	4	-2	4	-2	4
101	0	0	1	1	1	1
102	-1	1	-2	4	-1	1
103	1	1	-2	4	-2	4
104	1	1	1	1	2	4
105	-2	4	-2	4	-2	4
106	0	0	0	0	2	4
107	0	0	-2	4	-2	4
108	-2	4	-1	1	-2	4
109	-1	1	1	1	0	0
110	2	4	2	4	2	4
111	0	0	-2	4	-2	4
112	-1	1	2	4	2	4
113	1	1	-2	4	-2	4
114	0	0	-2	4	-2	4
115	-1	1	-2	4	-2	4
116	1	1	-1	1	-2	4
117	-2	4	-2	4	-2	4
118	2	4	1	1	2	4
119	-2	4	-2	4	-2	4
120	-2	4	-2	4	-2	4

第六章　时间和能力因素与花园幽径句阅读效果的方差分析

续表

n	5S1（X1）	(X1)²	7S1（X2）	(X2)²	10S1（X3）	(X3)²
121	−2	4	−2	4	−2	4
122	2	4	0	0	2	4
123	−2	4	2	4	2	4
124	−2	4	−2	4	−2	4
125	2	4	−2	4	−2	4
126	−1	1	0	0	2	4

由以上表格，我们可以得到如下数值：

$n = 126$（单组被试个数）

$N = 378$（三组的总个数）

$N'_{within} = 126 - 3 = 123$（组内自由度）

$N'_{between} = 3 - 1 = 2$（组间自由度）

$\sum X1 = 5$（5 秒组评分总和）

$\sum X2 = -104$（7 秒组评分总和）

$\sum X3 = -75$（10 秒组评分总和）

$\sum\sum X = \sum X1 + \sum X2 + \sum X3 = 5 - 104 - 75 = -174$（三个组的评分总和）

$(\sum\sum X)^2 / N = (-174)^2 / 378 = 80.10$（三个组评分总和的平方与总个数之比）

$\sum (X1)^2 = 239$（5 秒组评分平方的总和）

$\sum (X2)^2 = 386$（7 秒组评分平方的总和）

$\sum (X3)^2 = 381$（10 秒组评分平方的总和）

$\sum\sum (X^2) = \sum (X1)^2 + \sum (X2)^2 + \sum (X3)^2 = 239 + 386 + 381 = 1006$（三组评分平方总和相加）

$(\sum X1)^2 = 5 \times 5 = 25$（5 秒组评分和的平方）

$(\sum X2)^2 = (-104) \times (-104) = 10816$（7 秒组评分和的平方）

$(\sum X3)^2 = (-75) \times (-75) = 5625$（10 秒组评分和的平方）

$(\sum X1)^2/n = 25/126 = 0.20$（5秒组评分和的平方与单组个数之比）

$(\sum X2)^2/n = 10816/126 = 85.84$（7秒组评分和的平方与单组个数之比）

$(\sum X3)^2/n = 5625/126 = 44.64$（10秒组评分和的平方与单组个数之比）

$\sum(\sum X)^2/n = (\sum X1)^2/n + (\sum X2)^2/n + (\sum X3)^2/n = 0.20 + 85.84 + 44.64 = 130.68$

把如上的值代入公式：

$$\text{MS}_{between} = \frac{\sum[(\sum X)^2/n] - [(\sum\sum X)^2/N]}{N'_{between}} = (130.68 - 80.10)/2 = 50.58/2 = 25.29$$

$$\text{MS}_{within} = \frac{\sum\sum(X^2) - \sum(\sum X)^2/n}{N'_{within}} = (1006 - 130.68)/123 = 875.32/123 = 7.12$$

$$F = \frac{\text{MS}_{between}}{\text{MS}_{within}} = 25.29/7.12 = 3.55$$

$F_{(2, 123)} = 3.55$，$p < .05$

根据统计量表可知：在.05水平下，分子自由度为2，分母为无穷大（>100），方差临界值为3.0。此处计算的F值大于临界值，说明组间差距大于组内差距，因此被试在5秒—7秒—10秒的反应时状态下进行的阅读效果评分，具有显著性差异，即时间因素的确改变了被试组的阅读效果。这个方差分析的结果进一步验证了上一章非独立t检验中的事实：S1测试句的阅读因反应时变量的变化出现了显著性的阅读偏差。

第二节 时间因素与花园幽径句阅读效果的方差分析

通过在不同反应时状态下，被试对100个花园幽径句和对照句的阅读效果研究，我们发现时间因素的影响不是整体和全局的，而是部分和局部的。也就是说，我们无法得出一个一概而论的结果。对于有些句子，反应时变化影响了阅读效果。而对于有些句子而言，反应时的调整并没有给被试的认知产生影响，时间和效果不敏感。我们对这些测试结果进行了方差分析（具体请见附录三）。下面将深入分析时间因素与效果的内在联系，以便找出两者间的系统性关联。126个被试的方差分析结果（由小到大排序）见表6-2。

表6-2　　反应时分组与阅读效果的 ANOVA 分析列表

N	F	N	F
S16	0.01	S56	0.77
S30	0.01	S65	0.8
S53	0.01	S51	0.89
S25	0.02	S71	0.91
S54	0.03	S52	0.94
S93	0.04	S15	0.95
S86	0.05	S46	1.01
S91	0.05	S50	1.03
S11	0.07	S82	1.1
S24	0.08	S3	1.11
S79	0.08	S26	1.16
S100	0.09	S38	1.17
S69	0.09	S43	1.17
S23	0.11	S89	1.24
S73	0.11	S36	1.28
S32	0.12	S8	1.28
S74	0.12	S81	1.3
S60	0.14	S42	1.5
S35	0.15	S4	1.52
S77	0.18	S33	1.53
S21	0.19	S96	1.53

续表

N	F	N	F
S94	0.24	S48	1.55
S34	0.26	S62	1.58
S75	0.29	S80	1.58
S92	0.29	S98	1.6
S17	0.3	S7	1.63
S97	0.31	S39	1.7
S70	0.32	S84	1.7
S47	0.33	S63	1.75
S83	0.35	S45	1.78
S12	0.36	S40	1.8
S72	0.36	S14	1.91
S20	0.37	S18	1.92
S44	0.44	S29	1.95
S66	0.45	S61	2.07
S68	0.45	S67	2.16
S37	0.47	S58	2.23
S5	0.47	S76	2.27
S49	0.48	S19	2.29
S22	0.49	S78	2.62
S64	0.5	S28	2.7
S85	0.5	S57	2.92
S31	0.53	S41	3.36
S55	0.57	S88	3.36
S9	0.57	S1	3.55
S27	0.63	S10	4.09
S59	0.65	S6	4.49
S99	0.73	S13	6.29
S87	0.76	S2	12.31
S95	0.76	S90	13.63

在.05水平下,分子自由度为2,分母为无穷大(>100),方差临界值为3.0

第六章　时间和能力因素与花园幽径句阅读效果的方差分析

从上表的数值分析可以看出，作为组别的反应时变化在大多情况下没有引起 F 值的显著性差异。能够达到或超过临界值的测试句选项只有 8 个（$p < .05$），其他的均不具有显著性差异（$p > .05$）。根据 F 检验的临界值量表，当分子为 2、分母大于 100 时，其 F 值的临界为 3.0。满足该临界值的测试句和具体值请见表 6-3。

表 6-3　　反应时分组与阅读效果 $p < .05$ 的 ANOVA 列表

N	F
S41	3.36
S88	3.36
S1	3.55
S10	4.09
S6	4.49
S13	6.29
S2	12.31
S90	13.63

*S41 – The dog that I had really loved bones.

*S88 – The teacher told the children the ghost story had frightened that it wasn't true.

*S1 – Because he always jogs a mile seems a short distance to him.

*S10 – I told the girl the cat scratched that Bill would help her.

*S6 – I convinced her that children are noisy.

*S13 – Mary gave the child that the dog bit a cake.

*S2 – Because he always jogs, a mile seems a short distance to him.

*S90 – The tomcat curled itself up on the cushion and seemed friendly.

对比产生 F 值显著性差异的 8 个测试句可以看出：它们都是在非独立 t 检验中具有显著性差异的项。这说明在非独立 t 检验中不具有显著性差异的项，其在方差分析中也是一如既往地没有系统差异性。

而对于在非独立 t 检验中出现显著性差异的项,其 F 值是否达到临界值尚需重新考虑。

时间因素与阅读效果的方差分析出现了尚无法完全解释的现象,即在非独立 t 检验中产生显著性差异的 51 个测试句,却只有 8 个在后期的三组反应时的方差分析中出现了显著性差异,其他的 43 个没有达到临界值。而且,这 8 个选项并不具有统一的特征。这种情况说明,在方差分析中,仅仅采用反应时作为分组变量来分析阅读效果尚达不到多层立体的效果,各测试句选项无法实现有效区分。为此,我们考虑是否存在另外的可以引起这些测试句出现层次性差异的方差分析。从被试的角度,如果我们将他们按照前面分析的高考总成绩、高考英语成绩或英语专业四级英语成绩进行分类划组,再重新对他们的得分以成绩分组为变量来研究方差分析,是否可以获得较明确的研究思路?下面我们将讨论英语成绩组别因素与花园幽径句阅读效果的方差分析,即探讨被试阅读能力与效果的方差分析。

第三节　英语能力与花园幽径句阅读效果的方差分析

在前面的被试能力研究方面,我们分析了三个主要的代表值:高考总成绩代表被试入校前的综合能力;高考英语成绩代表了被试入校前的英语能力;英语专业四级成绩代表的是被试测试时的英语能力。其中,高考总成绩与英语专业四级成绩以 0.42 的相关系数呈现了中度相关性,高考英语成绩与英语专业四级成绩以 0.59 的相关系数呈现了强相关性。前者共享方差为 17.64%,后者为 34.81%。两个英语成绩的关联性更高,且具有更好的方差拟合。

英语专业四级成绩更适合作为被试分组依据。从前面讨论可以看出,三个成绩均在某种程度上代表了被试的能力。考虑到我们的研究主要是对英语测试句的阅读效果研究,所以,高考总成绩不适合作为分组依据。两个英语成绩的选择方面,我们认为,如果讨论的是预期性的研究，即从被试入校时的英语成绩来推断未来1—2年其能力的变化，采用高考英语成绩较为合适。但在这里，我们需要的是按照测试结果进行的语言能力分组，不涉及预期问题，所以，高考英语成绩也不太适合作为我们英语能力的分组依据。由此，我们确定以英语专业四级成绩作为被试能力的划组标准。

根据统计学知识，如果我们将被试按照英语专业四级成绩划分能力组之后，在方差分析之前，必须进行是否齐性的讨论。方差分析有三个假定的前提条件：总体呈正态分布；变异的可加性；各处理组的方差一致。在最重要的正态分布方面，需要对能力组进行卡方检验。如果卡方值出现了显著性差异，则代表我们的分组是非正态分布，则无法进行方差齐性分析。相反，如果经过卡方检验证明我们的分组不具有显著性差异，则证明分组的个数差异达不到引起组别显著性差异的程度，分组呈现正态分布特征，因此，可以使用方差分析来讨论能力分组与花园幽径句阅读效果之间的F值检验。被试依据英语专业四级成绩进行分组划分后的卡方检验如下。

一 英语专业四级成绩分组的卡方检验

卡方检验是非正态分布时进行的非参数检验，是自由分布统计。在正态分布时，参数统计的方差都是齐性或者类似的。对于非参数的方差是否齐性，则可以根据频数数据进行分析。卡方检验可以很好地根据频数测定统计中是否存在偏好，即选择的分组项是否出现了较大的偏差。

英语专业四级成绩分组属于单样本卡方检验范畴。我们在对被试进行分组时，需要考虑分组是否是等量的分布，以便后期进行验证时根据结果决定是否采用方差分析。如果卡方值证明分组不具有显著性差异，则各组的频数选择就是我们随机预期的结果，方差就是齐性的，我们就可以根据分组的具体情况进行简单的方差分析ANOVA。

频数需要考虑随机预期数量和实际观察数量的差异。从逻辑上来说，如果我们预计分组频数和实际得到的频数之间没有差异，那么，这种情况就不存在偏差问题,频数分布就是正态的,卡方值就是0。相反,如果我们预期的频数和实际频数之间差异较大,而且达到或超过了临界值,那么,这种频数分布就不是正态的,方差也就不是齐性的,卡方值也就会很高。所以,比较随机预期数量和实际观察数量则是计算卡方值的必选。具体的卡方统计公式如下:

$$X^2 = \sum \frac{(O-E)^2}{E} \qquad (6-4)$$

式中:X^2 为卡方值;

Σ 为连加求和符号;

O 为观察频数;

E 为预期频数。

根据以上公式我们可以看出:频数的计算是分类的,即被试归于哪一个组必须是排他的。归于1组将不能同时归于2组或者3组。这说明卡方检验本质上是分类检验。我们下面将根据被试的英语专业四级成绩划分能力组。具体的成绩见表6-4。

表6-4　　　　　　被试的英语专业四级成绩列表

N	TEM	N	TEM	N	TEM
1	46	43	60	85	68
2	47	44	60	86	68
3	47	45	60	87	68
4	48	46	60	88	68
5	49	47	60	89	68
6	50	48	60	90	68
7	50	49	60	91	68
8	50	50	61	92	68
9	51	51	61	93	69
10	51	52	61	94	69
11	51	53	61	95	69
12	52	54	62	96	69

第六章　时间和能力因素与花园幽径句阅读效果的方差分析

续表

N	TEM	N	TEM	N	TEM
13	52	55	62	97	70
14	52	56	62	98	70
15	53	57	62	99	70
16	54	58	62	100	70
17	54	59	62	101	70
18	54	60	62	102	70
19	55	61	62	103	71
20	56	62	63	104	71
21	56	63	63	105	71
22	56	64	63	106	71
23	56	65	64	107	72
24	56	66	64	108	72
25	56	67	64	109	72
26	56	68	64	110	73
27	56	69	64	111	73
28	56	70	64	112	73
29	57	71	64	113	74
30	57	72	64	114	74
31	58	73	64	115	74
32	58	74	64	116	74
33	58	75	64	117	74
34	58	76	65	118	75
35	60	77	65	119	76
36	60	78	65	120	76
37	60	79	65	121	77
38	60	80	66	122	77
39	60	81	66	123	78
40	60	82	67	124	79
41	60	83	67	125	79
42	60	84	67	126	81

由上表可以看出，被试组的英语专业四级成绩最低46，最高81，极差为81－46＝35。通过计算，可得到均值（63.25）和中位数

(63)。均值和中位数的偏度幅度 0.25（63.25 - 63），该数据呈现正偏度特征。根据这个特征，我们的分组中线将靠近均值和中位数。综合考虑，我们认为该成绩列表以 64 为中线分成四类能力组较为合适，即 60—64 和 65—69 各为一组，两头的 <60 和 ≥70 的各为一组。这样，我们就根据被试的英语专业四级成绩得到了四个能力组：弱能力组（<60），较弱能力组（60—64），较强能力组（65—69）和强能力组（≥70）。

根据前面的讨论，如果我们需要对这四个组进行方差分析以求证被试能力和阅读效果之间的关联性，就必须证明分组项具有方差齐性的特征，即它们的频数应该是随机分布且没有偏好模型的，也就是需要证明它们的预期频数和观察频数差异没有达到系统性偏差的程度。如果我们能够从卡方值与临界值的比较中得出分组数据的显著性与否的特征，就可以证明我们的分组频数是否是正态分布。我们对 126 个被试分成四个组后的卡方检验见表 6 - 5。

表 6 - 5　　　　　英语专业四级成绩分组的卡方检验

Category	<60	60—64	65—69	≥70
O	34.00	41.00	21.00	30.00
E	32.25	32.25	32.25	32.25
O - E	1.75	8.75	- 11.25	- 2.25
$(O - E)^2$	3.06	76.56	126.56	5.06
$(O - E)^2/E$	0.09	2.37	3.92	0.16
X^2	\multicolumn{4}{c}{6.55（p <.05）}

备注：在 .05 水平下，df = 3，临界值为 7.82
结论：被试按照以上 TEM 分数划分的组别不具有显著差异

从上表可以看出，我们得到的卡方值为 6.55，远未达到临界值 7.82（在 .05 水平下且 df = 3），即这种分组不具有显著性差异，属于正态分布。因此，在我们根据该成绩进行的分类中，分组项在预期频数和实际观察频数之间的差异没有达到显著性差异的临界值，各组之间不存在偏好,分组呈现正态分布特征,方差是齐性的。我们可以根据简单方差分析的公式对这四个能力组与花园幽径句阅读效果进行分析。

二 英语能力与阅读效果的方差分析

以测试句 S1 为例,我们对四个不同能力组的阅读效果评分进行了统计,同时计算了各组被试效果评分的平方值。在列表中,N1—N4 分别代表弱能力 A 组(<60),较弱能力 B 组(60—64),较强能力 C 组(65—69)和强能力 D 组(≥70)的被试频数。X1—X4 代表四个组的阅读效果评分值。$(X1)^2$—$(X4)^2$代表效果评分的平方。具体数值请见表 6-6。

表 6-6　　　　英语能力组与阅读效果评分及平方列表

N1	X1	$(X1)^2$	N2	X2	$(X2)^2$	N3	X3	$(X3)^2$	N4	X4	$(X4)^2$
1	1	1	1	-2	4	1	-2	4	1	-2	4
2	-2	4	2	-2	4	2	-2	4	2	-2	4
3	-1	1	3	-2	4	3	-2	4	3	-2	4
4	-1	1	4	-2	4	4	-1	1	4	-2	4
5	1	1	5	-2	4	5	-2	4	5	-2	4
6	-2	4	6	-2	4	6	1	1	6	1	1
7	-2	4	7	-2	4	7	-2	4	7	-2	4
8	1	1	8	-2	4	8	-2	4	8	-2	4
9	-1	1	9	-2	4	9	2	4	9	0	0
10	1	1	10	-1	1	10	-2	4	10	1	1
11	2	4	11	1	1	11	-2	4	11	-2	4
12	-2	4	12	2	4	12	-2	4	12	-1	1
13	-1	1	13	2	4	13	-2	4	13	1	1
14	2	4	14	2	4	14	-2	4	14	-2	4
15	-2	4	15	2	4	15	-2	4	15	2	4
16	-2	4	16	-2	4	16	-2	4	16	2	4
17	-2	4	17	-2	4	17	1	1	17	-2	4
18	1	1	18	-2	4	18	-2	4	18	-2	4

续表

N1	X1	(X1)²	N2	X2	(X2)²	N3	X3	(X3)²	N4	X4	(X4)²
19	-2	4	19	-2	4	19	0	0	19	-2	4
20	-2	4	20	-2	4	20	1	1	20	-2	4
21	-2	4	21	-2	4	21	2	4	21	-1	1
22	-2	4	22	-2	4				22	1	1
23	-2	4	23	-2	4				23	-2	4
24	-1	1	24	-2	4				24	-2	4
25	1	1	25	-2	4				25	-2	4
26	2	4	26	-1	1				26	0	0
27	2	4	27	1	1				27	2	4
28	2	4	28	-2	4				28	-2	4
29	-1	1	29	-2	4				29	-2	4
30	1	1	30	2	4				30	0	0
31	-2	4	31	-2	4						
32	-1	1	32	-2	4						
33	-1	1	33	-2	4						
34	2	4	34	-2	4						
			35	-1	1						
			36	-1	1						
			37	-1	1						
			38	-1	1						
			39	1	1						
			40	2	4						
			41	2	4						

根据方差分析公式法要求,我们计算了如下项:

$n_1 = 34$

$n_2 = 41$

$n_3 = 21$

$n_4 = 30$

$N = n_1 + n_2 + n_3 + n_4 = 126$

$\sum X_1 = -15$

$\sum X2 = -39$

$\sum X3 = -22$

$\sum X4 = -28$

$\sum\sum X = \sum X1 + \sum X2 + \sum X3 + \sum X4 = -104$

$(\sum\sum X)^2/N = (-104)^2/126 = 85.84$

$\sum (X1)^2 = 91$

$\sum (X2)^2 = 137$

$\sum (X3)^2 = 68$

$\sum (X4)^2 = 90$

$\sum\sum X^2 = \sum(X1)^2 + \sum(X2)^2 + \sum(X3)^2 + \sum(X4)^2 = 386$

$(\sum X1)^2/n1 = (-15)^2/34 = 6.62$

$(\sum X2)^2/n2 = (-39)^2/41 = 37.10$

$(\sum X3)^2/n3 = (-22)^2/21 = 23.05$

$(\sum X4)^2/n4 = (-28)^2/30 = 26.13$

$\sum(\sum X)^2/n = (\sum X1)^2/n1 + (\sum X2)^2/n2 + (\sum X3)^2/n3 + (\sum X4)^2/n4 = 92.90$

$N'_{between} = 4 - 1 = 3$

$N'_{within} = 126 - 4 = 122$

$\sum(\sum X)^2/n - (\sum\sum X)^2/N = 92.90 - 85.84 = 7.06$

$\sum\sum X^2 - \sum(\sum X)^2/n = 386 - 92.90 = 293.10$

根据以上计算，得到表6-7。

表6-7　　　　　能力分组和阅读效果的方差分析列表

来源	平方和	df	平方和均值	F
组间	7.06	3	2.35	
组内	293.10	122	2.4	0.98
总和	300.16	125		

在.05风险水平，分子为3，分母infinity（频数>100为无穷大），F值临界为2.61

结论：p>.05，能力分组和阅读效果不具有显著性差异从上表结论可以看出，我们在对花园幽径句 S1 测试时，被试的英语能力水平并没有影响到阅读效果。传统的认知"能力越强的被试会在阅读中具有越高的效果评分"并没有得到我们的实验证明。相反，实验却证明在对具有行进错位的花园幽径句的理解过程中，四个不同的能力组并没有出现显著的评分差异，即能力并没有在花园幽径句评分中得到体现。我们推论是该局部歧义句在某些方面阻碍了高能力组的认知能力显现。这个结果是对传统认知的一个反例。

是否其余的花园幽径句和对照句也具有相同的特征？如果答案是肯定的话，这个特征还将包括哪些特点？如果答案是否定的话，为什么有的会出现该特征而有的却没有出现，根源是什么？表 6-8 中，我们将对其他 99 个测试句进行能力分组和阅读效果的方差分析，以期找到系统性偏差的原因（方差分析值由小到大排序）。

表 6-8　　能力分组与效果评分的 100 个测试句 F 值列表

N	F	N	F
S46	0.02	S30	1.23
S35	0.10	S37	1.23
S11	0.12	S28	1.26
S99	0.19	S2	1.27
S29	0.22	S89	1.32
S79	0.23	S40	1.38
S75	0.26	S14	1.42
S91	0.26	S8	1.46
S77	0.30	S32	1.49
S87	0.31	S92	1.50
S98	0.39	S54	1.53
S74	0.41	S95	1.63
S55	0.42	S96	1.64
S57	0.43	S20	1.68
S60	0.47	S62	1.72

第六章 时间和能力因素与花园幽径句阅读效果的方差分析

续表

N	F	N	F
S66	0.48	S47	1.74
S48	0.49	S51	1.78
S27	0.52	S36	1.85
S100	0.56	S61	1.85
S85	0.57	S94	1.87
S33	0.57	S13	1.90
S97	0.58	S6	1.95
S86	0.61	S76	2.08
S58	0.63	S84	2.11
S7	0.67	S45	2.39
S65	0.77	S25	2.42
S93	0.79	S68	2.43
S23	0.80	S67	2.50
S34	0.86	S73	2.52
S9	0.87	S52	2.55
S22	0.87	S4	2.57
S17	0.89	S81	2.68
S31	0.89	S44	2.77
S69	0.91	S71	2.78
S38	0.93	S80	2.89
S72	0.93	S3	3.06
S63	0.94	S59	3.12
S1	0.98	S53	3.20
S90	0.98	S43	3.20
S12	1.00	S88	3.29
S24	1.01	S82	3.41
S21	1.01	S70	3.53
S18	1.02	S19	3.56
S5	1.03	S83	3.79
S49	1.06	S39	3.81

续表

N	F	N	F
S56	1.07	S41	4.24
S64	1.12	S78	4.58
S16	1.15	S10	4.66
S26	1.18	S15	4.73
S42	1.19	S50	5.29

在.05风险水平,分子为3,分母infinity(频数>100为无穷大),F值临界为2.61

从上表的F值列表可以看出,100个测试句的能力分组和效果评分的方差分析呈现不平衡分布的特征。从S81（F=2.68）以下至S50（5.29）的测试句出现了能力分组和效果评分的显著性差异。这19个测试句的方差分析值由小到大从2.68升至5.29,具体请见表6-9。

表6-9　能力分组与效果评分的显著性差异项F值列表

N	F	N	F
S81	2.68	S70	3.53
S44	2.77	S19	3.56
S71	2.78	S83	3.79
S80	2.89	S39	3.81
S3	3.06	S41	4.24
S59	3.12	S78	4.58
S53	3.20	S10	4.66
S43	3.20	S15	4.73
S88	3.29	S50	5.29
S82	3.41		

对于没有引起显著性差异的能力分组来说,他们的评分研究价值相对来说较弱,即组间的差异没有达到系统性偏差的地步。对于具有显著性差异的能力分组来说,各组之间的差异则具有研究的价值。下

第六章 时间和能力因素与花园幽径句阅读效果的方差分析

面我们将引起系统偏差的 19 个测试句分别进行讨论。为便于分析，我们将四个分组的评分总和情况在括号中体现出来，从左到右依次为弱能力组、较弱能力组、较强能力组和强能力组总得分。具体分类如下。

多组阅读效果异质项（6 个）：

*S10 – I told the girl the cat scratched that Bill would help her. （5, 4, -25, -17）

*S39 – The cotton that clothing is usually made of grows in Mississippi. （-8, 12, 10, 33）

*S50 – The government plans to raise taxes were defeated. （2, -34, -32, -31）

*S59 – The man who hunts ducks out on weekends. （8, -17, -6, 21）

*S82 – The statue stands in the park are rusty. （35, 11, -10, 13）

*S88 – The teacher told the children the ghost story had frightened that it wasn't true. （2, -17, -15, -34）

多组阅读效果负同质项（3 个）：

S44 – The fat that people eat accumulates. （-29, -31, -27, -1）

*S71 – The prime people number few. （-41, -30, -1, -14）

*S81 – The sour drink from the ocean. （-31, -17, -26, -42）

多组阅读效果正同质项（10 个）：

*S3 – Fat people eat accumulates. （45, 44, 13, 7）

*S15 – Please have the students who failed the exam take the supplementary. （23, 41, 21, 56）

*S19 – Single and married soldiers and their families are housed in the complex. （36, 26, 31, 42）

*S41 – The dog that I had really loved bones. （47, 74, 41, 60）

*S43 – The fact that Jill is never here hurts me. （4, 29, 24, 38）

S53 – The man came back to his house and was happy. （39, 41, 35,

· 135 ·

53）

  S70 – The prime number is forty. （60, 53, 41, 57）
  *S78 – The sniper guards the victim in the woods. （13, 48, 23, 48）
  *S80 – The sniper pins were rusty from the rain. （26, 37, 17, 48）
  S83 – The statue stands in the park. （46, 76, 40, 55）

  对上述19个引起方差分析显著性差异的测试句来说，有一个非常有趣的现象，即占比78.95%（15/19）的项在非独立 t 检验中也出现了显著性差异（具体请见附录一）。为了便于比较，我们用星号表示在非独立 t 检验中有显著差异的项。

  （一）多组阅读效果异质项研究

  在多组阅读效果异质项中，6个项全部同时具有方差分析和非独立 t 检验的显著性差异。也就是说，这6个项具有非常强烈的行进错位的顿悟效果。从方差分析和非独立 t 检验两个差异性对比中可以找到反差强烈的原因。

  （1）*S10 – I told the girl the cat scratched that Bill would help her. （非独立 t 检验83；-10）（方差分析5, 4, -25, -17）

  在上面的数据中，我们可以看到：（1）当阅读时间从5秒延长至10秒后，原来的被试组总体评分从83转为-10，即从原来"该句完全正确"的整体偏向转为"该句可能错误"的认知。这次转向导致了错位的出现。（2）在四个能力分组中，弱能力组和较弱能力组均认为该句是正确的，而较强能力组与强能力组则一致性认为该句是错误的。这种泾渭分明的阅读效果是花园幽径效应的强体现。请见该句在 Stanford parser 中的机器自动剖析的结果。

  Your query
  I told the girl the cat scratched that Bill would help her.
  Tagging
  I/PRP
  told/VBD

the/DT
girl/NN
the/DT
cat/NN
scratched/VBZ
that/IN
Bill/NNP
would/MD
help/VB
her/PRP
./.
Parse
(ROOT
　(S
　　(NP (PRP I))
　　(VP (VBD told)
　　　(NP
　　　　(NP (DT the) (NN girl))
　　　　(SBAR
　　　　　(S
　　　　　　(NP (DT the) (NN cat))
　　　　　　(VP (VBZ scratched)
　　　　　　　(SBAR (IN that)
　　　　　　　　(S
　　　　　　　　　(NP (NNP Bill))
　　　　　　　　　(VP (MD would)
　　　　　　　　　　(VP (VB help)
　　　　　　　　　　　(NP (PRP her))))))))))))
　　(. .)))

Universal dependencies
nsubj（told－2，I－1）主谓关系
root（ROOT－0，told－2）根节点
det（girl－4，the－3）限定关系
dobj（told－2，girl－4）动宾关系
det（cat－6，the－5）限定关系
nsubj（scratched－7，cat－6）主谓关系
acl：relcl（girl－4，scratched－7）修饰关系
mark（help－11，that－8）引导性关系
nsubj（help－11，Bill－9）主谓关系
aux（help－11，would－10）助动关系
ccomp（scratched－7，help－11）句补关系
dobj（help－11，her－12）动宾关系

句补关系错位的花园幽径句依存图如图6－1所示。

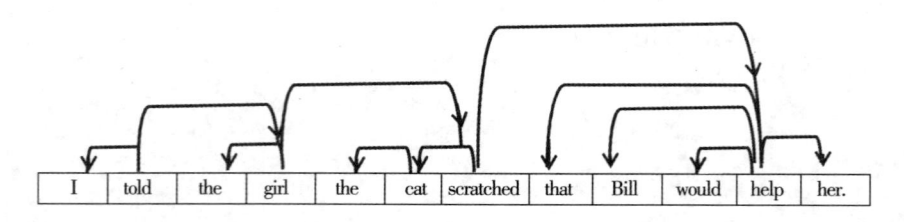

图6－1　句补关系错位的花园幽径句依存图

由上面的句法结构和依存关系分析可知，系统剖析在句补关系时出现了错误。真正的句补关系不是在ccomp（scratched－7，help－11）之间，而应该在ccomp（told－2，help－11）之间。请见删除了作为girl的定语嵌套成分the cat scratched之后的剖析结果：

Your query

I told the girl that Bill would help her.

Tagging

第六章 时间和能力因素与花园幽径句阅读效果的方差分析

I/PRP
told/VBD
the/DT
girl/NN
that/IN
Bill/NNP
would/MD
help/VB
her/PRP
./.
Parse
(ROOT
　(S
　　(NP (PRP I))
　　(VP (VBD told)
　　　(NP (DT the) (NN girl))
　　　(SBAR (IN that)
　　　　(S
　　　　　(NP (NNP Bill))
　　　　　(VP (MD would)
　　　　　　(VP (VB help)
　　　　　　　(NP (PRP her)))))))
　　(. .)))
Universal dependencies
nsubj (told-2, I-1) 主谓关系
root (ROOT-0, told-2) 根节点
det (girl-4, the-3) 限定关系
dobj (told-2, girl-4) 动宾关系
mark (help-8, that-5) 引导性关系

nsubj（help – 8，Bill – 6）主谓关系
aux（help – 8，would – 7）助动关系
ccomp（told – 2，help – 8）句补关系
dobj（help – 8，her – 9）动宾关系

上面普通句的剖析很成功，系统没有产生错位效应。系统能够非常准确地认定 that 引导的从句是动词 told 的宾语结构。

比较系统对两个句子剖析所形成的句法结构和依存关系，我们可以看出：在 girl 后面出现深层次的嵌套结构之后，原来顺畅的理解被阻断。系统不再认为 that 引导的从句归属于 told，而就近认为是归属于动词 scratched 的宾语结构。如果从句法节点来说，错位的系统剖析将 that 引导的从句降低了一个节点层次。这个系统自动剖析的错误也预示了被试组在理解过程中可能出现的关键节点。

在非独立 t 检验中，被试组总体评分从 5 秒状态下的 83 转为 10 秒状态下的 – 10，从认可该句的存在转变为否定该句的正确性。其间，被试的认知经历了行进式错位。我们认为 girl 后面的嵌套结构 the cat scratched 让被试耗费了较多的认知资源，反而在有了充足的时间进行理解时倾向性认为 the cat scratched that Bill would help her 是 told 的宾语结构（这已经通过上面的系统剖析得到验证），但是这在语义上无法接受，因此才会出现理解由正变负的反转情况。为什么一开始被试认为该句是正确的呢？这可以通过被试能力组的方差分析进行解释。

在四个能力分组的方差分析中，两个弱能力组和两个强能力组形成鲜明对照。其方差分析的得分轨迹呈现阅读效果的勺柄状特征。

能力弱的被试倾向于接受该句可能因为其阅读能力尚达不到多层嵌套解读的程度，所以仅仅凭借前面的简单结构认定该句合乎语法，这与被试组在仓促反应时（5 秒）状态下的第一感是一致的。

而能力强的被试能够深入解读嵌套结构，但是却被句法结构之外的语义所困扰，在无法跨越语义鸿沟的情况下，只能得出该句不被接受的结论。这个解读过程与系统自动剖析错误认定的 ccomp

第六章 时间和能力因素与花园幽径句阅读效果的方差分析

（scratched – 7，help – 11）句补关系一致。所以说，能力强的被试反倒因为能力较强在跨越句法障碍后却掉进了语义的壕沟。这种能力越强越容易受到花园幽径效应影响的观点与伊斯特威克和菲利普斯（Eastwick and Phillips，1999）的观点一致。

发表在苏格兰爱丁堡大学（University of Edinburgh）期刊《语言处理的结构与机制》（*Architectures and Mechanisms for Language Processing*）上的文章《句法歧义解读中语义线索有效性的变量研究》（*Variability in semantic cue effectiveness on syntactic ambiguity resolution*）中，作者伊斯特威克和菲利普斯认为：在简单句解码中，能力强者阅读时间总体上比能力弱者耗时较少。但在复杂句理解中，能力强者受到语义干扰较严重，解码时间相对延长。能力弱者对复杂句中的潜存信息不敏感，解码时间未产生显著变化。总之，阅读难度加大之后，句法外的蕴含语义信息对能力强者有显著性影响。

我们上面的分析从计算和统计的角度验证了伊斯特威克和菲利普斯的观点：在一定的认知范围内，相对能力弱的被试而言，能力强的被试更可能受到复杂结构（例如花园幽径句）的语义信息影响。

（2）＊S39 – The cotton that clothing is usually made of grows in Mississippi.（非独立 t 检验 27；104）（方差分析 – 8，12，10，33）

Your query

The cotton that clothing is usually made of grows in Mississippi.

Tagging

The/DT

cotton/NN

that/IN

clothing/NN

is/VBZ

usually/RB

made/VBN

of/IN

grows/VBZ
in/IN
Mississippi/NNP
./.
Parse
(ROOT
　　(S
　　　(NP
　　　　(NP (DT The) (NN cotton))
　　　　(SBAR (IN that)
　　　　　(S
　　　　　　(NP (NN clothing))
　　　　　　(VP (VBZ is)
　　　　　　　(ADVP (RB usually))
　　　　　　　(VP (VBN made)
　　　　　　　　(PP (IN of)))))))
　　　(VP (VBZ grows)
　　　　(PP (IN in)
　　　　　(NP (NNP Mississippi))))
　　　(. .)))

Universal dependencies
det (cotton-2, The-1)
nsubj (grows-9, cotton-2)
mark (made-7, that-3)
nsubjpass (made-7, clothing-4)
auxpass (made-7, is-5)
advmod (made-7, usually-6)
dep (cotton-2, made-7)
nmod (made-7, of-8)

第六章 时间和能力因素与花园幽径句阅读效果的方差分析

root（ROOT-0，grows-9）

case（Mississippi-11，in-10）

nmod（grows-9，Mississippi-11）

该句的系统剖析是成功的。在句法结构和依存关系的分析中，系统把 that clothing is usually made of 解码为 cotton 的定语从句，并完成了对主句结构根动词 root（ROOT-0，grows-9）的认定。该句是只有一个嵌套层级的结构，句法和语义难度都不是很大。

从非独立 t 检验结果来看，被试组在延长阅读时间之后，认为该句正确的比例具有较大攀升，从 5 秒状态下的 27 提升到了 104，这说明越来越多的被试在对较简单的句式进行解读时，充裕的阅读时间可以增强阅读效果。时间是影响效果的一个不可忽视的因素。

从能力分组的方差分析来看，从弱到强四个组的得分分别为 -8，12，10，33。该结果基本呈现阅读能力与效果的正相关，即能力越弱，解读效果越差；能力越强，解读效果越好。其阅读效果轨迹基本呈现斜率线性特征。

（3）＊S50-The government plans to raise taxes were defeated.（非独立 t 检验 -38；-95）（方差分析 2，-34，-32，-31）

Your query

The government plans to raise taxes were defeated.

Tagging

The/DT

government/NN

plans/VBZ

to/TO

raise/VB

taxes/NNS

were/VBD

defeated/VBN

./.

Parse
（ROOT
　　（S
　　　　（NP（DT The）（NN government））
　　　　（VP（VBZ plans）
　　　　　（S
　　　　　　（VP（TO to）
　　　　　　　（VP（VB raise）
　　　　　　　　（SBAR
　　　　　　　　　（S
　　　　　　　　　　（NP（NNS taxes））
　　　　　　　　　　（VP（VBD were）
　　　　　　　　　　　（VP（VBN defeated））））））))))
　　　　（..）))

Universal dependencies
　　det（government-2, The-1）限定关系
　　nsubj（plans-3, government-2）主谓关系
　　root（ROOT-0, plans-3）根节点
　　mark（raise-5, to-4）引导性关系
　　xcomp（plans-3, raise-5）开放性句补关系
　　nsubjpass（defeated-8, taxes-6）被动性主谓关系
　　auxpass（defeated-8, were-7）助动关系
　　ccomp（raise-5, defeated-8）句补关系

该句的系统剖析出现了较大错误。

从句法结构来说，系统认为形成的是［The government］NP +［plans to raise taxes were defeated］VP结构。

从依存关系来说，系统剖析逻辑更为混乱。

首先，系统认为 xcomp（plans-3, raise-5）形成的是开放性句补关系，即 clausal complement with external subject 或 open clausal complement，是附属句自身没有主语但却被外在主语所限制的一种关系。如"He says that you like to swim"可表示为 xcomp（like，swim），"I am ready to leave"可表示为 xcomp（ready，leave）。

其次，系统认为（defeated－8，taxes－6）形成的是被动性主谓关系 nsubjpass，即 passive nominal subject，如"Dole was defeated by Mike"可表示为 nsubjpass（defeated，Dole）。

最后，系统认为（raise－5，defeated－8）形成的是句补关系 ccomp，即 clausal complement，是指从句中具有内在主谓关系，整个从句充当补语，如"He says that you like to swim"可表示为 ccomp（says，like），"I am certain that he did it"可表示为 ccomp（certain，did），"I admire the fact that you are honest"可表示为 ccomp（fact，honest）。

为便于理解，我们删除中间的干扰项 to raise taxes，可以看到系统正确的句法和语义剖析。具体如下：

Your query

The government plans were defeated.

Tagging

The/DT

government/NN

plans/NNS

were/VBD

defeated/VBN

./.

Parse

(ROOT
　(S
　　(NP (DT The) (NN government) (NNS plans))
　　(VP (VBD were)
　　　(VP (VBN defeated)))

（. .）））

Universal dependencies

det（plans – 3，The – 1）

compound（plans – 3，government – 2）

nsubjpass（defeated – 5，plans – 3）

auxpass（defeated – 5，were – 4）

root（ROOT – 0，defeated – 5）

比较两次剖析，我们可以看出：出现歧义的地方在 plans/NNS 和 plans/VBZ 的认定上。如果认为 plans 是名词复数 NNS 形式，则得到的是正确的剖析结果。如果认为 plans 是第三人称单数现在时 VBZ 形式，得到的将是无法完成解读的错误剖析。被试的认知倾向于哪个选择将决定他们的阅读效果。

从非独立 t 检验来看，被试组在 5 秒和 10 秒反应时的得分均为负数，分别是 – 38 和 – 95。这说明给予的阅读时间越长，被试组越认为该句是无法接受的。这种无法自拔的状态与系统把 plans 认定是 VBZ 形式的状况相同。

从能力组方差分析来看，最弱的组得分为 2，其他三个组差别不大，分别是 – 34，– 32 和 – 31。方差分析分组的阅读效果轨迹呈现 L 状形态。

能力较强的三个组受到了 plans 的歧义影响，并认为该句是无法接受的错误句。而能力最弱的组受到的影响相对较小。这个结果也符合伊斯特威克和菲利普斯的观点：在一定的认知范围内，相对能力弱的被试而言，能力强的被试更可能受到复杂结构的语义信息影响。该句的结构虽然并不是很复杂，但是歧义项的存在加剧了结构的复杂度。中国英语学习者对 to do 结构有很深的认知认同感，当歧义项与后续的 to 同时出现时，极易产生认知共振，并倾向于将歧义项与 to 自动结合。这就使原来歧义效果不是非常明显的选择项变得具有明显的倾向性：to do 模式倾向。为了验证推断是否正确，我们可以进行数据库的统计分析。

第六章　时间和能力因素与花园幽径句阅读效果的方差分析

在 British National Corpus（BNC）中，我们可以利用语料库免费提供的 50 个随机项进行相关频数统计：（1）plan 频数统计；（2）plan to 频数统计。

如表 6-10 所示，在 BNC 随机抽样中，单词 plan 的动词义项并不占有频数优势，即当出现 plan 这个词时，国外的母语使用者更多的选择是认为它是名词类，即在没有 to 后续的情况下，倾向于缺省认为名词义项为优选结构，动词义项的选择是次选结构。但是，如果我们把后续的 to 构成的搭配结构作为检索项，情况发生了变化，我们获得了与前面不同的结构倾向。具体的频数卡方检验见表 6-11。

表 6-10　频数观察中的 plan 和 plan to 差异性列表

分类	观察频数	分类	观察频数
plan（名词）	43	plan to（补语）	27
plan（动词）	7	plan to（不定式）	23
总计	50	总计	50

表 6-11　在 BNC 语料库中 plan 和 plan to 的频数卡方检验

分类	观察频数 O	预期频数 E	偏差 O-E	$(O-E)^2/E$
plan（名词）	43	25	18	12.96
plan（动词）	7	25	-18	12.96
总计	50	50	\multicolumn{2}{c}{$X^2=25.92$}

在 .05 水平下，df=1，显著性水平临界值为 3.84

plan to（补语）	27	25	2	0.16
plan to（不定式）	23	25	-2	0.16
总计	50	50	\multicolumn{2}{c}{$X^2=0.32$}

如表 6-11 所示，单词 plan 动名词义项频数的情况是 $X^2=25.92$，$p<.05$，具有显著性差异。plan to 的补语和不定式结构频数的情况是 $X^2=0.32$，$p>.05$，不具有显著性差异。这说明结构 plan to

所形成的不定式信息搭配模式与补语信息搭配模式没有显著性差异。信息搭配改变了词汇本身的频率分布，给句子解码带来了一定的困难。而中国学习者从英语学习之初就开始反复背诵的 to do 模式最终形成了中国特色的不定式倾向。从该句分析可以看出，花园幽径句不是自足的，会受到外在搭配信息的干扰和影响。信息搭配不平衡将导致解码结构的不平衡。

（4） ＊S59 – The man who hunts ducks out on weekends.（非独立 t 检验 –17；36）（方差分析8，–17，–6，21）

Your query

The man who hunts ducks out on weekends.

Tagging

The/DT

man/NN

who/WP

hunts/VBZ

ducks/VBZ

out/RP

on/IN

weekends/NNS

./.

Parse

（ROOT

　（S

　　（NP

　　　（NP（DT The）（NN man））

　　　（SBAR

　　　　（WHNP（WP who））

　　　　（S

　　　　　（VP（VBZ hunts）)))))

第六章　时间和能力因素与花园幽径句阅读效果的方差分析

```
（VP（VBZ ducks）
    （PRT（RP out））
    （PP（IN on）
        （NP（NNS weekends））））
    （. .）））
```

Universal dependencies

det（man－2，The－1）

nsubj（ducks－5，man－2）

nsubj（hunts－4，who－3）

acl：relcl（man－2，hunts－4）

root（ROOT－0，ducks－5）

compound：prt（ducks－5，out－6）

case（weekends－8，on－7）

nmod（ducks－5，weekends－8）

该句的系统剖析非常准确。从上面的句法和依存关系可知，系统认为全句的核心动词是root（ROOT－0，ducks－5）。从句成分who hunts是对man的嵌套。虽然系统成功完成了剖析，但是，被试组却因受到hunts ducks的组合困扰无法取得一致的解码效果。

从非独立t检验来说，在反应时间延长一倍之后，被试组评分从原来的－17转变为36，即由原来的负面评价转为正面，认为该句是可以接受的。我们分析，在时间有限的情况下，被试组惯性认为ducks是名词，并作为动词hunts的宾语。随着阅读时间的延长，被试发现按照原来的思路无法完成该句的解码。但是，回溯后接受ducks是动词的选项却可以实现成功解码。这个回溯的过程在方差分析中得到验证。

从方差分析来说，四个能力组得分分别是8，－17，－6，21。能力最弱和最强的两组得分为正数。能力较弱和较强的两组受到干扰较大。方差分析四组得分的阅读效果呈现反抛物线特征。

我们推断认为，中间的两个能力组由于介于能力最强和最弱之间，他们比最弱组有更强的能力捕捉到有效的信息（如 out 不可能是动词，所以 ducks 就不可能是名词，hunts 只能是不及物选项），同时又不具有最强组的快速回溯整合能力，所以，这两个中间组在 hunts 的及物/不及物和 ducks 名/动词选项间摇摆，导致了解码错误。而最弱组能力有限，仅捕捉到 hunts 的不及物信息以及 ducks 的动词选项，所受干扰因能力较弱反而较小，因此成功解码。最强组经历了中间两个组所经历的一切，但该组以其超强的回溯效率和重新解码能力，跨越了句法和语义的双重障碍，实现了成功解码。

该句是具有花园幽径效应的句式，其行进式错位效应对最强和最弱的能力组影响较小，而对中等能力的两个组影响较大。这个结论为伊斯特威克和菲利普斯"强能力被试比弱能力被试更可能受到复杂结构影响"的观点提供了补充实例。

（5）＊S82 – The statue stands in the park are rusty.（非独立 t 检验 68；－2）（方差分析 35，11，－10，13）

Your query

The statue stands in the park are rusty.

Tagging

The/DT

statue/NN

stands/VBZ

in/IN

the/DT

park/NN

are/VBP

rusty/JJ

./.

Parse

(ROOT

(S

第六章　时间和能力因素与花园幽径句阅读效果的方差分析

```
    (NP (DT The) (NN statue))
    (VP (VBZ stands)
      (SBAR (IN in)
        (S
          (NP (DT the) (NN park))
          (VP (VBP are)
            (ADJP (JJ rusty))))))
    (. .)))
```

Universal dependencies
det (statue-2, The-1)
nsubj (stands-3, statue-2)
root (ROOT-0, stands-3)
mark (rusty-8, in-4)
det (park-6, the-5)
nsubj (rusty-8, park-6)
cop (rusty-8, are-7)
advcl (stands-3, rusty-8)

该句的解码出现了系统性错误。

从句法结构来说，系统认为 stands 的标注是 VBZ（第三人称单数动词），介词 in 充当的是引导词，the park are rusty 形成的是从句形式。整个句子的结构类似"The boy finds that the parks are clean."请看系统对这个句子的剖析结果，并请比较上句和该句的异同。

Parse
```
(ROOT
  (S
    (NP (DT The) (NN boy))
    (VP (VBZ finds)
      (SBAR (IN that)
        (S
```

　　　　　　（NP（DT the）（NNS parks））
　　　　　　（VP（VBP are）
　　　　　　　（ADJP（JJ clean））))))
　　　　（. .）))

　　比较两个剖析可以看出，除了前句（NP（DT the）（NN park））和后句（NP（DT the）（NNS parks））的差异之外，其他都相同。前句中 NN 代码为名词单数，后句中 NNS 代码为名词复数。前句的系统剖析不符合语法，因为后续的 are 要求前句应该是 NNS 而不是 NN。此外，前句的结构与剖析一致性的后句相比，明显具有句法结构的错误：in 的引导词功能让人生疑。句法剖析错误预示着该剖析是失败的，或者说系统没有找到成功剖析的关键节点。仔细分析可以看出，主要的错误出现在对 stands 的词性判断上。系统将 stands 剖析为第三人称单数的动词，导致了后续一连串错误。其内在的语义错误可见下面的依存分析。

　　从依存关系来说，系统的剖析出现多处错误。首先是系统将 stands 剖析为动词之后，介词 in 只能是引导词，并形成了错误的 mark（rusty-8，in-4）的引导性关系。其次，系统认定（stands-3，rusty-8）的关系是 advcl，即 adverbial clause modifier 副词性从句修饰关系，指用来修饰动词的附属成分，包括条件从句、时间从句等。如"The accident happened as the night was falling"可表示为 advcl（happened，falling），"If you know who did it, you should tell the teacher"可表示为 advcl（tell，know）。

　　如果我们将具有歧义的 stands 替换为 carriers，便会形成没有回溯效果的普通句。其潜在的句法和依存关系都没有发生变化。为了便于对照，我们将替换后的句子"The statue carriers in the park are rusty"的剖析展示如下：

Your query

The statue carriers in the park are rusty.

Tagging

· 152 ·

第六章 时间和能力因素与花园幽径句阅读效果的方差分析

The/DT
statue/NN
carriers/NNS
in/IN
the/DT
park/NN
are/VBP
rusty/JJ
./.
Parse
(ROOT
　(S
　　(NP
　　　(NP (DT The) (NN statue) (NNS carriers))
　　　(PP (IN in)
　　　　(NP (DT the) (NN park))))
　　(VP (VBP are)
　　　(ADJP (JJ rusty)))
　　(. .)))
Universal dependencies
det (carriers－3, The－1)
compound (carriers－3, statue－2)
nsubj (rusty－8, carriers－3)
case (park－6, in－4)
det (park－6, the－5)
nmod (carriers－3, park－6)
cop (rusty－8, are－7)
root (ROOT－0, rusty－8)

从上面花园幽径句"The statue stands in the park are rusty"和对照

句"The statue carriers in the park are rusty"在句法与依存分析上的对照可知,该花园幽径句剖析错误主要源于对 stands 的词性判断错误。当系统根据统计概率认为 stands 应是动词 VBZ 而不是名词复数 NNS 时,句法分析便出现了较大偏差,随之而来的就是语义上的不和谐。如果想成功剖析,系统必须回溯后重新解码。否则,得到的结果只能是句法和语义错误。

这种词性选择的归类错误在被试组的阅读效果评分中也得到了反映。

从非独立 t 检验来看,5 秒反应时状态下,被试组普遍认为该句是正确的,得分为 68。而在 10 秒反应时状态下,被试组反而推翻前期的认定,并给予该句不可接受的评分 -2。我们认为这个反转源于对该句的深度理解。在延长反应时后,被试从前期的囫囵吞枣的认知转变到精耕细作的理解,但是却受到句法和语义双重错位效应影响,最后偏离正确值。这说明:对花园幽径句的理解,延长反应时在某种程度上会加剧被试的认知延宕,并使被试误入语言的陷阱。

从方差分析来看,四个能力组在该句的理解上具有显著性差异。能力组由弱到强的得分为 35,11,-10,13。能力弱的 A 组得分远远超出其他三个能力组。四个组方差分析得分的阅读效果轨迹呈现反对钩状特征。

我们分析,这与伊斯特威克和菲利普斯的"弱能力被试可能受到复杂结构影响较小"的观点相一致。他们可能只选定 stands 为名词项,而较快得出可以接受的结论。得分为负数的较强能力 C 组受到的干扰最大,被试们最终被语言陷阱所俘获,认为该句不可接受。能力最强的 D 组得分较高,可能在于该组被试完成了回溯整合,重新选定 stands 为名词项的结论,推进了正确解码的进度。

(6) *S88 - The teacher told the children the ghost story had frightened that it wasn't true. (非独立 t 检验 16;-92)(方差分析 2,-17,-15,-34)

Your query

第六章 时间和能力因素与花园幽径句阅读效果的方差分析

The teacher told the children the ghost story had frightened that it wasn't true.

Tagging

The/DT

teacher/NN

told/VBD

the/DT

children/NNS

the/DT

ghost/NN

story/NN

had/VBD

frightened/VBD

that/IN

it/PRP

was/VBD

n't/RB

true/JJ

./.

Parse

(ROOT
　(S
　　(NP (DT The) (NN teacher))
　　(VP (VBD told)
　　　(NP
　　　　(NP (DT the) (NNS children))
　　　　(SBAR
　　　　　(S
　　　　　　(NP (DT the) (NN ghost) (NN story))

```
              (VP (VBD had)
                (VP (VBD frightened)
                  (SBAR (IN that)
                    (S
                      (NP (PRP it))
                      (VP (VBD was) (RB n't)
                        (ADJP (JJ true))))))))))))
          (. .)))
```

Universal dependencies

det (teacher-2, The-1)

nsubj (told-3, teacher-2)

root (ROOT-0, told-3)

det (children-5, the-4)

dobj (told-3, children-5)

det (story-8, the-6)

compound (story-8, ghost-7)

nsubj (frightened-10, story-8)

aux (frightened-10, had-9)

acl: relcl (children-5, frightened-10)

mark (true-15, that-11)

nsubj (true-15, it-12)

cop (true-15, was-13)

neg (true-15, n't-14)

ccomp (frightened-10, true-15)

该句的系统剖析是错误的。其错误主要在于对 the ghost story had frightened 成分的分析上。从句法结构分析可知，系统认为该成分属于宾语从句范畴，句子的整体结构是 The teacher told the children + SBAR。但是，实际上该成分是 the children 的定语从句。真正的结构应该是 The teacher told the children (the ghost story had frightened) that it wasn't true。直接宾语从句的范畴是 that it wasn't true，其控制动词不是 frightened 而是 told。由于对嵌套成分 the ghost story had frightened 的剖析错误，系统的依存分析必然导致语义上的不可接受。

依存关系中最关键的部分出现在 frightened/told 与 true 的句补关系 ccomp（clausal complement）的选择上。如果形成的是 ccomp（frightened－10，true－15），则认为控制 that it wasn't true 成分的是 frightened。如果形成的是 ccomp（told－3，true－15），则认为该从句被 told 所控制。系统出现了显著性错误，得到的依存关系是 ccomp（frightened－10，true－15）。这说明系统受到了干扰成分 the ghost story had frightened 的影响。如果我们将干扰项的嵌套结构去除，系统可以得到正确的剖析结果。

Your query

The teacher told the children that it wasn't true.

Tagging

The/DT

teacher/NN

told/VBD

the/DT

children/NNS

that/IN

it/PRP

was/VBD

n't/RB

true/JJ

./.

Parse

（ROOT

　（S

　　（NP（DT The）（NN teacher））

```
           （VP（VBD told）
              （NP（DT the）（NNS children））
              （SBAR（IN that）
                 （S
                    （NP（PRP it））
                    （VP（VBD was）（RB n't）
                       （ADJP（JJ true））))))
      （..）))
```

Universal dependencies
det（teacher – 2，The – 1）
nsubj（told – 3，teacher – 2）
root（ROOT – 0，told – 3）
det（children – 5，the – 4）
dobj（told – 3，children – 5）
mark（true – 10，that – 6）
nsubj（true – 10，it – 7）
cop（true – 10，was – 8）
neg（true – 10，n't – 9）
ccomp（told – 3，true – 10）

  比较干扰项去除前后的剖析结果可以看出，系统更愿意选择就近的动词作为 that it wasn't true 的控制项。这种系统倾向在被试组阅读测试中也存在。

  从非独立 t 检验来看，被试组 5 秒和 10 秒状态下的得分分别为 16 和 – 92。他们从初期的快速给定的正评价转到了充分阅读后给定的负评价。这个正确的花园幽径句不被接受的根本原因，与系统剖析错误的原因一致：受到了干扰项的影响并将 that it wasn't true 的控制项就近选择为 frightened 而不是远距离的 told。这说明在前期阅读时间不足的情况下，被试组倾向于"秒定"结果，而没有时间更深入地从语义上进行解读，选择接受的被试较多。当时间充裕时，被试从前期粗略的句法结构进入细致的语义分析层面，因受到花园幽径效应影响，遂得出不可接受的结果。由于该句字符串较长而且嵌套结构较复杂，真正的控制词 told 又距离较远，超出了被试的认知能力所能达到的距离，所以，被试后期认定该句不可接受。我们认为，被试前期的接受是对句法结构的大概理解，而后期的拒绝是对内在语义的深入解读，因误入语言陷阱而难以自拔。这种越深入分析，可能在语言陷阱中越陷越深的状况可以从方差分析中得到验证。

从能力组方差分析来看，错误的句法结构划分让能力高的被试深受语义困扰。四个由弱到强的能力组得分分别为 2，-17，-15，-34。阅读效果得分的轨迹呈现反斜率状态。

被试能力越强，受到的困惑越重。而能力最弱的组却可能因为自身能力所限在解码字串较长和结构较复杂的句式时无法深入，因而未进入语义困惑阶段，给出了该句可以接受的评分。这个测试结果再次验证了伊斯特威克和菲利普斯的观点：在一定的认知范围内，相对能力弱的被试而言，能力强的被试更可能受到复杂结构（例如花园幽径句）的语义信息影响。

（二）多组阅读效果负同质项研究

多组阅读效果负同质项共有 3 个。四个被试组均认为这些测试句不被接受，各个组之间不具有质的区别，但具有量的不同。下面我们具体分析这 3 个负同质项在四个组之间的量的差异。

（1）S44 - The fat that people eat accumulates.（非独立 t 检验 -54；-49）（方差分析 -29，-31，-27，-1）

Your query

The fat that people eat accumulates.

Tagging

The/DT

fat/NN

that/IN

people/NNS

eat/VBP
accumulates/VBZ
./.
Parse
(ROOT
　(S
　　(NP
　　　(NP (DT The) (NN fat))
　　　(SBAR (IN that)
　　　　(S
　　　　　(NP (NNS people))
　　　　　(VP (VBP eat)))))
　　(VP (VBZ accumulates))
　　(. .)))

Universal dependencies
det (fat-2, The-1)
nsubj (accumulates-6, fat-2)
mark (eat-5, that-3)
nsubj (eat-5, people-4)
dep (fat-2, eat-5)
root (ROOT-0, accumulates-6)

该花园幽径句的解读出现了跨语言的不同。首先，我们在基于母语是英语的 Stanford parser 的人工标注中发现，以概率上下文无关文法为支撑的系统认为该句的理解没有障碍。其句法结构符合嵌套特征，形成的主要结构是 [The fat that people eat] NP [accumulates] VP。其语义分析也符合依存关系的特征。根节点为动词 root (ROOT-0, accumulates-6)，另一个主谓关系分别是主句的 nsubj (accumulates-6, fat-2) 和嵌套句的 nsubj (eat-5, people-4)，引导性关系是 mark (eat-5, that-3)。限定关系是 det (fat-2, The-1)。唯一有一点小缺陷的是 dep（fat-2，eat-5）的关系认定。dep 代码是 dependent 依附关系的意思，是系统由于各种原因无法在两词间判定它们清晰的依存关系时采用的标注关系。如"Then, as if to show that he could, …"可表示为 dep（show, if）等。如果把 fat/NN 理解为宾语会更好一些。

我们的被试理解则出现了中国特色。

从非独立 t 检验的结果来看，延长的反应时并未带来根本的解码不同。被试们统统将该句列为不可接受的行列。两次的得分分别为-54和-49。这说明被试的解码呈现稳定错位状态。

从方差分析结果来看，四个由弱到强能力组的得分依次为-29,-31,-27,-1。阅读效果得分的轨迹呈现反 L 状态。

能力最强的组具有最好的解码结果，他们倾向于接受该句的状态。这个结果与母语国家的标注结果有差距，但相对来说差距较小（母语国家的标注表明该句是处于强接受的程度）。其他的三个较弱的能力组则认为该句不可以接受，他们的解码能力与母语国家的标注结果相去甚远。

我们推断出现该现象的原因在于：

词汇认知程度不够。单词 accumulates 是动词现在时的第三人称单数形式，系统代码是 accumulates/VBZ。其不及物动词在 LDOCE 中的释义为："to gradually increase in numbers or amount until there is a large quantity in one place"，配例为"Fat tends to accumulate around the hips and thighs."这说明作为动词"积累"的意义，通常与名词脂肪 fat 搭配。如果被试对该词缺乏认知，会导致理解和认知上的偏误。

受动词 eat 的影响。该动词在表示义项"to put food in your mouth and chew and swallow it"时有及物和不及物两类。当被试对 accumulates 没有认知并可能认为该词汇是动词 eat 的宾语时，将会产生极大的错位效应。通过对 BNC 语料库的随机查询可知，eat 后续宾语时共有三种情况，分别是 eat+NN0（48），eat+NN1（422）和 eat+NN2（221）。这三种的频数共计是691。当动词 eat 后续第三人称单数动词时只有一种情况，即 eat + VVZ （7）。从频数对比可知，7 与 691 明显处于卡方检验的显著性差异范围。这说明被试组受到了解码构式的影响，他们极有可能把 [eat + X] VP 当成了认知构式并受其驱动。

从方差分析结果轨迹来看，四个组得分呈现对钩状的阅读效果状态：能力最弱的得分较好，能力较弱的组得分较差，能力较强的组回归到较好，能力强的组得分最好。

（2） *S71 – The prime people number few.（非独立 t 检验 – 129；– 75）（方差分析 – 41, – 30, – 1, – 14）

  Your query
  The prime people number few.
  Tagging
The/DT
prime/JJ
people/NNS
number/NN
few/JJ
./.
  Parse
（ROOT
  （NP
   （NP（DT The）（JJ prime）（NNS people）（NN number））
   （NP（JJ few））
   （. .）））
  Universal dependencies
  det（number – 4, The – 1）
  amod（number – 4, prime – 2）
  compound（number – 4, people – 3）
  root（ROOT – 0, number – 4）
  dep（number – 4, few – 5）

该句的解码难点在于动词的认定上。解码中的相关字符串分别是 The，prime，people，number 和 few。而能够充当动词的只有 number。在 BNC 语料库中我们统计该动词的名词义项频数为 48716，而动词义项频数为 83。从认知上来说，动词义项是非显著性的低概率选项。所以，以概率上下文无关文法构建的解析器不可能将该词列为动词义项。所以，系统只能将该词解读为符合概率的 number/NN 形式，其句法结构和依存关系均告剖析失败。如果我们把容易产生歧义的 number 换成没有多义项的动词 achieve，相应的句法和语义关系便可以得到较好的理顺。换句话说，句子 The prime people number few 与 The prime people achieve few 具有相同的句法结构和语义关系，除了动词发生替换之外。具体如下：

Your query

The prime people achieve few.

Tagging

The/DT

prime/JJ

people/NNS

achieve/VBP

few/JJ

./.

Parse

(ROOT

　(S

　　(NP (DT The) (JJ prime) (NNS people))

　　(VP (VBP achieve)

　　　(ADJP (JJ few)))

　　(. .)))

Universal dependencies

det (people－3, The－1)

amod（people – 3，prime – 2）

nsubj（achieve – 4，people – 3）

root（ROOT – 0，achieve – 4）

xcomp（achieve – 4，few – 5）

被试组的解读也与系统一样，受到了多义项的很大干扰。

从非独立 t 检验来看，两次得分是 – 129 和 – 75。虽然也都是不认可该句，但程度有较大减轻，表明时间延长之后，部分被试开始尝试接受该句。但是，在 126 个被试中，接受该句的人数尚未达到从量变到质变并接受该句的程度。

从分组的方差分析来看，得分具有较为明显的倾向：能力弱和能力较弱的两个组分别是 – 41 和 – 30。这表明他们均程度较相似地拒绝承认该句。而能力较强和能力强的两组得分为 – 1 和 – 14，能力强的组反倒受到较大的认知干扰。我们认为出现这种局面的原因是多方面的，但总体来说，能力在该句中得到一定正相关的体现，但能力达到一定的程度之后却会因为错位效应影响而下降，四个组的解码效应呈现典型的抛物线特征，能力较强的组达到了抛物线的顶点。

（3）＊S81 – The sour drink from the ocean.（非独立 t 检验 – 67；– 135）（方差分析 – 31，– 17，– 26，– 42）

Your query

The sour drink from the ocean.

Tagging

The/DT

sour/JJ

drink/NN

from/IN

the/DT

ocean/NN

./.

Parse

（ROOT
　　（NP
　　　　（NP（DT The）（JJ sour）（NN drink））
　　　　（PP（IN from）
　　　　　　（NP（DT the）（NN ocean）））
　　　　（. .）））

Universal dependencies

det（drink – 3, The – 1）
amod（drink – 3, sour – 2）
root（ROOT – 0, drink – 3）
case（ocean – 6, from – 4）
det（ocean – 6, the – 5）
nmod（drink – 3, ocean – 6）

该句是我们出于测试需要设定的干扰句，从句法和语义上来说都是不可以接受的。

系统的分析非常准确，无论句法和语义均完成得很好。

被试组的解码效果也呈现了与系统剖析的一致性。5 秒和 10 秒反应时状态下的得分为 – 67 和 – 135。时间延长后，更多的被试发现该句是错误的，遂给予较多的负值评分。在分组的方差分析中，四个组也均认为该句错误，得分较为集中，即 – 31，– 17，– 26，– 42。能力很弱和很强的两个组阅读效果较好，中间两个组相对较弱，呈现枕木状阅读效果轨迹。

（三）多组阅读效果正同质项研究

多组阅读效果正同质项共包括 10 个测试句。这些句子被试各组均认为是可以接受的，但在保持同质的基础上，各组之间的认知程度却呈现显著性差异的特点。我们尝试从这些迥异的特征中找寻到中国学习者对英语复杂句理解的规律并总结其特征，以便于为后期的研究抛砖引玉。

（1）　*S3 – Fat people eat accumulates.（非独立 t 检验 136；74）

（方差分析 45，44，13，7）

该句是我们设定的四个对照组中的一个，各个对照组的解码出现了较为明显的差异。请比较下面四个句子（星号表示非独立 t 检验具有显著性差异，两个数代表先后两次测试的得分；方差分析的临界值是 2.61，我们提供了方差显著项由弱到强四个组的测试得分）：

*S3 – Fat people eat accumulates.（非独立 t 检验显著，先后得分 136；74）（方差分析显著，F = 3.06 > 2.61；能力四组 45，44，13，7）

S4 – Fat that people eat accumulates.（非独立 t 检验不显著，先后得分 –31；–28）（方差分析不显著，F = 2.57 < 2.61）

S44 – The fat that people eat accumulates.（非独立 t 检验不显著，先后得分 –54；–49）（方差分析显著，F = 2.77 > 2.61；能力四组 –29，–31，–27，–1）

*S45 – The fat that people eat accumulates in their bodies.（非独立 t 检验显著，先后得分 –10；68）（方差分析不显著，F = 2.39 < 2.61）

在句子结构关系对照方面，第一组 S3 和 S4 的组内区别在于引导词 that 的存在与否。第二组 S44 和 S45 的组内区别在于状语 in their bodies 的有无。两组组间的主要差异在于 fat 有无限定词 the 的存在。具体的统计结果和结构对照请见表 6–12。

表 6–12　四个对照句的结构对比与显著性差异对比

组别	句编号	结构差异	非独立 t 检验	方差分析	难易程度
第一组 fat	S3	people eat	显著	显著	难
	S4	that people eat	不显著	不显著	易
第二组 the fat	S44	无状语	不显著	显著	中等
	S45	in their bodies	显著	不显著	中等

从表中可以看出：

第一，名词 fat 前有限定词 the 的第二组总体来说比没有限定词

the 的第一组更容易一些，究其原因在于限定词 the 提示了 fat 的词性，这样就部分化解了 fat 的名词和形容词的潜在歧义，减轻了被试的解码难度。

第二，在第一组中，有嵌套结构提示词 that 的 S4 要比没有提示词提示的 S3 容易很多，其 t 值和 F 值的测试中均显示为非显著。

第三，在第二组中，有状语成分 in their bodies 的 S45 要比没有状语成分的 S44 容易理解，原因在于该状语成分提示了前面的动词 accumulates 为不及物动词。

第四，从对照中可以看出，花园幽径句 S3 在三个关键歧义点上都没有得到相应的提示，既没有出现提示 fat 词性的限定词 the，也没有出现提示嵌套结构的引导词 that，更没有出现提示动词 accumulates 及物与否的状语成分 in their bodies。这就导致该花园幽径句承载了较重的认知负载。请见系统对 S3 的错误剖析：

Your query

Fat people eat accumulates.

Tagging

Fat/NNP

people/NNS

eat/VBP

accumulates/NNS

./.

Parse

(ROOT
   (S
     (NP (NNP Fat) (NNS people))
     (VP (VBP eat)
       (NP (NNS accumulates)))
     (. .)))

Universal dependencies

compound（people – 2，Fat – 1）
nsubj（eat – 3，people – 2）
root（ROOT – 0，eat – 3）
dobj（eat – 3，accumulates – 4）

从上面的系统剖析可以看出，出现错误的部分也主要在于前面分析的三个地方：第一，没有词性提示下，系统将 Fat/NNP 分析为单数专有名词，并将其与后续的 people/NNS 复数名词构成名词短语 NP（NNP Fat）（NNS people）。第二，没有嵌套结构指示词提示，系统把 people eat 拆分开来，并认为 eat 为主句的主动词。第三，没有状语成分提示，动词被分析成 accumulates/NNS 的复数名词结构。这三个主要的错误使整个系统分析漏洞百出，语义上的依存分析更是难以理解。

被试在理解该句时，在非独立 t 检验和方差分析两方面都出现了显著性差异的阅读效果。

从非独立 t 检验来说，5 秒和 10 秒状态下的得分依次为 136 和 74。这说明在给予了充分的阅读时间后，被试组得分反倒降低，认为可以接受该句的得分甚至降至接近一半的程度。时间因素制约了被试的理解。这种状况大概源于时间在提供给被试足够的思考机会的同时，也带给了被试更多的歧义空间，阻碍了他们较快且较准确地获得正确的阅读结果。

从方差分析角度来说，四个由弱到强的能力组得分依次为 45，44，13，7。其阅读效果轨迹基本呈现反斜率线性特征。能力越强的组受到的干扰越大得分越低，能力越弱的组受到的干扰越小得分越高。这个花园幽径句测试结果再次验证了伊斯特威克和菲利普斯（1999）的观点：相对能力弱的被试而言，能力强的被试更可能受到复杂结构影响。

对系统自动剖析而言，如果想要获得正确的句法和语义剖析结果，系统必须具备快速准确地处理上述三个歧义节点项的能力。

通过在 Stanford parser 中试误的方法，我们发现在这三个歧义点

第六章 时间和能力因素与花园幽径句阅读效果的方差分析

上，系统最难理解的项在于对嵌套结构的划分上，即系统很难在提示词 that 缺失的情况下把 people eat 划分为嵌套结构。我们为了减轻系统的剖析压力，明确指出首词是名词词性，尾词是不及物动词，但系统仍然无法得到正确的剖析。如在"The food people eat reduces."和"The food people eat reduces during the period."的剖析中，系统剖析均告失败。具体的失败剖析如下：

在首词添加了限定词 the（the food）之后，people eat 没有嵌套结构提示词 that 时的失败剖析：

Your query

The food people eat reduces.

Tagging

The/DT

food/NN

people/NNS

eat/VBP

reduces/VBZ

./.

Parse

(ROOT
　　(S
　　　(NP (DT The) (NN food) (NNS people))
　　　(VP (VBP eat)
　　　　(SBAR
　　　　　(S
　　　　　　(VP (VBZ reduces))))))
　　(. .)))

Universal dependencies

det (people - 3, The - 1)

compound (people - 3, food - 2)

nsubj（eat－4，people－3）

root（ROOT－0，eat－4）

ccomp（eat－4，reduces－5）

在首词添加了限定词 the（the food）并在尾词添加了提示前动词是不及物属性的状语（during the period）之后，people eat 没有嵌套结构提示词 that 时的失败剖析：

Your query

The food people eat reduces during the period.

Tagging

The/DT

food/NN

people/NNS

eat/VBP

reduces/VBZ

during/IN

the/DT

period/NN

./.

Parse

(ROOT
　(S
　　(NP (DT The) (NN food) (NNS people))
　　(VP (VBP eat)
　　　(SBAR
　　　　(S
　　　　　(VP (VBZ reduces)
　　　　　　(PP (IN during)
　　　　　　　(NP (DT the) (NN period)))))))
　　(. .)))

第六章 时间和能力因素与花园幽径句阅读效果的方差分析

Universal dependencies
det（people – 3，The – 1）
compound（people – 3，food – 2）
nsubj（eat – 4，people – 3）
root（ROOT – 0，eat – 4）
ccomp（eat – 4，reduces – 5）
case（period – 8，during – 6）
det（period – 8，the – 7）
nmod（reduces – 5，period – 8）

从上面的两次失败剖析我们可以看出，真正的系统性错误在于对嵌套结构的认定上。一旦系统失去了认定嵌套结构的引导词 that 的帮助，系统便陷入全面的剖析错误。从另一个角度说，如果我们补足了这个系统缺陷，在其他两个歧义点不进行系统标示的情况下（不提示首词是名词，即不添加限定词 the；不提示尾动词是不及物动词，即不添加状语成分），是否就可以得到正确的剖析呢？如果按照我们的分析思路进行剖析，且其结果证明都是正确的，那么系统性缺陷就可以确定是指向嵌套结构的：添加嵌套提示词 that 就可以解决局部歧义句的句法和语义问题；省略嵌套提示词 that 系统甚至无法解决正常句的句法和语义剖析。

请看对三个句子"Food that people eat reduces."、"The food that people eat reduces."和"The food that people eat reduces during the period."的系统剖析：

仅提供嵌套提示词 that 时的"Food that people eat reduces."的正确剖析如下：

Your query
Food that people eat reduces.
Tagging
Food/NNP
that/IN

· 171 ·

people/NNS

eat/VBP

reduces/VBZ

./.

Parse

(ROOT

　(S

　　(NP

　　　(NP (NNP Food))

　　　(SBAR (IN that)

　　　　(S

　　　　　(NP (NNS people))

　　　　　(VP (VBP eat)))))

　　(VP (VBZ reduces))

　　(. .)))

Universal dependencies

nsubj (reduces-5, Food-1)

mark (eat-4, that-2)

nsubj (eat-4, people-3)

dep (Food-1, eat-4)

root (ROOT-0, reduces-5)

提供嵌套提示词 that 和首词限定词 the 时的"The food that people eat reduces."的正确剖析如下：

Your query

The food that people eat reduces.

Tagging

The/DT

food/NN

that/IN

people/NNS

eat/VBP

reduces/VBZ

./.

Parse

（ROOT

　（S

　　（NP

　　　（NP（DT The）（NN food））

　　　（SBAR（IN that）

　　　　（S

　　　　　（NP（NNS people））

　　　　　（VP（VBP eat）)))))

　　（VP（VBZ reduces））

　　（..）))

Universal dependencies

det（food-2，The-1）

nsubj（reduces-6，food-2）

mark（eat-5，that-3）

nsubj（eat-5，people-4）

dep（food-2，eat-5）

root（ROOT-0，reduces-6）

提供嵌套提示词 that，首词限定词 the 以及状语成分时的"The food that people eat reduces during the period."的正确剖析如下：

Your query

The food that people eat reduces during the period.

Tagging

The/DT

food/NN

that/IN
people/NNS
eat/VBP
reduces/VBZ
during/IN
the/DT
period/NN
./.
Parse
(ROOT
　(S
　　(NP
　　　(NP (DT The) (NN food))
　　　(SBAR (IN that)
　　　　(S
　　　　　(NP (NNS people))
　　　　　(VP (VBP eat)))))
　　(VP (VBZ reduces)
　　　(PP (IN during)
　　　　(NP (DT the) (NN period))))
　　(. .)))
Universal dependencies
det (food-2, The-1)
nsubj (reduces-6, food-2)
mark (eat-5, that-3)
nsubj (eat-5, people-4)
dep (food-2, eat-5)
root (ROOT-0, reduces-6)
case (period-9, during-7)

第六章　时间和能力因素与花园幽径句阅读效果的方差分析

det（period－9，the－8）

nmod（reduces－6，period－9）

在提供了嵌套结构的提示词 that 之后，系统对三类分项的句子都完成了正确解码。这个结果验证了我们之前的推断：系统的最薄弱环节在于对缺失提示词 that 下的嵌套结构认定。系统剖析的这三个句子都是普通句。那么，既然系统的缺陷在普通句剖析中能够得到补足，是否意味着这个补足后的系统也能够用于纠错性折返花园幽径句的理解呢？也就是说花园幽径句 S3 的错误理解是否也可以在提示词 that 补足之后得到更正呢？如果答案是肯定的，即系统可以在其他条件不变的情况下仅仅添加嵌套结构提示词就可以化解局部歧义，那么说明嵌套结构提示词在宾语嵌套从句结构中至关重要，不仅影响到相对简单的普通句解码，甚至还影响到复杂的花园幽径句的解码。后期我们就可以重点提示中国英语学习者对嵌套结构的关注。请见下面的剖析：

花园幽径句 S3 在其他条件不变时，仅仅添加嵌套结构提示词 that 时的正确剖析：

Your query

Fat that people eat accumulates.

Tagging

Fat/NNP

that/IN

people/NNS

eat/VBP

accumulates/VBZ

./.

Parse

(ROOT

　(S

　　(NP

```
            (NP(NNP Fat))
            (SBAR(IN that)
              (S
                (NP(NNS people))
                (VP(VBP eat)))))
            (VP(VBZ accumulates))
            (..)))
```
Universal dependencies
nsubj(accumulates-5,Fat-1)
mark(eat-4,that-2)
nsubj(eat-4,people-3)
dep(Fat-1,eat-4)
root(ROOT-0,accumulates-5)

从上面的正确剖析可以看出，花园幽径句 S3 原来面临的三个歧义节点都随着嵌套结构提示词 that 的出现迎刃而解。具体的变化对照请见表 6-13。

表6-13 嵌套结构引导词 that 对花园幽径句 S3 的系统剖析对照

分项	正确解码（that 提示）	行进错位（无 that 提示）
词类标注	Fat/NNP	Fat/NNP
	that/IN	
	people/NNS	people/NNS
	eat/VBP	eat/VBP
	accumulates/VBZ	accumulates/NNS
句法结构	NP(NNP Fat)	NP(NNP Fat)(NNS people)
	SBAR(IN that)	
	S 　　(NP(NNS people)) 　　(VP(VBP eat))	VP 　　(VBP eat) 　　(NP(NNS accumulates))
	VP(VBZ accumulates)	

续表

分项	正确解码（that 提示）	行进错位（无 that 提示）
依存关系	nsubj（accumulates – 5，Fat – 1）	compound（people – 2，Fat – 1）
	mark（eat – 4，that – 2）	
	nsubj（eat – 4，people – 3）	nsubj（eat – 3，people – 2）
	dep（Fat – 1，eat – 4）	dobj（eat – 3，accumulates – 4）
	root（ROOT – 0，accumulates – 5）	root（ROOT – 0，eat – 3）
结论：嵌套结构引导词 that 有无是影响系统成功解码与否的关键		

从上面剖析的对照可以看出，花园幽径句 S3 最关键的歧义节点在于嵌套结构提示词 that 的有无。如果借助该提示词帮助，系统有足够的能力成功剖析其他节点的歧义结构。如果系统中没有提示词 that 出现，系统将进入行进错位花园幽径效应的回溯状态。

花园幽径句 S3 的被试组语言测试和系统剖析结果说明：第一，时间因素对该花园幽径句起到了负相关作用，提供给被试的时间越长，被试受到的干扰越大；第二，能力强弱与该句的测试结果呈现负相关，并再次验证"能力强的被试更易受到复杂结构影响"的论证；第三，宾语从句中嵌套结构提示词 that 具有至关重要的作用，如果缺失将导致花园幽径句（甚至是普通句）的解码错位。

（2）＊S15 – Please have the students who failed the exam take the supplementary.（非独立 t 检验 98；146）（方差分析 23，41，21，56）

S15 的核心解码信息在于嵌套结构 who failed the exam 的划分上。如果动词 failed 被认为是及物动词，那么形成的结构就是［the students［who failed the exam］CP］NP +［take the supplementary］VP。如果认定该动词是不及物动词，形成的就是［the students［who failed］CP］NP +［the exam take the supplementary］IP 结构。通过语料库分析这两个选项哪一个是高频选项将有助于我们进行分析。

在 BNC 中，我们统计了动词 fail 的频次约是 3215，其中充当及物动词的频次约是 169，不及物动词的频次约为 3046。不及物动词以绝

· 177 ·

对优势的频次作为优选项。这个统计结果将证明在以概率上下文无关文法为理论支撑的 Stanford parser 中，系统将采用［the students［who failed］CP］NP +［the exam take the supplementary］IP 结构，即将 the exam 划分为后一句的主语，最终导致解码错误。请见系统对 S15 的错误剖析：

Your query

Please have the students who failed the exam take the supplementary.

Tagging

Please/UH

have/VB

the/DT

students/NNS

who/WP

failed/VBD

the/DT

exam/NN

take/VBP

the/DT

supplementary/NN

./.

Parse

(ROOT

　(S

　　(INTJ (UH Please))

　　(VP (VB have)

　　　(NP

　　　　(NP (DT the) (NNS students))

　　　　(SBAR

　　　　　(WHNP (WP who))

```
( S
    ( VP ( VBD failed)
    ( SBAR
        ( S
            ( NP ( DT the) ( NN exam))
            ( VP ( VBP take)
            (NP(DT the)(NN supplementary))))))))))
( . . )))
```

Universal dependencies

discourse (have – 2 , Please – 1)

root (ROOT – 0 , have – 2)

det (students – 4 , the – 3)

dobj (have – 2 , students – 4)

nsubj (failed – 6 , who – 5)

acl：relcl (students – 4 , failed – 6)

det (exam – 8 , the – 7)

nsubj (take – 9 , exam – 8)

ccomp (failed – 6 , take – 9)

det (supplementary – 11 , the – 10)

dobj (take – 9 , supplementary – 11)

上面的剖析验证了我们之前的分析。系统按照概率将动词 fail 采纳为不及物动词。由此，系统产生了对句法和语义双重的错误剖析。如果我们能够变换符合系统预期的动词，将可以解决此类问题。请见我们将嵌套结构调整为 who were absent 后得到的正确剖析：

Your query

Please have the students who were absent take the supplementary.

Tagging

Please/UH

have/VB

the/DT
students/NNS
who/WP
were/VBD
absent/JJ
take/VB
the/DT
supplementary/NN
./.
Parse
(ROOT
　　(S
　　　　(INTJ (UH Please))
　　　　(VP (VB have)
　　　　　　(S
　　　　　　　　(NP
　　　　　　　　　　(NP (DT the) (NNS students))
　　　　　　　　　　(SBAR
　　　　　　　　　　　　(WHNP (WP who))
　　　　　　　　　　　　(S
　　　　　　　　　　　　　　(VP (VBD were)
　　　　　　　　　　　　　　　　(ADJP (JJ absent))))))
　　　　　　　　(VP (VB take)
　　　　　　　　　　(NP (DT the) (NN supplementary)))))
　　　　(. .)))
Universal dependencies
discourse (have-2, Please-1)
root (ROOT-0, have-2)
det (students-4, the-3)

第六章 时间和能力因素与花园幽径句阅读效果的方差分析

nsubj（take－8，students－4）

nsubj（absent－7，who－5）

cop（absent－7，were－6）

acl：relcl（students－4，absent－7）

ccomp（have－2，take－8）

det（supplementary－10，the－9）

dobj（take－8，supplementary－10）

在对S15的测试统计中，被试组出现的变化是同质性变化，即不论是非独立t检验还是方差分析，均接受该句的正确性，只是在程度上有较大差异。

从非独立t检验来看，两次测试成绩分别是98和146。在反应时从5秒延长到10秒后，被试组认为该句正确的得分显著性得到了提升。时间因素与阅读效果呈现正比例状态。

从方差分析来看，能力组由弱到强的得分分别为23，41，21，56。其阅读效果得分轨迹呈现波浪形。较强能力组仅为21分，其得分甚至比最弱的能力组还低。之所以出现如此状况，我们推断可能是这一能力阶段的被试受到的干扰是最大的。其干扰源应该来自failed的及物与否的属性判定上。但为什么偏偏较强能力组受到的干扰最大，而不是最弱组或者最强组？目前我们无法得到合理解释，希望将来有更多的学者关注此类非对称性的认知效果研究。不过，该句部分验证了国外学者关于"能力较强的被试更容易被复杂句影响"的论断。对S15的理解，能力最强的被试组获得了最高的得分，这说明他们具有很强的阅读能力。

（3）﹡S19－Single and married soldiers and their families are housed in the complex.（非独立t检验77；143）（方差分析36，26，31，42）

Your query

Single and married soldiers and their families are housed in the complex.

Tagging

Single/JJ
and/CC
married/JJ
soldiers/NNS
and/CC
their/PRP$
families/NNS
are/VBP
housed/VBN
in/IN
the/DT
complex/NN
./.
Parse
(ROOT
　(S
　　(NP
　　　(NP (JJ Single)
　　　　(CC and)
　　　　(JJ married) (NNS soldiers))
　　　(CC and)
　　　(NP (PRP$ their) (NNS families)))
　　(VP (VBP are)
　　　(VP (VBN housed)
　　　　(PP (IN in)
　　　　　(NP (DT the) (NN complex)))))
　　(. .)))
Universal dependencies
amod (soldiers-4, Single-1)

第六章 时间和能力因素与花园幽径句阅读效果的方差分析

cc（Single – 1, and – 2）
conj（Single – 1, married – 3）
nsubjpass（housed – 9, soldiers – 4）
cc（soldiers – 4, and – 5）
nmod：poss（families – 7, their – 6）
conj（soldiers – 4, families – 7）
auxpass（housed – 9, are – 8）
root（ROOT – 0, housed – 9）
case（complex – 12, in – 10）
det（complex – 12, the – 11）
nmod（housed – 9, complex – 12）

系统对 S19 的剖析很正确。该句的关键点在于主语的选定上。系统成功地剖析出句子的主语是 Single and married soldiers and their families，并在句法和语义方面得到了体现。

从非独立 t 检验来看，5 秒和 10 秒状态得分分别为 77 和 143。更多的反应时帮助被试更清楚地认知，得分更高。时间因素正向影响阅读效果。

从方差分析来看，四个能力组的得分为 36, 26, 31, 42。阅读效果得分轨迹呈现对勾状。最弱能力组得分出乎意料的高，最强的能力组得分最高。由于该句的主语字串过长，需要耗费被试较多的认知资源，最弱能力组表现抢眼。我们认为，之所以出现这样的局面，应该是最弱能力组采用的阅读策略是囫囵吞枣的 good enough（Ferreira and Patson, 2007）。这些能力最弱的被试跳跃性阅读，对句法和语义浮光掠影并未深入，这种粗读让他们节省了阅读时间，释放了较多的认知资源，补充了自身语言能力不足的缺陷。

（4）﹡S41 – The dog that I had really loved bones.（非独立 t 检验 166; 229）（方差分析 47, 74, 41, 60）

在 S41 的解码中，关键节点在于 had 是否是助动词的认定上。通常后续动词时；had 习惯性被认定是助动词。而在这个句子的解码中，恰好形成的是对传统认知的颠覆。had 作为实义动词出现，是嵌套结构的主动词过去式。如果不能将该歧义点正确解读，将无法实现正确剖析。请见系统误将 had 分析成助动词后形成的错误剖析：

Your query

The dog that I had really loved bones.

Tagging

The/DT

dog/NN

that/IN

I/PRP

had/VBD

really/RB

loved/VBN

bones/NNS

./.

Parse

（ROOT

　　（NP（DT The）（NN dog）

　　（SBAR（IN that）

　　　　（S

　　　　　（NP（PRP I））

　　　　　（VP（VBD had）

　　　　　（ADVP（RB really））

　　　　　（VP（VBN loved）

　　　　　（NP（NNS bones））））））

　　（. .）））

Universal dependencies

det（dog－2，The－1）

root（ROOT－0，dog－2）

第六章 时间和能力因素与花园幽径句阅读效果的方差分析

mark（loved – 7，that – 3）

nsubj（loved – 7，I – 4）

aux（loved – 7，had – 5）

advmod（loved – 7，really – 6）

ccomp（dog – 2，loved – 7）

dobj（loved – 7，bones – 8）

从系统句法和语义剖析可以看出，关键节点的解码失败导致了剖析的错误。在依存关系中 aux（loved – 7，had – 5）的语义关系验证了我们的推断。代码 aux（auxiliary）表示在句中起到助动词作用的助动关系，如"Reagan has died"可表示为 aux（died，has），"He should leave"可表示为 aux（leave，should）。系统将 S41 的 had 剖析为助动词成为整个解码错误的根源。如果我们通过换词的方式化解 had 歧义，将有助于系统得到正确剖析。请见将 had 更换为没有歧义的 hit 之后系统的正确剖析结果：

Your query

The dog that I hit really loved bones.

Tagging

The/DT

dog/NN

that/IN

I/PRP

hit/VBD

really/RB

loved/VBD

bones/NNS

./.

Parse

(ROOT

  (S

```
(NP
  (NP (DT The) (NN dog))
  (SBAR (IN that)
    (S
      (NP (PRP I))
      (VP (VBD hit)
        (ADVP (RB really))))))
(VP (VBD loved)
  (NP (NNS bones)))
(. .)))
```

Universal dependencies
det (dog-2, The-1)
nsubj (loved-7, dog-2)
mark (hit-5, that-3)
nsubj (hit-5, I-4)
dep (dog-2, hit-5)
advmod (hit-5, really-6)
root (ROOT-0, loved-7)
dobj (loved-7, bones-8)

如果我们在 had 和后面的动词之间添加状语成分以隔断两者的惯性搭配，这种花园幽径效应是否就能够得到缓解呢？为了配合测试，我们推出了一个对照句 S40："The dog that I had as a pet really loved bones."请见两个句子的结果对比：

从非独立 t 检验来看，S40 和 S41 都出现了显著性差异，而且两次测试的成绩得分几乎一致。S40 的 5 秒和 10 秒的两次得分分别为 169 和 218。S41 的得分是 166 和 229。这说明反应时延长一倍后，更多的被试接受了两个句子的正确性评估。

从方差分析来看，两个句子出现了较为明显的组间差异。

S40 中，状语成分 as a pet 的存在隔断了 had 和动词 loved 的习惯性搭配，这种距离感让被试有时间思考 had 的归属（助动词或实义动词），并据此得出正确的结论。所以，在方差分析中，S40 的 F 值为 1.38＜2.61，不具有显著性差异。

S41 中缺少较长状语成分的隔断，组间差异较大，其 F 值为 4.24，大于临界值 2.61，具有显著性差异。能力由弱到强的四个组得分为 47，74，41，60。阅读效果的得分轨迹呈现波浪形。能力较弱的组得到了最高分 74 分。这个测试结果表明能力强弱在某些复杂句的理解上并不是决定性因素。

（5）＊S43 – The fact that Jill is never here hurts me.（非独立 t 检验 85；147）（方差分析 4，29，24，38）

该句的剖析相对容易，没有较难的关键点，剖析没有障碍。请见系统形成的正确的剖析结果：

Your query

The fact that Jill is never here hurts me.

Tagging

The/DT

fact/NN

that/IN

Jill/NNP

is/VBZ

never/RB

here/RB

hurts/VBZ

me/PRP

./.

Parse

(ROOT

　(S

　　(NP

                 （NP（DT The）（NN fact））
               （SBAR（IN that）
                 （S
                   （NP（NNP Jill））
                   （VP（VBZ is）
                     （ADVP（RB never））
                     （ADVP（RB here））))))
             （VP（VBZ hurts）
               （NP（PRP me）))
             （. .）))

Universal dependencies

det（fact – 2, The – 1）

nsubj（hurts – 8, fact – 2）

mark（is – 5, that – 3）

nsubj（is – 5, Jill – 4）

dep（fact – 2, is – 5）

neg（is – 5, never – 6）

advmod（is – 5, here – 7）

root（ROOT – 0, hurts – 8）

dobj（hurts – 8, me – 9）

在被试组的测试中，形成的也是类似系统剖析的一边倒的正确模式。从非独立 t 检验来看，两次得分是 85 和 147。给予的阅读时间越长，被试越容易理解，正确率得分就越高。从方差分析来看，四个组的得分是 4, 29, 24, 38，基本呈现了能力大小与得分多少的正相关模式。这说明对于相对简单的句子来说，阅读效果与阅读时间和阅读能力都呈现正比率模式。这个结果与我们传统的认知是符合的：充足的阅读时间带来更精确的阅读效果；阅读能力的强弱决定阅读效果的好坏。

（6）S53 – The man came back to his house and was happy.（非独立

第六章 时间和能力因素与花园幽径句阅读效果的方差分析

t 检验 167;171)（方差分析 39,41,35,53）

该句是作为对照句出现的一个并列的简单句，系统剖析没有问题。请见系统的正确剖析结果：

Your query

The man came back to his house and was happy.

Tagging

The/DT

man/NN

came/VBD

back/RP

to/TO

his/PRP$

house/NN

and/CC

was/VBD

happy/JJ

./.

Parse

(ROOT
　　(S
　　　(NP (DT The) (NN man))
　　　(VP
　　　　(VP (VBD came)
　　　　　(PRT (RP back))
　　　　　(PP (TO to)
　　　　　　(NP (PRP$ his) (NN house))))
　　　　(CC and)
　　　　(VP (VBD was)
　　　　　(ADJP (JJ happy))))

(..)))

Universal dependencies

det（man－2，The－1）

nsubj（came－3，man－2）

root（ROOT－0，came－3）

compound：prt（came－3，back－4）

case（house－7，to－5）

nmod：poss（house－7，his－6）

nmod（came－3，house－7）

cc（came－3，and－8）

cop（happy－10，was－9）

conj（came－3，happy－10）

对被试组来说，这个简单句的解码符合阅读效果与时间因素和阅读能力的正相关比率关系。从非独立 t 检验来看，5 秒和 10 秒两次测试的得分比较接近，分别是 167 和 171。这两个得分说明绝大多数的被试都认为该句是可以接受的，两次得分不具有显著性差异。从方差分析来看，四个能力组的得分分别是 39，41，35，53。前三组得分显著性差异较少，但对于能力最强的被试组来说，后者得分远远超出前三组，体现了该组极强的阅读能力。这个简单句的理解基本符合传统认知中"阅读效果可以通过阅读能力体现"的观点，但能力较弱的前三组阅读效果差异不大，显著性差异出现在能力最强的被试组，这个结果与传统认知略有差异。

（7）S70 – The prime number is forty.（非独立 t 检验 213；228）（方差分析 60，53，41，57）

该句是作为花园幽径句 S69 – The prime number few 和 S71 – The prime people number few 而出现的对照句，系统剖析正常，请见结果：

Your query

The prime number is forty.

Tagging

第六章　时间和能力因素与花园幽径句阅读效果的方差分析

The/DT
prime/JJ
number/NN
is/VBZ
forty/JJ
./.
Parse
（ROOT
　（S
　　（NP（DT The）（JJ prime）（NN number））
　　（VP（VBZ is）
　　　（ADJP（JJ forty）））
　　（..）））
Universal dependencies
det（number – 3，The – 1）
amod（number – 3，prime – 2）
nsubj（forty – 5，number – 3）
cop（forty – 5，is – 4）
root（ROOT – 0，forty – 5）

　　对花园幽径句 S71 来说，它具有阅读效果的负同质项特点。无论是非独立 t 检验得分（ – 129；– 75），还是方差分析得分（ – 41，– 30，– 1，– 14），S71 都呈现了显著性差异的特征。被试组无一例外均受到花园幽径效应影响，其中能力最弱的组得分最低，其他组随能力提高而逐渐获得较高分值，但是能力最强的组受到了较大干扰，并未得到最高分值，其得分低于能力较强组的得分。我们分析，是在辨别 number 的词性方面耗费了大量的认知资源。所有组最后倾向于拒绝承认该句的正确性。

　　如果说对于 S71 的解码还有部分被试犹豫不决的话，那么对于花园幽径句 S69 – The prime number few 的理解则完全被缴械了。在 S69

· 191 ·

中，非独立 t 检验两次得分竟高达 -151 和 -161，这说明绝大多数被试认为 S69 不可接受。而且，在方差分析中，四个组得分差异性不大，分别为 -45，-50，-36，-35。这也从另一个侧面说明了对于出现概率极低的花园幽径句来说，时间因素和能力因素都无法提升被试的阅读效果，也就是说对于这类极端的花园幽径模式，阅读效果是完全独立于时间和能力的。这个观点颠覆了传统中有关时间、能力与阅读效果正相关的观点，也颠覆了国外学者关于能力强的被试更容易受到复杂结构影响的观点。换句话说，当花园幽径句的难度达到一定程度时，不管是延长时间还是更换能力组，该句的阅读效果均不会有显著性提高。难度一旦超出被试们的认知强度，时间因素和能力因素均告失效了。

与 S69 和 S71 不同，普通句 S70 的解码有其自身的特点。从非独立 t 检验来看，5 秒和 10 秒状态下的得分分别是 213 和 228，不具有显著性差异，这说明大多数被试都能够正确解码。

从方差分析来看，四个能力组的得分分别为 60，53，41，57，均接受该句，但具有组间得分的显著性差异。阅读效果和得分轨迹呈现 V 形。其中，能力最弱的组和能力最强的组得分较高而且比较接近。中间的两个组受到的干扰较大，尤其是能力较强的组得分最低。我们分析认为可能是受到 number 词性的影响。不过，普通句中间的两个组得分竟然远不及能力最差组的得分这个结果是我们始料不及的，因何出现这种局面有待今后进行深入研究。

(8) *S78 – The sniper guards the victim in the woods.（非独立 t 检验 91；172）（方差分析 13，48，23，48）

该句是普通句，系统可以正常解码，具体如下：

Your query

The sniper guards the victim in the woods.

Tagging

The/DT

sniper/NN

第六章　时间和能力因素与花园幽径句阅读效果的方差分析

guards/VBZ

the/DT

victim/NN

in/IN

the/DT

woods/NNS

./.

Parse

(ROOT

　(S

　　(NP (DT The) (NN sniper))

　　(VP (VBZ guards)

　　　(NP

　　　　(NP (DT the) (NN victim))

　　　　(PP (IN in)

　　　　　(NP (DT the) (NNS woods)))))

　　(. .)))

Universal dependencies

det (sniper-2, The-1)

nsubj (guards-3, sniper-2)

root (ROOT-0, guards-3)

det (victim-5, the-4)

dobj (guards-3, victim-5)

case (woods-8, in-6)

det (woods-8, the-7)

nmod (victim-5, woods-8)

对于被试组来说，该句理解没有问题，均承认其正确性。在非独立 t 检验和方差分析方面的显著性差异源自时间因素与组间能力差异。在 5 秒和 10 秒反应时状况下，得分分别为 91 和 172，即时间因素促进了阅读效果的提升。在四个能力组中，得分分别为 13，48，23，48。阅读效果和得分轨迹呈现波浪形。能力最弱的组得分显著性最低，我们分析主要原因在于 sniper 和 victim 是较为生僻的单词，能力最弱的被试或受到此类词汇干扰。能力较强的组缘何受到较大干扰，而能力最强的组和能力较弱的组却能够获得等同的最高分？此类问题或许只有引入脑认知实验数据才能得到更好的解释。

（9）＊S80 – The sniper pins were rusty from the rain.（非独立 t 检验 102；165）（方差分析 26，37，17，48）

Your query

The sniper pins were rusty from the rain.

Tagging

The/DT

sniper/NN

pins/NNS

were/VBD

rusty/VBN

from/IN

the/DT

rain/NN

./.

Parse

(ROOT
　(S
　　(NP (DT The) (NN sniper) (NNS pins))
　　(VP (VBD were)
　　　(VP (VBN rusty)
　　　　(PP (IN from)
　　　　　(NP (DT the) (NN rain)))))
　　(. .)))

第六章 时间和能力因素与花园幽径句阅读效果的方差分析

Universal dependencies

det（pins – 3，The – 1）

compound（pins – 3，sniper – 2）

nsubjpass（rusty – 5，pins – 3）

auxpass（rusty – 5，were – 4）

root（ROOT – 0，rusty – 5）

case（rain – 8，from – 6）

det（rain – 8，the – 7）

nmod（rusty – 5，rain – 8）

从上面的系统剖析可以看出，S80 是正确的句子，系统无论是句法还是语义都成功完成了剖析。从非独立 t 检验来看，两次的测试得分分别为 102 和 165，时间延长后被试得到了更好的阅读效果，具有显著性差异。从方差分析来看，四个组得分为 26，37，17，48。每个组都接受该句的正确性。阅读效果和得分轨迹呈现波浪形。这种状况与 S78 的分析比较接近。简单句解码中，能力最强的组得分处于高分状态。这个结果与传统认知相符合。

（10）S83 – The statue stands in the park.（非独立 t 检验 196；211）（方差分析 46，76，40，55）

Your query

The statue stands in the park.

Tagging

The/DT

statue/NN

stands/VBZ

in/IN

the/DT

park/NN

./.

Parse

```
(ROOT
  (S
    (NP (DT The) (NN statue))
    (VP (VBZ stands)
      (PP (IN in)
        (NP (DT the) (NN park))))
    (. .)))
```

Universal dependencies

det（statue-2, The-1）

nsubj（stands-3, statue-2）

root（ROOT-0, stands-3）

case（park-6, in-4）

det（park-6, the-5）

nmod（stands-3, park-6）

S83也是一个简单句，其非独立t检验的得分为196和211，不具有显著性差异，被试组认可该句的比率很高。从方差分析来看，四个组得分为46，76，40，55，具有显著性差异。与前两个简单句类似，阅读效果和得分轨迹也呈现波浪形。唯一不同的是能力较弱的组取得了76的高分峰值。该分比能力最强的组得分还高出很多。这个现象我们无法从常规进行解释。随着语言科学的脑认知化，我们相信这种从常规统计和计算角度无法得到满意分析的局面会得到较好解决。

本章小结

本章主要从时间因素与花园幽径句阅读效果的方差分析，以及能力因素与花园幽径句阅读效果的方差分析两个角度展开讨论。

首先，在讨论前我们设定分析方法是简单方差分析，即一元方差分析。我们的分析逻辑是：随机因素产生的组内差异如果在统计学意义上大于刻意分组所造成的组间差异的话，那么组间差异就是无意义的。这种状况下，组间差异与组内差异之比值 F 等于或小于 1，随机因素的组内差异起到决定性作用，分组效果差异不具有显著性。相反，如果组间差异远远大于组内差异的话，组间差异就是有统计学意义的。此时，组间差异与组内差异的比值 F 大于或远远大于 1，不同的分组效果具有显著性差异，即随机因素之外的因素起到了决定性效果。为了便于计算，我们引入了三个公式：组间均方公式 $MS_{between}$，组内均方公式 MS_{within}，以及前后两项之比的简单方差分析 F 值公式。

其次，在时间因素与花园幽径句阅读效果的方差分析中，我们进行了不同反应时的测试，共得到 5 秒—7 秒—10 秒的实验结果。在 .05 水平下，分子自由度为 2，分母为无穷大（>100），方差临界值为 3.0。我们的 100 个测试句中，能达到或者超过方差临界值的只有 8 个测试句，这说明对这些测试句来说，时间因素的确改变了被试组的阅读效果，而且，它们在非独立 t 检验中都具有显著性差异。具体包括 S1、S2、S6、S10、S13、S41、S88 和 S90。

最后，在能力因素与花园幽径句阅读效果的方差分析中，我们按照英语专业四级成绩把被试组分成了四个能力组：弱能力组（<60），较弱能力组（60—64），较强能力组（65—69）和强能力组（≥70）。在考虑方差是否齐性方面，我们对分组项进行了卡方检验。四个能力组的卡方值为 6.55，小于临界值 7.82（在 .05 水平下且 df = 3）。这说明我们分组不具有显著性差异，属于正态分布，方差也是齐性的。这为我们进行能力组阅读效果的方差分析奠定了基础。

在对不同能力组阅读效果研究中，我们共得到具有显著性方差差异的项 19 个，其中占比 78.95%（15/19）的项在非独立 t 检验中也出现了显著性差异。这说明不同能力组对这 19 个测试句出现了强烈的组间差异。根据各组阅读效果的接受程度，我们进行了如下三类区分：（1）多组阅读效果异质项共 6 个，包括 S10、S39、S50、S59、S82、S88；（2）多组阅读效果负同质项共 3 个，包括 S44、S71、S81；（3）多组阅读效果正同质项共 10 个，包括 S3、S15、S19、S41、S43、S53、S70、S78、S80、S83。通过借助 Stanford parser 的自动剖析系统，我们对照性研究了这三类测试句。

对于多组阅读效果异质项来说，不同能力组出现了组间颠覆性阅读效果，即有的组高分值接受测试句的正确性，而有的组却对此坚决拒绝接受，组间差异是质的不同。这些异质项全部同时具有方差分析和非独立 t 检验的显著性差异，具有非常强烈的行进错位的顿悟效果。这些特点在系统的自动剖析和各组折返性分析中可以得到体现。对于多组阅读效果负同质项来说，不同能力组均承认测试句不可接受，但组间差异源于程度的不同，是量的变化。这个特点与多组阅读效果正同质项相似，只不过后者中被试均不同程度承认测试句可以接受。

我们的研究结果证明（有特例存在）：

（1）对于不构成被试困惑的简单句来说，时间因素和能力因素基本上与阅读效果正相关：给予的阅读时间越长，阅读效果越好；阅读能力越强，阅读效果越好。这个结论与我们的传统认知具有一致性。

（2）对于难度可控并在被试认知理解范围内的花园幽径句解码，呈现与阅读效果的负相关特征。给予的反应时越长，被试受到的干扰越大；被试能力越强，受到的干扰越大。这个结论与"能力强的被试更易受到复杂结构影响"的论证相一致（Just and Carpenter, 1992; Eastwick and Phillips, 1999）。

（3）对于难度较大并超出被试组可接受范围的花园幽径句解码，时间因素和能力因素都无法提升被试的阅读效果。阅读效果独立于时间和能力因素。这个观点颠覆了传统中有关时间与能力与阅读效果正相关的观点，也颠覆了国外学者关于能力强的被试更容易受到复杂结构影响的观点。这说明花园幽径句解码与影响因素的正负相关是有限度的阶段性相关，难度一旦超出被试的认知强度，时间因素和能力因素便均告失效。

结　　语

　　花园幽径句是一种复杂的语言结构，蕴含休克性解码特性，并具有信息不对称所引发的认知困惑和超负荷。其"循旧—破旧—立新"的解码模式会激发行进式错位回溯并导致塌陷式认知更迭。

　　从国内外研究特点来看，学者们主要有三个学术观点：（1）结构中心论认为，花园幽径现象是句法结构调整所产生的启动机制变化；（2）认知容量核心论认为，认知容量的有限性促使大脑快速构建理解模式，这种相对粗糙的模糊匹配易产生错位效应；（3）实践性经验策略认为，解码者语言经验的多寡是诱发花园幽径现象的关键，基于实践的多经验者更容易捕捉解码所需的有用信息，同样，也更容易被提供的虚假信息所干扰。这些观点的存在相互补充了各自理论的不足，推动了英语复杂句研究。

　　此外，还有学者提出了一些观点：（1）基于词频的词汇期待观点；（2）常规语义属性被边缘语义属性所取代的语义决定性观点；（3）语境的多元限定和化解的观点。

　　除了传统的语言定性分析方法，越来越多的学者开始关注量化和脑认知的研究。统计学、计算语言学以及心理学的多种方法和理论的交叉带来了英语复杂句研究的多维性。

　　花园幽径现象具有层级存在性、理解折返性、认知顺序性和纠错控制性，系统中程序算法的顺序、选择和循环结构反映了认知的先后性、条件性和螺旋性。基于概率上下文无关文法构建的 Stanford parser

被证明是分析花园幽径句自动剖析的有力工具。该解析器所提供的句法结构剖析和依存语义关系的解读为中国学习者英语复杂句的学习过程分析和结果分析提供了系统支持。

在被试组数据锚的选定上，我们从偏度和相关系数角度分析了三种主要的被试成绩：（1）代表被试综合能力的高考总成绩；（2）代表单项能力的高考英语成绩；（3）代表被试测试时能力的英语专业四级成绩。结果显示：被试组的高考总成绩和高考英语成绩呈现负偏度特征，英语专业四级成绩呈现正偏度特征。英语专业四级成绩较其他两个成绩来说变异性更小，数据分布更集中，符合正态分布的特征。在相关系数方面，英语专业四级成绩具有更好的方差拟合，两个英语成绩的关联性更高。在三个数据组对比中，英语专业四级成绩更适合作为后期研究的来源数据。

在针对5秒和10秒反应时变化而进行的非独立t检验测试中，我们发现100个测试句中有51个具有显著性差异，被试组在延长阅读时间后超过一半的测试句出现了阅读效果的调整。其效果变化共分三种类型：（1）阅读结果发生颠覆的相反项。其中包括由错误评分向正确评分转化的趋正性相反项和由正值向负值变化的趋负性相反项。（2）前后两次测试均为负数的负数项。包括从完全错误端向不完全错误端评分转化的回归性落差项，以及从不完全错误理解向完全错误理解的离心性落差项。（3）前后评分均为正数的正数项。包括阅读得分由小到大的渐强性效果项，以及认知效果由强到弱的渐弱性效果项。

经过对非独立t检验差异项的分析，我们认为显著性差异原因在于五个方面：错位效应影响、字符串长短与嵌套影响、生僻表达方式影响、干扰成分影响和莫名因素影响。对于非显著性差异项，我们认为虽然它们评分差异较小尚不足以引起系统性偏差，但在产生原因方面却仍然有自身的特点，如简单效应、复杂效应、标记效应和纠偏泛化效应。

在针对5秒—7秒—10秒的时间因素与花园幽径句阅读效果的方

结　语

差分析中，我们统计后发现具有显著性差异的有 8 个测试句，包括 S1，S2，S6，S10，S13，S41，S88 和 S90。对于这些测试句来说，时间因素主导了阅读效果的显著性变化。这个结果比 5 秒和 10 秒反应时变化的非独立 t 检验结果更精确，而且这些测试句均源于非独立 t 检验的显著性差异集合。它们具有强烈的时间效应变化曲线。

在能力因素与花园幽径句阅读效果的方差分析中，我们把被试组分成了四个能力组：弱能力组（<60），较弱能力组（60—64），较强能力组（65—69）和强能力组（≥70）。该分组方差齐性，经卡方检验不具有组别频数显著性差异，属于正态分布。在能力组的阅读效果研究中，我们共得到 19 个出现了强烈组间差异的测试句。根据多组阅读效果，我们对它们进行了区分：效果异质项 6 个（S10，S39，S50，S59，S82，S88），效果负同质项 3 个（S44，S71，S81），效果正同质项 10 个（S3，S15，S19，S41，S43，S53，S70，S78，S80，S83）。

我们通过多组阅读效果与系统剖析结果对照分析后认为：（1）效果异质项具有非常强烈的行进错位的顿悟效果，不同能力组得分具有质的不同，且组间能产生颠覆性阅读效果，并可导致系统自动剖析出现崩溃。人工阅读强于系统剖析。（2）效果负同质项均拒绝接受正确的测试句，其效果源于组间接受程度的不同，是量的变化，不同被试组均无法达到正确解读测试句的程度。系统对负同质项的剖析分歧较大，总体而言机器剖析效果优于被试组。（3）效果正同质项解码较为简单，能力组均对正确的测试句给出正面评价。系统剖析以绝对优势超过人工解码。

由以上的语言统计和计算分析可知，已经具有英语专业四级水平的中国英语学习者在阅读复杂结构的英语句时，会受到多重因素的影响。时间因素和能力因素将"多层立体"地对阅读效果产生影响，具体体现在以下几方面。

（1）已经进入英语句法结构和语义体系的中国英语学习者，在遇到具有局部歧义的花园幽径句时，均会像系统解析器一样受到干扰。

（2）从时间因素来说，当阅读时间短到我们无法全面理解复杂结构时，解码系统会像机器一样发生系统崩溃，而能力强的被试相对来说能获得较好的效果。但是，对于超出被试阅读能力的复杂结构，时间因素并不能带来阅读效果的改善。总体而言，对同一被试组，反应时延长一倍，有51%的可能产生阅读效果的变化。

（3）从能力因素来说，能力弱的被试不具有很强的捕捉潜在信息的能力，因此受到的句法和语义干扰较少，表现较稳定，与测试句难度基本呈现负相关（难度小，得分高；难度大，得分低）。能力强的被试在相对简单句中阅读速度快且解码效果好，但是在复杂句解码中表现不稳定。他们在具有局部歧义特点的复杂结构解码中深受影响，并常被引入行进式错位效应歧途。当测试句难度超出英语专业四级水平的认知范围的时候，阅读效果对能力因素不再敏感。

（4）在借助系统进行自动剖析时，我们应该关注词汇的同形歧义（如过去式和过去分词同形，名词和动词同形等），还要关注构式所产生的结构歧义（如 that 省略造成的宾语缺位，及物动词与非及物动词的结构认定等），以及深层次的题元和论元结构等，这些都能帮助我们找到歧义节点并据此为系统改良提供理论支撑。

综上所述，基于已经验证的语言统计数据和语言计算剖析结果，我们认为对于中国学习者来说，英语复杂结构的解码在某种程度可以独立于时间因素和能力因素，具有英语专业四级能力学习者与英语母语者一样具有认知的即时匹配效应。

语言加工并不总是创建理想化结构或构建完美的推断或推理，有时只是构建一个能满足基本解释的"尚好"模式（Christianson, et al., 2001; Ferreira, et al., 2002; Ferreira and Patson, 2007）。语言加工并不一定会完全奉行语法规则，如果能够达到交流的"尚好"条件就可以实现解码。这对传统语言研究中"语言处理就是对输入成分完整、详细和准确的加工"这种观点提出了反例，同时对英语教学中的"交际策略"提供了有力支撑。

参考文献

英文部分[①]

［1］ Abney S P. A computational model of human parsing［J］. Journal of Psycholinguistic Research, 1989, 18（1）: 129 – 144.

［2］ Allen K, Pereira F, Botvinick M, et al. Distinguishing grammatical constructions with fMRI pattern analysis［J］. Brain and Language, 2012.

［3］ Altmann G, Steedman M. Interaction with context during human sentence processing［J］. Cognition, 1988, 30（3）: 191 – 238.

［4］ Altmann G T M, Garnham A, Dennis Y. Avoiding the garden path: eye movements in context［J］. Journal of Memory and Language, 1992, 31（5）: 685 – 712.

［5］ Altmann G T M, Kamide Y. Incremental interpretation at verbs: restricting the domain of subsequent reference［J］. Cognition, 1999, 73（3）: 247 – 264.

［6］ Anderson M. Down the Garden Path and Up the Labyrinth［J］. Semiotics, 1996: 105 – 110.

［7］ Anick P G, Vaithyanathan S. Exploiting clustering and phrases for

---

① 为了便于检索，英文文献参照 GB/T 7714 格式编排。

context-based information retrieval [J]. Proceedings of the 20th ACM SIGIR Conference (SIGIR'97), 1997.

[8] Arai M. What can head-final languages tell us about syntactic priming (and vice versa)? [J]. Language and Linguistics Compass, 2012, 6 (9): 545-559.

[9] Arai M, Keller F. The use of verb-specific information for prediction in sentence processing [J]. Language and Cognitive Processes, 2013, 28 (4): 525-560.

[10] Arai M, Nakamura C, Mazuka R. Predicting the unbeaten path through syntactic priming [J]. Journal of Experimental Psychology. Learning, Memory, and Cognition, 2015, 41 (2): 482.

[11] Ashbaugh J W. Down the garden path of self-determination [J]. Mental Retardation, 2002, 40 (5): 416-417.

[12] Baddeley A D, Hitch G. Working memory [M]. England: Oxford University Press, 1986.

[13] Bader M. Prosodic influences on reading syntactically ambiguous sentences [M] //Reanalysis in sentence processing. Springer Netherlands, 1998: 1-46.

[14] Bader M, Meng M. Subject-object ambiguities in German embedded clauses: an across-the-board comparison [J]. Journal of Psycholinguistic Research, 1999, 28 (2): 121-143.

[15] Bader M, Häussler J. Resolving number ambiguities during language comprehension [J]. Journal of Memory and Language, 2009, 61 (3): 352-373.

[16] Bai Y. Incongruity-resolution in English humor [J]. Theory and Practice in Language Studies, 2011, 1 (1): 83-86.

[17] Bailey C J N. The garden path that historical linguistics went astray on [J]. Language & Communication, 1982, 2 (2): 151-160.

[18] Bailey K G D, Ferreira F. Disfluencies affect the parsing of garden-

path sentences [J]. Journal of Memory and Language, 2003, 49 (2): 183 - 200.

[19] Basili R, Pazienza M T, Velardi P. An empirical symbolic approach to natural language processing [J]. Artificial Intelligence, August 1996, 85 (1): 59 - 99.

[20] Beattie J D. Natural language processing by computer [J]. International Journal of Man-Machine Studies, July 1969, 1 (3): 311 - 329.

[21] Bencini G M L, Goldberg A E. The contribution of argument structure constructions to sentence meaning [J]. Journal of Memory and Language, 2000, 43 (4): 640 - 651.

[22] Berg T. The internal structure of four-noun compounds in English and German [J]. Corpus Linguistics and Linguistic Theory, 2006, 2 (2): 197 - 231.

[23] Berg T. Recursion introduces a left-branching bias (where possible) [J]. Linguistics, 2011, 49 (5): 977 - 990.

[24] Berg T. Branching direction in recursive structures [J]. English Language and Linguistics, 2012, 16 (03): 385 - 401.

[25] Bever T G. The cognitive basis for linguistic structures [A]. In J. R. Hayes (ed.), Cognition and the Development of Language. New York: John Wiley and Sons, 1970: 279 - 352.

[26] Biber D, Conrad S, Reppen R. Corpus linguistics: investigating language structure and use [M]. Cambridge: Cambridge University Press, 1998.

[27] Binder K S, Duffy S A, Rayner K. The effects of thematic fit and discourse context on syntactic ambiguity resolution [J]. Journal of Memory and Language, 2001, 44 (2): 297 - 324.

[28] Bock J K. Syntactic persistence in language production [J]. Cognitive Psychology, 1986, 18 (3): 355 - 387.

[29] Bodenhorn B. Calling into being: naming and speaking names on Alaska's North Slope [J]. The Anthropology of Names and Naming, 2006: 139-56.

[30] Boland J E, Tanenhaus M K, Garnsey S M, et al. Verb argument structure in parsing and interpretation: evidence from wh-questions [J]. Journal of Memory and Language, 1995, 34 (6): 774-806.

[31] Boland J E. The relationship between syntactic and semantic processes in sentence comprehension [J]. Language and Cognitive Processes, 1997, 12 (4): 423-484.

[32] Boland J E, Boehm-Jernigan H. Lexical constraints and prepositional phrase attachment [J]. Journal of Memory and Language, 1998, 39 (4): 684-719.

[33] Bornkessel I, et al. Multi-dimensional contributions to garden path strength: dissociating phrase structure from case marking [J]. Journal of Memory and Language, 2004, 51 (4): 495-522.

[34] Bornkessel I, Schlesewsky M. An alternative perspective on "semantic P600" effects in language comprehension [J]. Brain Research Reviews, 2008, 59 (1): 55-73.

[35] Bos L S, Dragoy O, Stowe L A, et al. Time reference teased apart from tense: Thinking beyond the present [J]. Journal of Neurolinguistics, 2012.

[36] Boston M F, Hale J T. Garden-pathing in a statistical dependency parser [C] //Proceedings of the Midwest Computational Linguistics Conference (MCLC), 2007.

[37] Branigan H P, Pickering M J, McLean J F. Priming prepositional-phrase attachment during comprehension [J]. Journal of Experimental Psychology: Learning, Memory, and Cognition, 2005, 31 (3): 468.

[38] Breen M, Clifton Jr C. Stress matters revisited: a boundary change

experiment [J]. The Quarterly Journal of Experimental Psychology, 2013: 1-30.

[39] Brennan J, Pylkkänen L. The time-course and spatial distribution of brain activity associated with sentence processing [J]. Neuroimage, 2012.

[40] Britt M A, Perfetti C A, Garrod S, et al. Parsing in discourse: context effects and their limits [J]. Journal of Memory and Language, 1992, 31 (3): 293-314.

[41] Britt M A. The interaction of referential ambiguity and argument structure in the parsing of prepositional phrases [J]. Journal of Memory and Language, 1994, 33 (2): 251-283.

[42] Brouwer H, Fitz H, Hoeks J. Getting real about Semantic Illusions: rethinking the functional role of the P600 in language comprehension [J]. Brain Research, 2012.

[43] Burgess C, Hollbach S C. A computational model of syntactic ambiguity as a lexical process [R]. Rochester University NY Dept Of Computer Science, 1989: 263-296.

[44] Caplan D, Waters G S. Aphasic disorders of syntactic comprehension and working memory capacity [J]. Cognitive Neuropsychology, 1995, 12 (6): 637-649.

[45] Caplan D, Waters G. Working memory and connectionist models of parsing: a reply to MacDonald and Christiansen (2002) [J]. Psychological Review, 2002, 109 (1): 66-74.

[46] Caplan D, Waters G. Memory mechanisms supporting syntactic comprehension [J]. Psychonomic Bulletin & Review, 2013, 20 (2): 243-268.

[47] Carlson K, Clifton C, Frazier L. Prosodic boundaries in adjunct attachment [J]. Journal of Memory and Language, 2001, 45 (1): 58-81.

[48] Carroll D W. Psychology of language [M]. 3rd ed. Beijing: Foreign Language Teaching and Research Press, 2000: 156.

[49] Carston R. Metalinguistic negation and echoic use [J]. Journal of Pragmatics, 1996, 25 (3): 309-330.

[50] Chan Y C, Chou T L, Chen H C, et al. Segregating the comprehension and elaboration processing of verbal jokes: an fMRI study [J]. NeuroImage, 2012, 61 (4): 899-906.

[51] Chang F R. Active memory processes in visual sentence comprehension: clause effects and pronominal reference [J]. Memory & Cognition, 1980, 8 (1): 58-64.

[52] Chaves R P. On the grammar of extraction and coordination [J]. Natural Language & Linguistic Theory, 2012, 30 (2): 465-512.

[53] Choi Y, Trueswell J C. Children's (in) ability to recover from garden paths in a verb-final language: evidence for developing control in sentence processing [J]. Journal of Experimental Child Psychology, 2010, 106 (1): 41-61.

[54] Chomsky N. Language and mind [M]. New York: Harcourt Brace Jovanovich, 1968.

[55] Christensen K R. Syntactic reconstruction and reanalysis, semantic dead ends, and prefrontal cortex [J]. Brain and Cognition, 2010, 73 (1): 41-50.

[56] Christensen K R, Kizach J, Nyvad A M. The processing of syntactic islands——an fMRI study [J]. Journal of Neurolinguistics, 2012.

[57] Christianson K, Hollingworth A, Halliwell J F, et al. Thematic roles assigned along the garden path linger [J]. Cognitive Psychology, 2001, 42 (4): 368-407.

[58] Christianson K, Williams C C, Zacks R T, et al. Younger and older adults' "good-enough" interpretations of garden-path sentences [J]. Discourse Processes, 2006, 42 (2): 205-238.

[59] Christianson K. Sensitivity to syntactic changes in garden path sentences [J]. Journal of Psycholinguistic Research, 2008, 37 (6): 391-403.

[60] Christianson K, Luke S G, Ferreira F. Effects of plausibility on structural priming [J]. Journal of Experimental Psychology: Learning, Memory, and Cognition, 2010, 36 (2): 538.

[61] Christianson K, Luke S G. Context strengthens initial misinterpretations of text [J]. Scientific Studies of Reading, 2011, 15 (2): 136-166.

[62] Christopher B. Statistics in linguistics [M]. Boston: Basil Blackwell, 1985.

[63] Clifton C, Frazier L, Connine C. Lexical expectations in sentence comprehension [J]. Journal of Verbal Learning and Verbal Behavior, 1984, 23 (6): 696-708.

[64] Clifton Jr C, Ferreira F. Ambiguity in context [J]. Language and Cognitive Processes, 1989, 4 (3-4): SI77-SI103.

[65] Clifton C, Speer S, Abney S P. Parsing arguments: phrase structure and argument structure as determinants of initial parsing decisions [J]. Journal of Memory and Language, 1991, 30 (2): 251-272.

[66] Clifton Jr C, Duffy S A. Sentence and text comprehension: roles of linguistic structure [J]. Annual Review of Psychology, 2001, 52 (1): 167-196.

[67] Clifton C, Staub A, Rayner K. Eye movements in reading words and sentences [J]. Eye Movements: A Window on Mind and Brain, 2007: 341-372.

[68] Clifton Jr C, Staub A. Parallelism and competition in syntactic ambiguity resolution [J]. Language and Linguistics Compass, 2008, 2 (2): 234-250.

[69] Clifton Jr C, Staub A. Teaching and learning guide for: parallelism

and competition in syntactic ambiguity resolution [J]. Language and Linguistics Compass, 2010, 4 (1): 61 – 63.

[70] Clifton C, Ferreira F, Henderson J M, et al. Eye movements in reading and information processing: Keith Rayner's 40year legacy [J]. Journal of Memory and Language, 2016, 86: 1 – 19.

[71] Collins A M & Quillian M R. Retrieval time from semantic memory [J]. Journal of Verbal Learning and Verbal Behavior, 1969, 8 (2): 240.

[72] Crain S, Steedman M. On not being led up the garden path: the use of context by the psychological parser [A]. In D. Dowty, L. Karttunen & A. Zwicky (eds.), Natural Language Processing: Psychological, Computational and Theoretical Perspectives, Cambridge University Press. Cambridge, U. K, 1985.

[73] Crocker M W. Mechanisms for sentence processing [M]. Centre for Cognitive Science, University of Edinburgh, 1996.

[74] Crocker M W, Brants T. Wide-coverage probabilistic sentence processing [J]. Journal of Psycholinguistic Research, 2000, 29 (6): 647 – 669.

[75] Daneman M, Carpenter P A. Individual differences in working memory and reading [J]. Journal of Verbal Learning and Verbal Behavior, 1980, 19 (4): 450 – 466.

[76] Dean Fodor J, Inoue A. Syntactic features in reanalysis: positive and negative symptoms [J]. Journal of Psycholinguistic Research, 2000, 29 (1): 25 – 36.

[77] DeDe G. Lexical and prosodic effects on syntactic ambiguity resolution in aphasia [J]. Journal of Psycholinguistic Research, 2012: 1 – 22.

[78] DeKeyser R M. The effect of error correction on L2 grammar knowledge and oral proficiency [J]. Modern Language Journal, 1993:

501-514.

[79] Den Y, Inoue M. Disambiguation with verb-predictability: evidence from Japanese garden-path phenomena [C] //Proceedings of the 19th Annual Conference of the Cognitive Science Society. 1997: 179-184.

[80] Diez Arroyo M. Interpretation and garden-path effect [J]. Pragmalinguistica, 1997, 5: 95-117.

[81] Doolittle J H. Using riddles and interactive computer games to teach problem-solving skills [J]. Teaching of Psychology, 1995, 22 (1): 33-36.

[82] DU Jia-Li, Ping-fang Y. Machine learning for second language learning: effects on syntactic processing in garden-path sentences [C] //Computational Intelligence and Software Engineering (CiSE), 2010 International Conference on. IEEE, 2010a: 1-5.

[83] DU Jia-Li, Ping-fang Y. Syntax-directed machine translation of natural language: Effect of garden path phenomenon on sentence structure [C] //Intelligent System Design and Engineering Application (ISDEA), 2010 International Conference on. IEEE, 2010b, 2: 535-539.

[84] DU Jia-Li, Ping-fang Y. Towards an algorithm-based intelligent tutoring system: computing methods in syntactic management of garden path phenomenon [C] //Intelligent Computing and Intelligent Systems (ICIS), 2010 International Conference on. IEEE, 2010c, 2: 521-525.

[85] DU Jia-Li, Ping-fang Y. A computational linguistic approach to natural language processing with applications to garden path sentences analysis [J]. International Journal of Advanced Computer Science and Applications, 2012, 9 (3): 61-75.

[86] DU Jia-Li, Ping-fang Y. Predicting garden path sentences based on

natural language understanding system [J]. International Journal of Advanced Computer Science and Applications, 2012, 11 (03): 1 – 7.

[87] DU Jia-Li, Ping-fang Y. Machine Learning from Garden Path Sentences: the Application of computational Linguistics [J]. International Journal of Emerging Technologies in Learning, 2014, 9 (6): 58 – 62.

[88] DU Jia-Li, Ping-fang Y. Towards GP sentence parsing of V + P + CP/NP structure: a perspective of computational linguistics [J]. International Journal of Advanced Computer Science and Applications, 2015, 6 (6): 37 – 44.

[89] DU Jia-Li, Ping-fang Y. Machine learning techniques for decoding GP sentences: effects of processing breakdown [J]. International Journal of Reasoning-Based Intelligent Systems, 2015, 7 (3): 177 – 185.

[90] DU Jia-Li, Alexandris C, et al. Controlling interaction in multilingual conversation revisited: a perspective for services and interviews in mandarin Chinese [J]. HCII 2017, Springer: 573 – 583.

[91] Dubey A. The influence of discourse on syntax: a psycholinguistic model of sentence processing [C] //Proceedings of the 48th Annual Meeting of the Association for Computational Linguistics. Association for Computational Linguistics, 2010: 1179 – 1188.

[92] Duffy J R. Stroke with dysarthria: evaluate and treat; garden variety or down the garden path? [C] //Seminars in Speech and Language. 1997, 19 (1): 93 – 8.

[93] Duffy J H. Up the garden path with Dubuffet [J]. Word & Image, 2014, 30 (4): 317 – 335.

[94] Dynel M. Garden paths, red lights and crossroads: on finding our way to understanding the cognitive mechanisms underlying jokes

[J]. Israeli Journal of Humor Research: An International Journal, 2012, 1: 6 - 28.

[95] Eastwick E C, Phillips C. Variability in semantic cue effectiveness on syntactic ambiguity resolution: inducing low-span performance in high-span readers [J]. Architectures and Mechanisms for Language Processing IV, University of Edinburgh, Scotland, 1999.

[96] Eberhard K M, Spivey-Knowlton M J, Sedivy J C, et al. Eye movements as a window into real-time spoken language comprehension in natural contexts [J]. Journal of Psycholinguistic Research, 1995, 24 (6): 409 - 436.

[97] Engle R W, Cantor J, Carullo J J. Individual differences in working memory and comprehension: a test of four hypotheses [J]. Journal of Experimental Psychology: Learning, Memory, and Cognition, 1992, 18 (5): 972.

[98] Ericsson K A, Kintsch W. Long-term working memory [J]. Psychological Review, 1995, 102 (2): 211 - 245.

[99] Esser J. Syntactic and prosodic closure in on-line speech production [J]. Anglia-Zeitschrift für Englische Philologie, 1998, 116 (4): 476 - 491.

[100] Farmer T A, Christiansen M H, Kemtes K A. Sentence processing in context: the impact of experience on individual differences [C]//Proceedings of the Twenty-Seventh Annual Conference of the Cognitive Science Society, 2005: 642 - 647.

[101] Farmer T A, Anderson S E, Spivey M J. Gradiency and visual context in syntactic garden-paths [J]. Journal of Memory and Language, 2007, 57 (4): 570 - 595.

[102] Farmer T A, Fine A B, Jaeger T F. Implicit context-specific learning leads to rapid shifts in syntactic expectations [C]//The 33rd Annual Meeting of the Cognitive Science Society (cogsci11). Bos-

ton, MA. 2011.

[103] Federmeier K D, Kutas M. A rose by any other name: long-term memory structure and sentence processing [J]. Journal of Memory and Language, 1999, 41 (4): 469 – 495.

[104] Feeney A, Coley J D, Crisp A. The relevance framework for category-based induction: evidence from garden-path arguments [J]. Journal of Experimental Psychology: Learning, Memory, and Cognition, 2010, 36 (4): 906.

[105] Ferrari-Bridgers F. Limits of on-line strategies of reanalysis [C] //Systems, Man, and Cybernetics, 2001 International Conference on. IEEE, 2001, 1: 187 – 192.

[106] Ferreira F, Clifton C. The independence of syntactic processing [J]. Journal of Memory and Language, 1986, 25 (3): 348 – 368.

[107] Ferreira F, Henderson J M. Use of verb information in syntactic parsing: evidence from eye movements and word-by-word self-paced reading [J]. Journal of Experimental Psychology: Learning, Memory, and Cognition, 1990, 16 (4): 555.

[108] Ferreira F, Henderson J M. Recovery from misanalyses of garden-path sentences [J]. Journal of Memory and Language, 1991, 30 (6): 725 – 745.

[109] Ferreira F, Henderson J M. Reading processes during syntactic analysis and reanalysis [J]. Canadian Journal of Experimental Psychology/Revue Canadienne de Psychologie Expérimentale, 1993, 47 (2): 247.

[110] Ferreira F, McClure K K. Parsing of garden-path sentences with reciprocal verbs [J]. Language and Cognitive Processes, 1997, 12 (2 – 3): 273 – 306.

[111] Ferreira F, Henderson J M. Syntactic reanalysis, thematic process-

ing, and sentence comprehension [A]. In J. D. Fodor & F. Ferreira (eds.), Reanalysis in Sentence Processing [C]. Dordrecht: Kluwer Academic Publishers, 1998: 73-100.

[112] Ferreira F, Bailey K G D, Ferraro V. Good-enough representations in language comprehension [J]. Current Directions in Psychological Science, 2002, 11 (1): 11-15.

[113] Ferreira F. The misinterpretation of noncanonical sentences [J]. Cognitive Psychology, 2003, 47 (2): 164-203.

[114] Ferreira F, Lau E F, Bailey K G D. Disfluencies, language comprehension, and tree adjoining grammars [J]. Cognitive Science, 2004, 28 (5): 721-749.

[115] Ferreira F, Patson N D. The "good enough" approach to language comprehension [J]. Language and Linguistics Compass, 2007, 1 (12): 71-83.

[116] Ferreira F, Foucart A, Engelhardt P E. Language processing in the visual world: effects of preview, visual complexity, and prediction [J]. Journal of Memory and Language, 2013, 69 (3): 165-182.

[117] Ferretti T R, McRae K, Hatherell A. Integrating verbs, situation schemas, and thematic role concepts [J]. Journal of Memory and Language, 2001, 44 (4): 516-547.

[118] Fine A B, Jaeger T F. Language comprehension is sensitive to changes in the reliability of lexical cues [C] //The 33rd Annual Meeting of the Cognitive Science Society (cogsci11). Boston, MA, 2011.

[119] Fine A B, Jaeger T F. Evidence for implicit learning in syntactic comprehension [J]. Cognitive science, 2013.

[120] Fine A B, Jaeger T F, Farmer T A, et al. Rapid expectation adaptation during syntactic comprehension [J]. Plos One, 2013, 8

(10).

[121] Florian Jaeger T. Redundancy and reduction: speakers manage syntactic information density [J]. Cognitive Psychology, 2010, 61 (1): 23-62.

[122] Fodor J A, Garrett M, Bever T G. Some syntactic determinants of sentential complexity, II: verb structure [J]. Attention, Perception, & Psychophysics, 1968, 3 (6): 453-461.

[123] Fodor J A, Bever T G, Garrett M F. The psychology of language: an introduction to psycholinguistics and generative grammar [M]. New York: McGraw-Hill, 1974.

[124] Fodor J D. Parsing strategies and constraints on transformations [J]. Linguistic Inquiry, 1978: 427-473.

[125] Fodor J A. The Modularity of Mind [M]. Cambridge, MA: MIT Press, 1983.

[126] Fodor J D, Inoue A. The diagnosis and cure of garden paths [J]. Journal of Psycholinguistic Research, 1994, 23 (5): 407-434.

[127] Fodor J D, Inoue A. Garden path repair: diagnosis and triage [J]. Language and Speech, 2000, 43 (3): 261-271.

[128] Fodor J D, Inoue A. Syntactic features in reanalysis: positive and negative symptoms [J]. Journal of Psycholinguistic Research, 2000, 29 (1): 25-36.

[129] Foltz A, Maday K, Ito K. Order Effects in Production and Comprehension of Prosodic Boundaries [M] //Prosodic Categories: Production, Perception and Comprehension. Springer Netherlands, 2011: 39-68.

[130] Ford M, Bresnan J W, Kaplan R M. A competence-based theory of syntactic closure [A]. In J. W. Bresnan (ed.), The Mental Representation of Grammatical Relations. Cambridge, Massachusetts: MIT Press, 1982: 727-796.

[131] Forster K I, Guerrera C, Elliot L. The maze task: measuring forced incremental sentence processing time [J]. Behavior Research Methods, 2009, 41 (1): 163-171.

[132] Foss D J, Jenkins C M. Some effects of context on the comprehension of ambiguous sentences [J]. Journal of Verbal Learning and Verbal Behavior, 1973, 12 (5): 577-589.

[133] Frazier L, Fodor J D. The Sausage Machine: a New Two-stage Parsing Model [J]. Cognition, 1978, 6 (4): 291-325.

[134] Frazier L. On comprehending sentences: syntactic parsing strategies [D]. ETD Collection for University of Connecticut, 1979: AAI7914150.

[135] Frazier L, Rayner K. Making and correcting errors during sentence comprehension: eye movements in the analysis of structurally ambiguous sentences [J]. Cognitive Psychology, 1982, 14 (2): 178-210.

[136] Frazier L, Rayner K. Resolution of syntactic category ambiguities: eye movements in parsing lexically ambiguous sentences [J]. Journal of Memory and Language, 1987, 26 (5): 505-526.

[137] Frazier L. Against lexical generation of syntax [C] //The First Part of this Paper was Originally Presented as Comments on Mark Steedman's talk "Sentence Processing from the Lexicon" at the Max-Planck-Institute in Nijmegen, Netherlands, in Jul 1986. The MIT Press, 1989.

[138] Frazier L, Rayner K. Taking on semantic commitments: processing multiple meanings vs. multiple senses [J]. Journal of Memory and Language, 1990, 29 (2): 181-200.

[139] Frazier L, Clifton Jr C. Sentence reanalysis, and visibility [M] // Reanalysis in Sentence Processing. Springer Netherlands, 1998: 143-176.

[140] Frazier L, et al. Scale structure: processing minimum standard and maximum standard scalar adjectives [J]. Cognition, 2008, 106 (1): 299 – 324.

[141] Friederici A D, Steinhauer K, Mecklinger A, et al. Working memory constraints on syntactic ambiguity resolution as revealed by electrical brain responses [J]. Biological Psychology, 1998, 47 (3): 193 – 221.

[142] Friederici A D. Diagnosis and reanalysis: two processing aspects the brain may differentiate [M] //Reanalysis in Sentence Processing. Springer Netherlands, 1998: 177 – 200.

[143] Friederici A D, Opitz B, Von Cramon D Y. Segregating semantic and syntactic aspects of processing in the human brain: an fMRI investigation of different word types [J]. Cerebral Cortex, 2000, 10 (7): 698 – 705.

[144] Friedmann N, Gvion A. As far as individuals with conduction aphasia understood these sentences were ungrammatical: garden path in conduction aphasia [J]. Aphasiology, 2007, 21 (6 – 8): 570 – 586.

[145] Frisson S, Pickering M J. The processing of metonymy: evidence from eye movements [J]. Journal of Experimental Psychology: Learning, Memory, and Cognition, 1999, 25 (6): 1366.

[146] Garnsey S M, Pearlmutter N J, Myers E, et al. The contributions of verb bias and plausibility to the comprehension of temporarily ambiguous sentences [J]. Journal of Memory and Language, 1997, 37 (1): 58 – 93.

[147] Gass S M. Learning and teaching: the necessary intersection [J]. Second Language Acquisition Theory and Pedagogy, 1995: 3 – 20.

[148] Gass S, Mackey A, Alvarez-Torres M J, et al. The effects of task repetition on linguistic output [J]. Language Learning, 1999, 49

(4): 549-581.

[149] Gebhart A L, Aslin R N, Newport E L. Changing structures in midstream: learning along the statistical garden path [J]. Cognitive Science, 2009, 33 (6): 1087-1116.

[150] George M S, Mannes S, Hoffinan J E. Global semantic expectancy and language comprehension [J]. Journal of Cognitive Neuroscience, 1994, 6 (1): 70-83.

[151] Gibson E A F. A computational theory of human linguistic processing: memory limitations and processing breakdown [D]. School of Computer Science, Carnegie Mellon University, 1991.

[152] Gibson E, Hickok G, Schütze C T. Processing empty categories: a parallel approach [J]. Journal of Psycholinguistic Research, 1994, 23 (5): 381-405.

[153] Gibson E, Pearlmutter N J. Constraints on sentence comprehension [J]. Trends in Cognitive Sciences, 1998, 2 (7): 262-268.

[154] Goeree R, O'Reilly D, Tarride J E, et al. Being led down the wrong garden PATH: the importance of knowledge and facts for the crossroads [J]. Pharmaco Economics, 2007, 25 (6): 528-532.

[155] Gompel R P G, Pickering M J, Pearson J, et al. The activation of inappropriate analyses in garden-path sentences: evidence from structural priming [J]. Journal of Memory and Language, 2006, 55 (3): 335-362.

[156] Gordon P C, Grosz B J, Gilliom L A. Pronouns, names, and the centering of attention in discourse [J]. Cognitive Science, 1993, 17 (3): 311-347.

[157] Gordon P C, Hendrick R, Johnson M. Memory interference during language processing [J]. Journal of Experimental Psychology: Learning, Memory, and Cognition, 2001, 27 (6): 1411-1423.

[158] Gorrell P G. Studies of human syntactic processing: ranked-parallel versus serial models [D]. Doctoral dissertation, University of Connecticut, Storrs, 1987.

[159] Gouvea A C, Phillips C, Kazanina N, et al. The linguistic processes underlying the P600 [J]. Language and Cognitive Processes, 2010, 25 (2): 149 – 188.

[160] Grain S, Steedman N. On not being led up the garden path: the use of context by the psychological parser [A]. In D. Dowty, L. Kartunnen & H. Zwicky (eds.), Natural Language Parsing [C]. Cambridge: Cambridge University Press, 1985: 320 – 358.

[161] Grodner D, Gibson E, Tunstall S. Syntactic complexity in ambiguity resolution [J]. Journal of Memory and Language, 2002, 46 (2): 267 – 295.

[162] Grodner D, Gibson E, Watson D. The influence of contextual contrast on syntactic processing: evidence for strong-interaction in sentence comprehension [J]. Cognition, 2005, 95 (3): 275 – 296.

[163] Grosjean F. Spoken word recognition processes and the gating paradigm [J]. Perception & Psychophysics, 1980, 28 (4): 267 – 283.

[164] Gurney J, Perlis D, Purang K. Interpreting presuppositions using active logic: from contexts to utterances [J]. Computational Intelligence, 1997, 13 (3): 391 – 413.

[165] Hagoort P, Brown C, Groothusen J. The syntactic positive shift (SPS) as an ERP measure of syntactic processing [J]. Language and Cognitive Processes, 1993, 8 (4): 439 – 483.

[166] Hagoort P. Interplay between syntax and semantics during sentence comprehension: ERP effects of combining syntactic and semantic violations [J]. Journal of Cognitive Neuroscience, 2003, 15 (6):

883 – 899.

[167] Hahne A, Friederici A D. Electrophysiological evidence for two steps in syntactic analysis: early automatic and late controlled processes [J]. Journal of Cognitive Neuroscience, 1999, 11 (2): 194 – 205.

[168] Harding-Pink D. Humanitarian medicine: up the garden path and down the slippery slope [J]. British Medical Journal, 2004, 329 (7462): 398.

[169] Hare M, McRae K, Elman J L. Sense and structure: meaning as a determinant of verb subcategorization preferences [J]. Journal of Memory and Language, 2003, 48 (2): 281 – 303.

[170] Hasher L, Quig M B, May C P. Inhibitory control over no-longer-relevant information: adult age differences [J]. Memory & Cognition, 1997, 25 (3): 286 – 295.

[171] Häussler J, Bader M. The assembly and disassembly of determiner phrases: minimality is needed, but not sufficient [J]. Lingua, 2009, 119 (10): 1560 – 1580.

[172] Hayes D P. Speaking and writing: distinct patterns of word choice [J]. Journal of Memory and Language, 1988, 27 (5): 572 – 585.

[173] Heider P M, Dery J E, Roland D. The processing of it object relative clauses: evidence against a fine-grained frequency account [J]. Journal of Memory and Language, 2014, 75: 58 – 76.

[174] Herron C. The garden path correction strategy in the foreign language classroom [J]. French Review, 1991: 966 – 977.

[175] Herron C, Tomasello M. Acquiring grammatical structures by guided induction [J]. French Review, 1992: 708 – 718.

[176] Hickok G. Parallel parsing: evidence from reactivation in garden-path sentences [J]. Journal of Psycholinguistic Research, 1993,

22 (2): 239-250.

[177] Hirose Y, Inoue A. Ambiguity of reanalysis in parsing complex sentences in Japanese [J]. Syntax and Semantics, 1998: 71-94.

[178] Holcomb P J. Semantic priming and stimulus degradation: implications for the role of the N400 in language processing [J]. Psychophysiology, 1993, 30 (1): 47-61.

[179] Holmes V M, Forster K I. Perceptual complexity and underlying sentence structure [J]. Journal of Verbal Learning and Verbal Behavior, 1972, 11 (2): 148-156.

[180] Holmes V M, O'Regan J K. Eye fixation patterns during the reading of relative-clause sentences [J]. Journal of Verbal Learning and Verbal Behavior, 1981, 20 (4): 417-430.

[181] Holmes V M. Parsing strategies and discourse context [J]. Journal of Psycholinguistic Research, 1984, 13 (3): 237-257.

[182] Holmes V M, Kennedy A, Murray W S. Syntactic structure and the garden path [J]. The Quarterly Journal of Experimental Psychology, 1987, 39 (2): 277-293.

[183] Holmes V M. Syntactic parsing: in search of the garden path [A]. In M. Coltheart (ed.), Attention and Performance XII: The Psychology of Reading. Hove: Erlbaum, 1987: 587-599.

[184] Holmes V M, Stowe L, Cupples L. Lexical expectations in parsing complement-verb sentences [J]. Journal of Memory and Language, 1989, 28 (6): 668-689.

[185] Hopf J M, Bayer J, Bader M, et al. Event-related brain potentials and case information in syntactic ambiguities [J]. Journal of Cognitive Neuroscience, 1998, 10 (2): 264-280.

[186] Hopf J M, Bader M, Meng M, et al. Is human sentence parsing serial or parallel?: evidence from event-related brain potentials [J]. Cognitive Brain Research, 2003, 15 (2): 165-177.

[187] Hu J, Gao S, Ma W, et al. Dissociation of tone and vowel processing in Mandarin idioms [J]. Psychophysiology, 2012.

[188] Huang H W, Federmeier K D. Dispreferred adjective orders elicit brain responses associated with lexico-semantic rather than syntactic processing [J]. Brain Research, 2012: 14-75.

[189] Hussey E K, Novick J M. The benefits of executive control training and the implications for language processing [J]. Frontiers in Psychology, 2012, 3.

[190] Hwang Y S, Finch A, Sasaki Y. Improving statistical machine translation using shallow linguistic knowledge [J]. Computer Speech & Language, April 2007, 21: 350-372.

[191] Hwang H, Schafer A J. Constituent length affects prosody and processing for a dative NP ambiguity in Korean [J]. Journal of Psycholinguistic Research, 2009, 38 (2): 151-175.

[192] Hwang H, Steinhauer K. Phrase length matters: the interplay between implicit prosody and syntax in Korean "garden path" sentences [J]. Journal of Cognitive Neuroscience, 2011, 23 (11): 3555-3575.

[193] Ito K, Speer S R. Anticipatory effects of intonation: eye movements during instructed visual search [J]. Journal of Memory and Language, 2008, 58 (2): 541-573.

[194] Ito K, Jincho N, Minai U, et al. Intonation facilitates contrast resolution: evidence from Japanese adults and 6-year olds [J]. Journal of Memory and Language, 2012, 66 (1): 265-284.

[195] Itzhak I, Pauker E, Drury J E, et al. Event-related potentials show online influence of lexical biases on prosodic processing [J]. Neuro Report, 2010, 21 (1): 8-13.

[196] Jacob G, Felser C. Reanalysis and semantic persistence in native and non-native garden-path recovery [J]. The Quarterly Journal

of Experimental Psychology, 2015: 1 – 19.

[197] Jaeger T F, Tily H. On language "utility": processing complexity and communicative efficiency [J]. Wiley Interdisciplinary Reviews: Cognitive Science, 2011, 2 (3): 323 – 335.

[198] Jaeger T F, Snider N E. Alignment as a consequence of expectation adaptation: syntactic priming is affected by the prime's prediction error given both prior and recent experience [J]. Cognition, 2013, 127 (1): 57 – 83.

[199] Jegerski J. The processing of subject-object ambiguities in native and near-native Mexican Spanish [J]. Bilingualism: Language and Cognition, 2012, 15 (04): 721 – 735.

[200] Jin Y H. Semantic analysis of Chinese garden-path sentences [J]. Proceedings of the Fifth SIGHAN Workshop on Chinese Language Processing (Sydney), 2006, 7: 33 – 39.

[201] Johnson P E, Thompson W B. Strolling down the garden path: detection and recovery from error in expert problem solving [C] // Seventh International Joint Conference on Artificial Intelligence, Vancouver, BC, 1981.

[202] Johnson P E, Thompson W B. Strolling down the garden path: error prone tasks in expert problem solving [C] //Proceedings of the 7th international joint conference on Artificial intelligence-Volume 1. Morgan Kaufmann Publishers Inc., 1981: 215 – 217.

[203] Juffs A, Harrington M. Garden path sentences and error data in second language sentence processing [J]. Language Learning, 1996, 46 (2): 283 – 323.

[204] Juffs A. The influence of first language on the processing of wh-movement in English as a second language [J]. Second Language Research, 2005, 21 (2): 121 – 151.

[205] Juliano C, Tanenhaus M K. A constraint-based lexicalist account of

the subject/object attachment preference [J]. Journal of Psycholinguistic Research, 1994, 23 (6): 459-471.

[206] Jun S A. Prosodic phrasing and attachment preferences [J]. Journal of Psycholinguistic Research, 2003, 32 (2): 219-249.

[207] Jun S A, Koike C. Default prosody and relative clause attachment in Japanese [J]. Japanese-Korean Linguistics, 2008, 13: 41-53.

[208] Jung H, Sontag S, Park Y B S, et al. Rhythmic effects of syntax processing in music and language [J]. Frontiers in Psychology, 2015, 6.

[209] Jurafsky D. A probabilistic model of lexical and syntactic access and disambiguation [J]. Cognitive Science, 1996, 20 (2): 137-194.

[210] Just M A, Carpenter P A. A theory of reading: from eye fixations to comprehension [J]. Psychological Review, 1980, 87 (4): 329-354.

[211] Just M A, Carpenter P A. A capacity theory of comprehension: individual differences in working memory [J]. Psychological Review, 1992, 99: 122-149.

[212] Just M A, Carpenter P A. A capacity-based theory of comprehension: new frontiers of evidence and arguments [J]. Psychological Review, 1992, 103: 773-780.

[213] Just M A, Carpenter P A, Keller T A, et al. Brain activation modulated by sentence comprehension [J]. Science, 1996, 274: 114-116.

[214] Just M A, Carpenter P A, Keller T A. The capacity theory of comprehension: new frontiers of evidence and arguments [J]. Psychological Review, 1996, 103: 773-780.

[215] Kaan E, Harris A, Gibson E, et al. The P600 as an index of syn-

tactic integration difficulty [J]. Language and Cognitive Processes, 2000, 15 (2): 159 - 201.

[216] Kaan E, Swaab T Y. Repair, revision, and complexity in syntactic analysis: an electrophysiological differentiation [J]. Journal of Cognitive Neuroscience, 2003, 15 (1): 98 - 110.

[217] Kamide Y, Scheepers C, Altmann G T M. Integration of syntactic and semantic information in predictive processing: cross-linguistic evidence from German and English [J]. Journal of Psycholinguistic Research, 2003, 32 (1): 37 - 55.

[218] Kamide Y. Anticipatory processes in sentence processing [J]. Language and Linguistics Compass, 2008, 2 (4): 647 - 670.

[219] Kaplan R M. Augmented transition networks as psychological models of sentence comprehension [J]. Artificial Intelligence, 1972 (3): 77 - 100.

[220] Kaplan R M. On process models for sentence analysis [A]. In D. A. Norman, D. E. Rumelhart & the LNR Research Group (eds.), Explorations in Cognition. San Francisco: Freeman, 1975.

[221] Kardes F R, Cronley M L, Pontes M C, et al. Down the garden path: the role of conditional inference processes in self-persuasion [J]. Journal of Consumer Psychology, 2001, 11 (3): 159 - 168.

[222] Karpicke J D, et al. False memories are not surprising: the subjective experience of an associative memory illusion [J]. Journal of Memory and Language, 2008, 58 (4): 1065 - 1079.

[223] Keller F, Zechner K. A connectionist model of lexical and contextual influences on ambiguity resolution in human sentence processing [A]. Proceedings of the 3rd Natural Language Processing Pacific-Rim Symposium, 1995: 592 - 597.

[224] Kempen G. Computational models of syntactic processing in human

language comprehension [A]. In T. Dijkstra & K. De Smedt (eds.), Computational Psycholinguistics: Symbolic and Subsymbolic Models of Language Processing. London: Taylor & Francis, 1996: 192 – 220.

[225] Kemper S, Crow A, Kemtes K. Eye-fixation patterns of high-and low-span young and older adults: down the garden path and back again [J]. Psychology and Aging, 2004, 19 (1): 157.

[226] Kemtes K A, Kemper S. Younger and older adults' on-line processing of syntactically ambiguous sentences [J]. Psychology and Aging, 1997, 12 (2): 362.

[227] Kielar A, Meltzer-Asscher A, Thompson C. Electrophysiological responses to argument structure violations in healthy adults and individuals with agrammatic aphasia [J]. Neuropsychologia, 2012, 50 (14): 3320 – 3337.

[228] Kim A E, Srinivas B, Trueswell J C. The convergence of lexicalist perspectives in psycholinguistics and computational linguistics [J]. University of Pennsylvania Working Papers in Linguistics, 2000, 6 (3): 8.

[229] Kimball J. Seven principles of surface structure parsing in natural language [J]. Cognition, 1973, 2 (1): 15 – 47.

[230] King J, Just M A. Individual differences in syntactic processing: the role of working memory [J]. Journal of Memory and Language, 1991, 30 (5): 580 – 602.

[231] Kjelgaard M M, Speer S R. Prosodic facilitation and interference in the resolution of temporary syntactic closure ambiguity [J]. Journal of Memory and Language, 1999, 40 (2): 153 – 194.

[232] Koh S. The resolution of the dative NP ambiguity in Korean [J]. Journal of Psycholinguistic Research, 1997, 26 (2): 265 – 273.

[233] Kohl J R. Improving translatability and readability with syntactic

cues [J]. Technical communication, 1999, 46 (2): 149 – 166.

[234] Kondo T, Mazuka R. Prosodic planning while reading aloud: online examination of Japanese sentences [J]. Journal of Psycholinguistic Research, 1996, 25 (2): 357 – 381.

[235] Kotz S A, Holcomb P J, Osterhout L. ERPs reveal comparable syntactic sentence processing in native and non-native readers of English [J]. Acta Psychologica, 2008, 128 (3): 514 – 527.

[236] Kromann M T. Optimality parsing and local cost functions in Discontinuous Grammar [J]. Electronic Notes in Theoretical Computer Science, 2004, 53: 163 – 179.

[237] Kurtzman H. Studies in syntactic ambiguity resolution [D]. Ph. D. dissertation, MIT, Cambridge, MA, 1985.

[238] Kutas M, Hillyard S A. Event-related brain potentials to semantically inappropriate and surprisingly large words [J]. Biological Psychology, 1980, 11 (2): 99 – 116.

[239] Kwon N, Sturt P. The use of control information in dependency formation: an eye-tracking study [J]. Journal of Memory and Language, 2014, 73: 59 – 80.

[240] Lassotta R, Omaki A, Franck J. Developmental changes in misinterpretation of garden-path wh-questions in French [J]. The Quarterly Journal of Experimental Psychology, 2015: 1 – 26.

[241] Lau E F, Ferreira F. Lingering effects of disfluent material on comprehension of garden path sentences [J]. Language and Cognitive Processes, 2005, 20 (5): 633 – 666.

[242] Lewis R L. Interference in short-term memory: the magical number two (or three) in sentence processing [J]. Journal of Psycholinguistic Research, 1996, 25 (1): 93 – 115.

[243] Lewis R L. Reanalysis and limited repair parsing: leaping off the

garden path [M] //Reanalysis in sentence processing. Springer Netherlands, 1998: 247-285.

[244] Lewis R L. Specifying architectures for language processing: process, control, and memory in parsing and interpretation [J]. Architectures and Mechanisms for Language Processing, 2000: 56-89.

[245] Lewis R L, Vasishth S. An activation-based model of sentence processing as skilled memory retrieval [J]. Cognitive Science, 2005, 29 (3): 375-419.

[246] Lewis G, Solomyak O, Marantz A. The neural basis of obligatory decomposition of suffixed words [J]. Brain and Language, 2011, 118 (3): 118-127.

[247] Lin C J C, Bever T G. Garden path and the comprehension of head-final relative clauses [J]. Processing and Producing Head-final Structures, 2011: 277-297.

[248] Lipka S. Reading sentences with a late closure ambiguity: does semantic information help? [J]. Language and Cognitive Processes, 2002, 17 (3): 271-298.

[249] Lyster R, Lightbown P, Spada N. A response to Truscott's "What's wrong with oral grammar correction" [J]. Canadian Modern Language Review, 1999, 55 (4): 457-467.

[250] MacDonald M C, Just M A, Carpenter P A. Working memory constraints on the processing of syntactic ambiguity [J]. Cognitive Psychology, 1992, 24 (1): 56-98.

[251] MacDonald M C, Pearlmutter N J, Seidenberg M S. The lexical nature of syntactic ambiguity resolution [J]. Psychological Review, 1994, 101 (4): 676-703.

[252] MacDonald M C. Probabilistic constraints and syntactic ambiguity resolution [J]. Language and Cognitive Processes, 1994, 9

(2): 157 – 201.

[253] MacDonald M C, Christiansen M H. Reassessing working memory: comment on Just and Carpenter (1992) and Waters and Caplan (1996) [J]. Psychological Review, 2002, 109: 35 – 54.

[254] Mak W M, Vonk W, Schriefers H. The influence of animacy on relative clause processing [J]. Journal of Memory and Language, 2002, 47 (1): 50 – 68.

[255] Malaia E, Wilbur R B, Weber-Fox C. ERP evidence for telicity effects on syntactic processing in garden-path sentences [J]. Brain and Language, 2009, 108 (3): 145 – 158.

[256] Marcus M P. Wait-and-see strategies for parsing natural language [J]. MIT Artificial Intelligence Laboratory, 1974, 08.

[257] Marcus M. A theory of syntactic recognition for natural languages [M]. Cambridge, MA: MIT Press, 1980.

[258] Marcus M P, Marcinkiewicz M A, Santorini B. Building a large annotated corpus of English: the Penn Treebank [J]. Computational Linguistics, 1993, 19 (2): 313 – 330.

[259] Marcus M, Kim G, Marcinkiewicz M A, et al. The Penn Treebank: annotating predicate argument structure [C] //Proceedings of the workshop on Human Language Technology. Association for Computational Linguistics, 1994: 114 – 119.

[260] Mauner G, Koenig J P. Linguistic vs. conceptual sources of implicit agents in sentence comprehension [J]. Journal of Memory and Language, 2000, 43 (1): 110 – 134.

[261] Maxfield N D, Lyon J M, Silliman E R. Disfluencies along the garden path: brain electrophysiological evidence of disrupted sentence processing [J]. Brain and Language, 2009, 111 (2): 86 – 100.

[262] May C P, Zacks R T, Hasher L, et al. Inhibition in the processing of garden-path sentences [J]. Psychology and Aging, 1999, 14

(2): 304.

[263] Mayerhofer B, Maier K, Schacht A. Priming interpretations: contextual impact on the processing of garden path jokes [J]. Discourse Processes, 2015: 1-20.

[264] Mayerhofer B, Schacht A. From incoherence to mirth: neuro-cognitive processing of garden-path jokes [J]. Frontiers in Psychology, 2015, 6.

[265] Mazuka R, Itoh K. Can Japanese speakers be led down the garden path [J]. Japanese sentence Processing, 1995: 295-329.

[266] Mazuka R, Itoh K, Kondo T. Processing down the garden path in Japanese: processing of sentences with lexical homonyms [J]. Journal of Psycholinguistic Research, 1997, 26 (2): 207-228.

[267] McCurdy K, Kentner G, Vasishth S. Implicit prosody and contextual bias in silent reading [J]. Journal of Eye Movement Research, 2013, 6 (2): 1-17.

[268] McElree B, Griffith T. Syntactic and thematic processing in sentence comprehension: evidence for a temporal dissociation [J]. Journal of Experimental Psychology: Learning, Memory, and Cognition, 1995, 21 (1): 134-157.

[269] McRae K, Ferretti T R, Amyote L. Thematic roles as verb-specific concepts [J]. Language and Cognitive Processes, 1997, 12 (2-3): 137-176.

[270] McRae K, Spivey-Knowlton M J, Tanenhaus M K. Modeling the influence of thematic fit (and other constraints) in on-line sentence comprehension [J]. Journal of Memory and Language, 1998, 38 (3): 283-312.

[271] McRae K, Cree G S, Seidenberg M S, et al. Semantic feature production norms for a large set of living and nonliving things [J]. Behavior Research Methods, 2005, 37 (4): 547-559.

[272] McRae K, Hare M, Elman J L, et al. A basis for generating expectancies for verbs from nouns [J]. Memory & Cognition, 2005, 33 (7): 1174 - 1184.

[273] Meng M, Bader M. Mode of disambiguation and garden-path strength: an investigation of subject-object ambiguities in German [J]. Language and Speech, 2000, 43 (1): 43 - 74.

[274] Meng M, Bader M. Ungrammaticality detection and garden path strength: evidence for serial parsing [J]. Language and Cognitive Processes, 2000, 15 (6): 615 - 666.

[275] Merlo P. A corpus-based analysis of verb continuation frequencies for syntactic processing [J]. Journal of Psycholinguistic Research, 1994, 23 (6): 435 - 457.

[276] Merrick H. Promoting sustainability and simple living online and offline: an Australian case study [J]. First Monday, 2012, 17 (12).

[277] Meseguer E, Carreiras M, Clifton C. Overt reanalysis strategies and eye movements during the reading of mild garden path sentences [J]. Memory & Cognition, 2002, 30 (4): 551 - 561.

[278] Mey J L. Pragmatic gardens and their magic [J]. Poetics, 1991, 20 (3): 233 - 245.

[279] Miller G A, McKean K O. A chronometric study of some relations between sentences [J]. The Quarterly Journal of Experimental Psychology, 1964, 16 (4): 297 - 308.

[280] Miller J. Semantics and syntax: parallels and connections [M]. Cambridge: Cambridge University Press, 1985.

[281] Milne R W. Predicting garden path sentences [J]. Cognitive Science, 1982, 6 (4): 349 - 373.

[282] Mings R C. Changing perspectives on the utility of error correction in second language acquisition [J]. Foreign Language Annals,

1993, 26 (2): 171 – 179.

[283] Mitchell D C, Holmes V M. The role of specific information about the verb in parsing sentences with local structural ambiguity [J]. Journal of Memory and Language, 1985, 24 (5): 542 – 559.

[284] Miyake A, Carpenter P A, Just M A. A capacity approach to syntactic comprehension disorders: making normal adults perform like aphasic patients [J]. Cognitive Neuropsychology, 1994, 11 (6): 671 – 717.

[285] Miyamoto E T, Nakamura M. Subject/object asymmetries in the processing of relative clauses in Japanese [C] //Proceedings of WCCFL, 2003, 22: 342 – 355.

[286] Mohamed M T, Clifton Jr C. Processing temporary syntactic ambiguity: the effect of contextual bias [J]. The Quarterly Journal of Experimental Psychology, 2011, 64 (9): 1797 – 1820.

[287] Mousty P, Bertelson P. Finger movements in braille reading: the effect of local ambiguity [J]. Cognition, 1992, 43 (1): 67 – 84.

[288] Muto H. The effects of linearity on sentence comprehension in oral and silent reading [J]. Japanese Psychological Research, 2015, 57 (3): 194 – 205.

[289] Nagata H. Reflexive resolution in nonlogophoric garden path sentences in Japanese [J]. Perceptual and Motor Skills, 1996, 82 (2): 563 – 569.

[290] Ni W. Sidestepping garden paths: assessing the contributions of syntax, semantics and plausibility in resolving ambiguities [J]. Language and Cognitive Processes, 1996, 11 (3): 283 – 334.

[291] Ni W, Fodor J D, Crain S, et al. Anomaly detection: eye movement patterns [J]. Journal of Psycholinguistic Research, 1998, 27 (5): 515 – 539.

[292] Nicol J L, Pickering M J. Processing syntactically ambiguous sentences: evidence from semantic priming [J]. Journal of Psycholinguistic Research, 1993, 22 (2): 207-237.

[293] Niikuni K, Muramoto T. Effects of punctuation on the processing of temporarily ambiguous sentences in Japanese [J]. Japanese Psychological Research, 2014, 56 (3): 275-287.

[294] Ning L H, Shih C. Prosodic effects on garden-path sentences [C] //Speech Prosody, 2012.

[295] Nitschke S, Kidd E, Serratrice L. First language transfer and long-term structural priming in comprehension [J]. Language and Cognitive Processes, 2010, 25 (1): 94-114.

[296] Novick J M, Kim A, Trueswell J C. Studying the grammatical aspects of word recognition: lexical priming, parsing, and syntactic ambiguity resolution [J]. Journal of Psycholinguistic Research, 2003, 32 (1): 57-75.

[297] Novick J M, Hussey E, Teubner-Rhodes S, et al. Clearing the garden-path: improving sentence processing through cognitive control training [J]. Language, Cognition and Neuroscience, 2014, 29 (2): 186-217.

[298] Oberauer K, Souza A S, Druey M D, et al. Analogous mechanisms of selection and updating in declarative and procedural working memory: experiments and a computational model [J]. Cognitive Psychology, 2013, 66 (2): 157-211.

[299] Osterhout L, Holcomb P J. Event-related brain potentials elicited by syntactic anomaly [J]. Journal of Memory and Language, 1992, 31 (6): 785-806.

[300] Osterhout L, Holcomb P J. Event-related potentials and syntactic anomaly: evidence of anomaly detection during the perception of continuous speech [J]. Language and Cognitive Processes, 1993, 8

(4): 413-437.

[301] Passonneau R J. Using centering to relax Gricean informational constraints on discourse anaphoric noun phrases [J]. Language and Speech, 1996, 39 (2-3): 229-264.

[302] Patson N D, Darowski E S, Moon N, et al. Lingering misinterpretations in garden-path sentences: evidence from a paraphrasing task [J]. Journal of Experimental Psychology: Learning, Memory, and Cognition, 2009, 35 (1): 280-285.

[303] Patson N D, Ferreira F. Conceptual plural information is used to guide early parsing decisions: evidence from garden-path sentences with reciprocal verbs [J]. Journal of Memory and Language, 2009, 60 (4): 464-486.

[304] Patson N D, Warren T. Eye movements when reading implausible sentences: investigating potential structural influences on semantic integration [J]. The Quarterly Journal of Experimental Psychology, 2010, 63 (8): 1516-1532.

[305] Patson N D, Warren T. Comparing the roles of referents and event structures in parsing preferences [J]. Language, Cognition and Neuroscience, 2014, 29 (4): 408-423.

[306] Pearlmutter N J, Daugherty K G, MacDonald M C, et al. Modeling the use of frequency and contextual biases in sentence processing [C]. In Proceedings of the 16th Annual Conference of the Cognitive Science Society, Urbana, 1994, 51: 699-704.

[307] Pearlmutter N J, MacDonald M C. Individual differences and probabilistic constraints in syntactic ambiguity resolution [J]. Journal of Memory and Language, 1995, 34 (4): 521-542.

[308] Perrin L, Deshaies D, Paradis C. Pragmatic functions of local diaphonic repetitions in conversation [J]. Journal of Pragmatics, 2003, 35 (12): 1843-1860.

[309] Perruchet P, Poulin-Charronnat B. Challenging prior evidence for a shared syntactic processor for language and music [J]. Psychonomic Bulletin & Review, 2013, 20 (2): 310-317.

[310] Pickering M J, Traxler M J, Crocker M W. Ambiguity resolution in sentence processing: evidence against frequency-based accounts [J]. Journal of Memory and Language, 2000, 43 (3): 447-475.

[311] Pozzan L, Trueswell J C. Second language processing and revision of garden-path sentences: a visual word study [J]. Bilingualism: Language and Cognition, 2015, 12: 1-8.

[312] Pritchett B L. Garden path phenomena and the grammatical basis of language processing [J]. Language, 1988: 539-576.

[313] Pulman S G. Chart parsing and well-formed substring tables [J]. Encyclopedia of Language & Linguistics, 2006: 302-306.

[314] Pynte J. Prosodic breaks and attachment decisions in sentence parsing [J]. Language and Cognitive Processes, 1996, 11 (1-2): 165-192.

[315] Rayner K. Eye movements in reading and information processing [J]. Psychological Bulletin, 1978, 85 (3): 618.

[316] Rayner K, Carlson M, Frazier L. The interaction of syntax and semantics during sentence processing: eye movements in the analysis of semantically biased sentences [J]. Journal of Verbal Learning and Verbal Behavior, 1983, 22 (3): 358-374.

[317] Rayner K, Frazier L. Parsing temporarily ambiguous complements [J]. The Quarterly Journal of Experimental Psychology, 1987, 39 (4): 657-673.

[318] Rayner K, Sereno S C. Regressive eye movements and sentence parsing: on the use of regression-contingent analyses [J]. Memory & Cognition, 1994, 22 (3): 281-285.

[319] Rayner K. Eye movements in reading and information processing: 20 years of research [J]. Psychological Bulletin, 1998, 124 (3): 372.

[320] Roark B. Robust garden path parsing [J]. Natural Language Engineering, 2004, 10 (1): 1-24.

[321] Roberts L, Felser C. Plausibility and recovery from garden paths in second language sentence processing [J]. Applied Psycholinguistics, 2011, 32 (2): 299-331.

[322] Rosszell H R, Takashima H. Down the garden path: another look at negative feedback [J]. Dealing with Profossional Topics in a Personal Way, 1994, 16 (1): 9.

[323] Rush B K, Barch D M, Braver T S. Accounting for cognitive aging: context processing, inhibition or processing speed? [J]. Aging, Neuropsychology, and Cognition, 2006, 13 (3-4): 588-610.

[324] Salamoura A, Williams J N. Lexical activation of cross-language syntactic priming [J]. Bilingualism: Language and Cognition, 2006, 9 (3): 299-307.

[325] Schlesewsky M, Bornkessel I. Ungrammaticality detection and garden path strength: a commentary on Meng and Bader's (2000) evidence for serial parsing [J]. Language and Cognitive Processes, 2003, 18 (3): 299-311.

[326] Schneider D, Phillips C. Grammatical search and reanalysis [J]. Journal of Memory and Language, 2001, 45 (2): 308-336.

[327] Schooler J W, Ohlsson S, Brooks K. Thoughts beyond words: when language overshadows insight [J]. Journal of Experimental Psychology: General, 1993, 122 (2): 166-183.

[328] Schubert L K. On parsing preferences [C] //Proceedings of the 10th International Conference on Computational Linguistics and

22nd annual Meeting on Association for Computational Linguistics. Association for Computational Linguistics, 1984: 247 - 250.

[329] Sedivy J C. Invoking discourse-based contrast sets and resolving syntactic ambiguities [J]. Journal of Memory and Language, 2002, 46 (2): 341 - 370.

[330] Shieber S M. Sentence disambiguation by a shift-reduce parsing technique [C] //Proceedings of the 21st Annual Meeting on Association for Computational Linguistics. Association for Computational Linguistics, 1983: 113 - 118.

[331] Sies C W, Cadwallader J, Florkowski C M, et al. Quartz renal calculi: were we being led up the garden path? [J]. Annals of Clinical Biochemistry, 2007, 44 (3): 312 - 314.

[332] Snedeker J, Thothathiri M. What lurks beneath: syntactic priming during language comprehension in preschoolers (and adults) [J]. Language Acquisition and Language Disorders, 2008, 44: 137.

[333] Snedeker J, Casserly E. Is it all relative? Effects of prosodic boundaries on the comprehension and production of attachment ambiguities [J]. Language and Cognitive Processes, 2010, 25 (7 - 9): 1234 - 1264.

[334] Solska A, Rojczyk A. Exploring interpretation and misinterpretation of garden-path sentences in polish [J]. International Review of Pragmatics, 2015, 7 (1): 98 - 127.

[335] Spivey M J, Tanenhaus M. Referential context and syntactic ambiguity resolution [A]. In C. Clifton, L. Frazier & K. Rayner (eds.), Perspectives on Sentence Processing [C]. Hillsdale, NJ: Erlbaum, 1994.

[336] Spivey-Knowlton M, Sedivy J C. Resolving attachment ambiguities with multiple constraints [J]. Cognition, 1995, 55 (3): 227 - 267.

[337] Spivey M J, Tanenhaus M K, Eberhard K M, et al. Eye movements and spoken language comprehension: effects of visual context on syntactic ambiguity resolution [J]. Cognitive Psychology, 2002, 45 (4): 447-481.

[338] Staub A, Rayner K, Pollatsek A, et al. The time course of plausibility effects on eye movements in reading: evidence from noun-noun compounds [J]. Journal of Experimental Psychology: Learning, Memory, and Cognition, 2007, 33 (6): 1162.

[339] Staub A. The return of the repressed: abandoned parses facilitate syntactic reanalysis [J]. Journal of Memory and Language, 2007, 57 (2): 299-323.

[340] Steinhauer K, Friederici A D. Prosodic boundaries, comma rules, and brain responses: the closure positive shift in ERPs as a universal marker for prosodic phrasing in listeners and readers [J]. Journal of Psycholinguistic Research, 2001, 30 (3): 267-295.

[341] Steinhauer K. Electrophysiological correlates of prosody and punctuation [J]. Brain and Language, 2003, 86 (1): 142-164.

[342] Sturt P. Incorporating unconscious reanalysis into an incremental, monotonic parser [C] //Proceedings of the Seventh Conference on European Chapter of the Association for Computational Linguistics. Morgan Kaufmann Publishers Inc., 1995: 291-296.

[343] Sturt P. Monotonic syntactic processing: a cross-linguistic study of attachment and reanalysis [J]. Language and Cognitive Processes, 1996, 11 (5): 449-494.

[344] Sturt P, Pickering M J, Crocker M W. Structural change and reanalysis difficulty in language comprehension [J]. Journal of Memory and Language, 1999, 40 (1): 136-150.

[345] Sturt P. Semantic re-interpretation and garden path recovery [J]. Cognition, 2007, 105 (2): 477-488.

[346] Swets B, Desmet T, Hambrick D Z, et al. The role of working memory in syntactic ambiguity resolution: A psychometric approach [J]. Journal of Experimental Psychology: General, 2007, 136 (1): 64.

[347] Tabor W, Juliano C, Tanenhaus M K. Parsing in a dynamical system: An attractor-based account of the interaction of lexical and structural constraints in sentence processing [J]. Language and Cognitive Processes, 1997, 12 (2-3): 211-271.

[348] Tabor W, Galantucci B, Richardson D. Effects of merely local syntactic coherence on sentence processing [J]. Journal of Memory and Language, 2004, 50 (4): 355-370.

[349] Tanenhaus M, Stowe K, Carlson G. Lexical expectations and pragmatics in parsing filler-gap constructions [C] //Proceedings of the Seventh Annual Meeting of the Cognitive Science Association, 1985.

[350] Tanenhaus M K, Carlson G, Trueswell J C. The role of thematic structures in interpretation and parsing [J]. Language and Cognitive Processes, 1989, 4 (3-4): 211-234.

[351] Thompson S A, Mulac A. The discourse conditions for the use of the complementizer that in conversational English [J]. Journal of Pragmatics, 1991, 15 (3): 237-251.

[352] Thornbury S. Reformulation and reconstruction: tasks that promote "noticing" [J]. ELT Journal, 1997, 51 (4): 326-335.

[353] Thothathiri M, Snedeker J. Give and take: syntactic priming during spoken language comprehension [J]. Cognition, 2008, 108 (1): 51-68.

[354] Tomasello M, Herron C. Down the garden path: inducing and correcting overgeneralization errors in the foreign language classroom [J]. Applied Psycholinguistics, 1988, 9 (3): 237-246.

[355] Tomasello M, Herron C. Feedback for language transfer errors [J]. Studies in Second Language Acquisition, 1989, 11 (4): 385-395.

[356] Tonso K, Roth W M. Of roads less traveled, trails blazed, and garden paths laid in walking [J]. Cultural Studies of Science Education, 2007, 2 (2): 309-317.

[357] Tooley K M, Traxler M J, Swaab T Y. Electrophysiological and behavioral evidence of syntactic priming in sentence comprehension [J]. Journal of Experimental Psychology: Learning, Memory, and Cognition, 2009, 35 (1): 19.

[358] Traxler M J, Morris R K, Seely R E. Processing subject and object relative clauses: evidence from eye movements [J]. Journal of Memory and Language, 2002, 47 (1): 69-90.

[359] Traxler M J, Williams R S, Blozis S A, et al. Working memory, animacy, and verb class in the processing of relative clauses [J]. Journal of Memory and Language, 2005, 53 (2): 204-224.

[360] Traxler M J, Tooley K M. Lexical mediation and context effects in sentence processing [J]. Brain Research, 2007, 1146: 59-74.

[361] Trueswell J C, Tanenhaus M K, Kello C. Verb-specific constraints in sentence processing: separating effects of lexical preference from garden-paths [J]. Journal of Experimental Psychology: Learning, Memory, and Cognition, 1993, 19 (3): 528-553.

[362] Trueswell J C, Tanenhaus M K, Garnsey S M. Semantic influences on parsing: use of thematic role information in syntactic ambiguity resolution [J]. Journal of Memory and Language, 1994, 33: 285-318.

[363] Trueswell J C. The role of lexical frequency in syntactic ambiguity resolution [J]. Journal of Memory and Language, 1996, 35 (4): 566-585.

[364] Trueswell J C, Kim A E. How to prune a garden path by nipping it in the bud: fast priming of verb argument structure [J]. Journal of Memory and Language, 1998, 39 (1): 102 – 123.

[365] Trueswell J C, Sekerina I, Hill N M, et al. The kindergarten-path effect: studying on-line sentence processing in young children [J]. Cognition, 1999, 73 (2): 89 – 134.

[366] Trueswell J C, Tanenhaus M K, Garnsey S M. Semantic influences on parsing [J]. Psycholinguistics: Critical Concepts in Psychology, 2002, 3: 172.

[367] Von der Malsburg T, Vasishth S. What is the scanpath signature of syntactic reanalysis? [J]. Journal of Memory and Language, 2011, 65 (2): 109 – 127.

[368] Von der Malsburg T, Vasishth S. Scanpaths reveal syntactic underspecification and reanalysis strategies [J]. Language and Cognitive Processes, 2013, 28 (10): 1545 – 1578.

[369] Vos S H, Gunter T C, Schriefers H, et al. Syntactic parsing and working memory: the effects of syntactic complexity, reading span, and concurrent load [J]. Language and Cognitive Processes, 2001, 16 (1): 65 – 103.

[370] Vos S H, Friederici A D. Intersentential syntactic context effects on comprehension: the role of working memory [J]. Cognitive Brain Research, 2003, 16 (1): 111 – 122.

[371] Vuong L C. The role of executive control in garden path reinterpretation [D]. PhD dissertation. RICE University, 2010.

[372] Vuong L C, Martin R C. The role of LIFG-based executive control in sentence comprehension [J]. Cognitive Neuropsychology, 2015, 32 (5): 243 – 265.

[373] Waltz D L, Pollack J B. Phenomenologically plausible parsing [C] //AAAI. 1984: 335 – 339.

[374] Waltz D L, Pollack J B. Massively parallel parsing: a strongly interactive model of natural language interpretation [J]. Cognitive Science, 1985, 9 (1): 51 – 74.

[375] Wang S, Mo D, Xiang M, et al. The time course of semantic and syntactic processing in reading Chinese: evidence from ERPs [J]. Language and Cognitive Processes, 2012, (1): 1 – 20.

[376] Warren T, McConnell K. Investigating effects of selectional restriction violations and plausibility violation severity on eye-movements in reading [J]. Psychonomic Bulletin & Review, 2007, 14 (4): 770 – 775.

[377] Waters G S, Caplan D. Processing resource capacity and the comprehension of garden path sentences [J]. Memory & Cognition, 1996, 24 (3): 342 – 355.

[378] Waters G S, Caplan D. The capacity theory of sentence comprehension: Critique of Just and Carpenter (1992) [J]. Psychological Review, 1996, 103 (4): 761 – 772.

[379] Waters G S, Caplan D. Working memory and on-line sentence comprehension in patients with Alzheimer's disease [J]. Journal of Psycholinguistic Research, 1997, 26 (4): 377 – 400.

[380] Waters G, Caplan D. Working memory and online syntactic processing in alzheimer's disease studies with auditory moving window presentation [J]. The Journals of Gerontology Series B: Psychological Sciences and Social Sciences, 2002, 57 (4): 298 – 311.

[381] Weber A, Grice M, Crocker M W. The role of prosody in the interpretation of structural ambiguities: a study of anticipatory eye movements [J]. Cognition, 2006, 99 (2): B63 – B72.

[382] Weber A, Crocker M W, Knoeferle P. Conflicting constraints in resource-adaptive language comprehension [J]. Resource-Adaptive Cognitive Processes, 2010: 119 – 141.

[383] Weighall A R. The kindergarten path effect revisited: children's use of context in processing structural ambiguities [J]. Journal of Experimental Child Psychology, 2008, 99 (2): 75 – 95.

[384] Weinberg, A. Parameters in the theory of sentence processing: minimal commitment theory goes east [J]. Journal of Psycholinguistic Research, 1993, 22 (3): 339 – 364.

[385] Wells J B, Christiansen M H, Race D S, et al. Experience and sentence processing: statistical learning and relative clause comprehension [J]. Cognitive Psychology, 2009, 58 (2): 250 – 271.

[386] Wilson M P, Garnsey S M. Making simple sentences hard: verb bias effects in simple direct object sentences [J]. Journal of Memory and Language, 2009, 60 (3): 368 – 392.

[387] Witzel J, Forster K. Lexical co-occurrence and ambiguity resolution [J]. Language, Cognition and Neuroscience, 2014, 29 (2): 158 – 185.

[388] Wonnacott E, Joseph H S S L, Adelman J S, et al. Is children's reading "good enough"? Links between online processing and comprehension as children read syntactically ambiguous sentences [J]. The Quarterly Journal of Experimental Psychology, 2015: 1 – 25.

[389] Woods W A. Transition network grammars for natural language analysis [J]. Communications of the ACM, 1970, 13 (10): 591 – 606.

[390] Woods A, Fletcher P, Hughes A. Statistics in language studies [M]. Cambridge: Cambridge University Press, 2000.

[391] Yamaguchi H. How to pull strings with words: deceptive violations in the garden-path joke [J]. Journal of Pragmatics, 1988, 12 (3): 323 – 337.

[392] Yek S. Leading hackers down the garden path [C] //Australian

Digital Forensics Conference, 2006: 40.

[393] Yu P F, Du J L. Automatic analysis of textual garden path phenomenon: a computational perspective [J]. Journal of Communication and Computer, 2008, 5 (10): 58 – 65.

[394] Yu P F, Du E J. Towards a syntactic structural analysis and an augmented transition explanation: a comparative study of the globally ambiguous sentences and garden path sentences [J]. Journal of Computers, 2012, 7 (1): 196 – 206.

[395] Yurchenko A, den Ouden D B, Hoeksema J, et al. Processing polarity: ERP evidence for differences between positive and negative polarity [J]. Neuropsychologia, 2012.

[396] Zervakis J, Mazuka R. Effect of repeated evaluation and repeated exposure on acceptability ratings of sentences [J]. Journal of Psycholinguistic Research, 2012: 1 – 21.

[397] Zervakis J, Mazuka R. Effect of repeated evaluation and repeated exposure on acceptability ratings of sentences [J]. Journal of Psycholinguistic Research, 2013, 42 (6): 505 – 525.

中文部分

[1] 曹贵康、杨东、张庆林：《顿悟问题解决的原型事件激活：自动还是控制》，《心理科学》2006年第5期。

[2] 常欣：《认知神经语言学视野下的句子理解》，科学出版社2009年版。

[3] 陈海叶：《汉语花园小径电子幽默：关联论的阐释》，《新乡师范高等专科学校学报》2005年第4期。

[4] 陈满华：《花园幽径句的层级、产生机制和修辞效果》，《修辞学习》2009年第4期。

[5] 程秀苹：《英语花园幽径现象研究》，《考试周刊》2008年第24

期。

［6］程燕华、吴本虎：《花园幽径句的认知加工模型探析》，《天津外国语大学学报》2011 年第 5 期。

［7］董安君、李世明：《直觉思维与灵感之异同刍见》，《心理学探新》1988 年第 1 期。

［8］窦东徽、金萍、蔡亮：《基于线索的顿悟问题解决：图式和表征操作的影响》，《心理发展与教育》2007 年第 4 期。

［9］窦东徽、沃建中：《顿悟问题解决过程中抑制解除理论有效性的实验研究》，《心理科学》2007 年第 2 期。

［10］杜家利、于屏方：《花园幽径现象顿悟性的认知解读》，《外语与外语教学》2011 年第 6 期。

［11］杜家利、于屏方：《花园幽径现象认知解读的程序化特性分析》，《计算机工程与应用》2011 年第 21 期。

［12］杜家利、于屏方：《花园幽径模式行进错位的量化研究：计算语言学视角》，《中文信息学报》2015 年第 5 期。

［13］杜家利、于屏方：《花园幽径句行进错位的计算语言学研究》，商务印书馆 2015 年版。

［14］杜家利：《非对称性信息补偿假说》，中国社会科学出版社 2015 年版。

［15］冯胜利：《论汉语的韵律结构及其对句法构造的制约》，《语言研究》1996 年第 1 期。

［16］冯志伟：《中文科技术语的结构描述及潜在歧义》，《中文信息学报》1989 年第 2 期。

［17］冯志伟：《论歧义结构的潜在性》，《中文信息学报》1995 年第 4 期。

［18］冯志伟：《花园幽径句的自动分析算法》，《当代语言学》2003 年第 4 期。

［19］冯志伟：《计算语言学基础》，商务印书馆 2008 年版。

［20］傅小兰：《探讨顿悟的心理过程与大脑机制——评罗劲的〈顿

悟的大脑机制〉》，《心理学报》2004 年第 2 期。

[21] 顾琦一、程秀苹：《中国英语学习者的花园路径句理解——与工作记忆容量和语言水平的相关研究》，《现代外语》2010 年第 3 期。

[22] 桂诗春：《新编心理语言学》，上海外语教育出版社 2004 年版。

[23] 韩宝成：《外语教学科研中的统计方法》，外语教学与研究出版社 2000 年版。

[24] 韩迎春、莫雷：《有关歧义消解的句子加工理论》，《广东教育学院学报》2008 年第 2 期。

[25] 韩玉花：《现代汉语中的"花园幽径"现象》，《成都大学学报（教育科学版）》2007 年第 2 期。

[26] 黄碧蓉：《幽默话语"花园路径现象"的关联论阐释》，《外语研究》2007 年第 6 期。

[27] 黄怀飞、李荣宝：《英语句法歧义句的认知模型》，《泉州师范学院学报》2008 年第 5 期。

[28] 黄洁、秦恺：《中国外语学习者 GP 句句法分析模型研究》，《山东外语教学》2010 年第 1 期。

[29] 黄洁：《GP 句重新分析难度与加工机制》，《天津外国语大学学报》2012 年第 4 期。

[30] 贾德林、秦洪林：《语义歧义研究》，江苏教育出版社 1991 年版。

[31] 姜德杰、尹洪山：《英语花园路径现象的触发性因素》，《青岛科技大学学报（社会科学版）》2006 年第 2 期。

[32] 蒋祖康：《"花园路径现象"研究综述》，《外语教学与研究：外国语文双月刊》2000 年第 4 期。

[33] 李瑞萍、康慧：《英语"花园小径"句的认知解读》，《河北理工大学学报（社会科学版）》2009 年第 2 期。

[34] 李绍山：《语言研究中的统计学》，西安交通大学出版社 2001 年版。

[35] 李宇明：《领属关系与双宾句分析》，《语言教学与研究》1996 年第 3 期。

[36] 林亚军：《汉语动词的语义句法特征与双宾语结构》，《外语学刊》2008 年第 3 期。

[37] 刘聪：《试论"渐修顿悟"与"格物贯通"的异同》，《江淮论坛》2007 年第 2 期。

[38] 刘国辉、石锡书：《花园幽径句的特殊思维激活图式浅析》，《外语学刊》2005 年第 5 期。

[39] 刘汉德、朱国前：《"足够好"理论下场认知方式与英语花园小径句理解的实验研究》，《江西理工大学学报》2012 年第 6 期。

[40] 刘菊华：《顿悟学习理论与阅读教学》，《西南科技大学学报（哲学社会科学版）》2005 年第 3 期。

[41] 刘儒德：《论问题解决过程的模式》，《北京师范大学学报（社会科学版）》1996 年第 1 期。

[42] 刘彦生、吕剑：《简论直觉顿悟的思维特征和形成基础》，《天津大学学报（社会科学版）》2005 年第 3 期。

[43] 刘莹：《叙事文本中"花园幽径句"的认知机制》，《外语学刊》2009 年第 5 期。

[44] 鲁忠义：《阅读理解的过程和影响理解的因素》，《外语教学与研究》1989 年第 4 期。

[45] 鲁忠义、彭聃龄：《故事阅读中句子加工时间与理解的研究》，《心理学报》1996 年第 4 期。

[46] 罗劲：《顿悟的大脑机制》，《心理学报》2004 年第 2 期。

[47] 罗劲、张秀玲：《从困境到超越：顿悟的脑机制研究》，《心理科学进展》2006 年第 4 期。

[48] 罗跃嘉：《揭开顿悟奥秘的一道曙光——评罗劲的〈顿悟的大脑机制〉》，《心理学报》2004 年第 2 期。

[49] 马广惠：《外国语言学及应用语言学统计方法》，西北农林科技大学出版社 2003 年版。

［50］马明：《论句子句法加工过程的模块性》，《东北大学学报（社会科学版）》2004年第2期。

［51］买晓琴、罗劲、吴建辉、罗跃嘉：《猜谜作业中顿悟的ERP效应》，《心理学报》2005年第1期。

［52］满在江：《生成语法理论与汉语双宾语结构》，《现代外语》2003年第3期。

［53］聂其阳、罗劲：《"啊哈！"和"哈哈！"：顿悟与幽默的脑认知成分比较》，《心理科学进展》2012年第2期。

［54］钱文、刘明：《顿悟研究及顿悟与智力超常的关系》，《心理科学》2001年第1期。

［55］邱江、罗跃嘉、吴真真、张庆林：《再探猜谜作业中"顿悟"的ERP效应》，《心理学报》2006年第4期。

［56］邱江、张庆林：《创新思维中原型激活促发顿悟的认知神经机制》，《心理科学进展》2011年第3期。

［57］曲涛、王准宁：《浅析花园幽径现象》，《吉林省教育学院学报》2006年第8期。

［58］任国防、邱江、曹贵康、张庆林：《顿悟：是进程监控还是表征转换》，《心理科学》2007年第5期。

［59］沈汪兵、刘昌、张小将等：《三字字谜顿悟的时间进程和半球效应：一项ERP研究》，《心理学报》2011年第3期。

［60］沈汪兵、刘昌、罗劲等：《顿悟问题思维僵局早期觉察的脑电研究》，《心理学报》2012年第7期。

［61］师保国、张庆林：《顿悟思维：意识的还是潜意识的》，《华东师范大学学报（教育科学版）》2004年第3期。

［62］石锡书：《花园幽径效应探析》，《山东外语教学》2005年第3期。

［63］孙肇春：《花园幽径句的最简方案解释》，《内蒙古民族大学学报》2006年第3期。

［64］田正玲：《花园小径句式歧义现象分析》，《唐山学院学报》

2007年第1期。

[65] 王丹、郑博、杨玉芳：《韵律特征对句法结构歧义解歧作用的实验研究》，《心理科学》2003年第4期。

[66] 王冬玲：《句法处理与花园幽径句》，《延安教育学院学报》2001年第2期。

[67] 王璠：《英汉花园幽径句与汉语相声小品中花园幽径初探》，《科教文汇（下旬刊）》2009年第1期。

[68] 王亚非、高越：《"花园幽径"在"拇指文学"中的应用浅析》，《北京邮电大学学报（社会科学版）》2008年第1期。

[69] 王云、郭智颖：《花园路径现象认知分析》，《四川教育学院学报》2008年第11期。

[70] 温宾利：《当代句法学导论》，外语教学与研究出版社2002年版。

[71] 吴红岩：《花园路径句的优选句法分析》，《广东外语外贸大学学报》2006年第4期。

[72] 吴先少、王利琳：《英语"花园小径句"刍议》，《郑州航空工业管理学院学报（社会科学版）》2007年第3期。

[73] 吴真真、邱江、张庆林：《顿悟的原型启发效应机制探索》，《心理发展与教育》2008年第1期。

[74] 吴真真、邱江、张庆林：《顿悟脑机制的实验范式探索》，《心理科学》2009年第1期。

[75] 肖瑶：《顿悟研究的两种取向》，《科技信息（科学教研）》2008年第17期。

[76] 邢强、曹贵康、张庆林：《顿悟认知机制研究述评》，《天水师范学院学报》2006年第3期。

[77] 邢强、黄伟东、张庆林：《顿悟研究述评及其展望》，《广州大学学报（社会科学版）》2006年第1期。

[78] 邢强、周雪雯：《时间知觉对顿悟问题解决的影响研究》，《广州大学学报（自然科学版）》2007年第5期。

[79] 邢强、黄伟东：《认知负荷对顿悟问题解决的影响》，《心理科学》2008 年第 4 期。

[80] 邢强：《顿悟：心理学的解释、困境与出路》，《宁波大学学报（教育科学版）》2008 年第 6 期。

[81] 徐杰：《"打碎了他四个杯子"与约束原则》，《中国语文》1999 年第 3 期。

[82] 徐列炯：《生成语法理论》，上海外语教育出版社 1998 年版。

[83] 徐艳红：《"花园路径现象"的原型范畴理论阐释》，《内蒙古民族大学学报》2010 年第 6 期。

[84] 徐艳红：《英汉语中的"花园路径现象"》，《西南科技大学学报（哲学社会科学版）》2012 年第 6 期。

[85] 徐章宏：《"花园路径现象"的认知语用学解释》，《广东外语外贸大学学报》2004 年第 3 期。

[86] 延俊荣：《双宾句研究述评》，《语文研究》2002 年第 4 期。

[87] 晏小琴：《中国大学生英语暂时句法歧义加工的定性研究》，《山东外语教学》2007 年第 5 期。

[88] 晏小琴：《英语花园路径句加工的定性研究》，《外国语言文学》2008 年第 1 期。

[89] 姚海娟、沈德立：《顿悟问题解决的心理机制的验证性研究》，《心理与行为研究》2005 年第 3 期。

[90] 姚海娟、沈德立：《启发信息对个体顿悟问题解决影响的眼动研究》，《心理与行为研究》2006 年第 3 期。

[91] 姚海娟、白学军、沈德立：《认知灵活性和顿悟表征转换：练习类型的影响》，《心理学探新》2008 年第 4 期。

[92] 尤肖南：《英语中的"花园幽径句"探析》，《高等函授学报（哲学社会科学版）》2005 年第 1 期。

[93] 于屏方、杜家利：《扩充转移网络在自然语言句法处理中的应用——以歧义句和花园幽径句对照分析为例》，《计算机工程与应用》2012 年第 17 期。

［94］于屏方、杜家利：《良构子串表在自然语言处理中的程序化应用——以花园幽径句为例》，《中文信息学报》2012 年第 5 期。

［95］曾萌芽：《图文广告"花园路径现象"的关联理论解读》，《新乡学院学报（社会科学版）》2012 年第 6 期。

［96］张伯江：《现代汉语的双及物结构式》，《中国语文》1999 年第 3 期。

［97］张殿恩：《英语"花园路径句"探究》，《涪陵师范学院学报》2006 年第 2 期。

［98］张帆：《"试误"与"顿悟"在外语教学过程中的运用》，《绵阳经济技术高等专科学校学报》1999 年第 S1 期。

［99］张福勇、杜家利、于屏方：《英语小说花园路径现象研究——以海明威和博尔赫斯为例》，外语教学与研究出版社 2011 年版。

［100］张奇、王霞：《顿悟与顿悟问题研究》，《宁波大学学报（教育科学版）》2006 年第 1 期。

［101］张庆林、邱江、曹贵康：《顿悟认知机制的研究述评与理论构想》，《心理科学》2004 年第 6 期。

［102］张庆林、邱江：《顿悟与源事件中启发信息的激活》，《心理科学》2005 年第 1 期。

［103］张庆林、田燕、邱江：《顿悟中原型激活的大脑自动响应机制：灵感机制初探》，《西南大学学报（自然科学版）》2002 年第 2 期。

［104］张亚旭、舒华、张厚粲等：《话语参照语境条件下汉语歧义短语的加工》，《心理学报》2002 年第 2 期。

［105］张志毅、张庆云：《词汇语义学》，商务印书馆 2001 年版。

［106］周韧：《汉语信息焦点结构的韵律解释》，《语言科学》2006 年第 3 期。

［107］朱德熙：《汉语句法中的歧义现象》，《中国语文》1980 年第 2 期。

[108] 朱海雪、杨春娟、李文福等:《问题解决中顿悟的原型位置效应的 fMRI 研究》,《心理学报》2012 年第 8 期。
[109] 朱智贤:《心理学的方法论问题》,《北京师范大学学报(社会科学版)》1987 年第 1 期。

附录一

花园幽径句和对照句测试样例

（星号表示非独立 t 检验中有显著差异的项，无标记表示为无显著差异项；括号内第一个和第二个值分别代表 5 秒和 10 秒反应时被试组测试总得分。）

*S1 – Because he always jogs a mile seems a short distance to him. （5；-75）

*S2 – Because he always jogs, a mile seems a short distance to him. （77；194）

*S3 – Fat people eat accumulates. （136；74）

S4 – Fat that people eat accumulates. （-31；-28）

S5 – I convinced her children are noisy. （53；27）

*S6 – I convinced her that children are noisy. （123；215）

*S7 – I know that the words to that song about the queen don't rhyme. （23；86）

*S8 – I know the words to that song about the queen don't rhyme. （71；130）

S9 – I told the girl that the cat that scratched Bill would help her. （57；58）

*S10 – I told the girl the cat scratched that Bill would help her. （83；-10）

S11 – I told the girl the cat that scratched Bill would help her. （117；113）

S12 – I told the girl who was scratched by the cat that Bill would help her. （143；117）

*S13 – Mary gave the child that the dog bit a cake. （13；-107）

S14 – Mary gave the child the dog bit a cake. （-49；-92）

*S15 – Please have the students who failed the exam take the supplementary. （98；146）

S16 – Returned to his house, the man was happy. （70；65）

S17 – She told me a little white lie will come back to haunt me. （5；19）

*S18 – She told me that a little white lie will come back to haunt me. （97；160）

*S19 – Single and married soldiers and their families are housed in the complex. （77；143）

S20 – The army stands on guard. （165；193）

S21 – The author composed the novel and was likely to be a best-seller. （111；90）

S22 – The author wrote that the novel in question was likely to be a best-seller. （71；61）

S23 – The author wrote the novel was likely to be a best-seller. （48；27）

S24 – The biggest rocks were by the seashore. （12；31）

S25 – The boat floated down the river quietly. （204；209）

*S26 – The boat floated down the river sank. （22；-34）

*S27 – The building blocks the sun faded are red. （-21；-66）

*S28 – The building blocks the sun shining on the house faded are red. （80；-16）

*S29 – The building blocks the sun shining on the house. （65；135）

S30 – The building blocks the sun. (152; 157)

S31 – The chestnut blocks are red. (156; 185)

S32 – The chestnut blocks the sink. (41; 25)

* S33 – The clothing, which is made of cotton, grows in Mississippi. (99; 11)

S34 – The complex houses married and single soldiers and their families. (-74; -101)

S35 – The cotton clothing is made in sunny Alabama. (190; 198)

S36 – The cotton clothing is made of grows in Mississippi. (32; 24)

S37 – The cotton clothing is usually made of grows in Mississippi. (37; 11)

* S38 – The cotton that clothing is made of grows in Mississippi. (-17; 53)

* S39 – The cotton that clothing is usually made of grows in Mississippi. (27; 104)

* S40 – The dog that I had as a pet really loved bones. (169; 218)

* S41 – The dog that I had really loved bones. (166; 229)

* S42 – The drink that was sour is from the ocean. (100; 154)

* S43 – The fact that Jill is never here hurts me. (85; 147)

S44 – The fat that people eat accumulates. (-54; -49)

* S45 – The fat that people eat accumulates in their bodies. (-10; 68)

* S46 – The girl told the story and cried. (152; 187)

S47 – The girl told the story cried. (-50; -46)

* S48 – The girl who was told the story cried. (156; 203)

S49 – The government is planning to raise taxes, which was defeated. (172; 136)

* S50 – The government plans to raise taxes were defeated. (-38; -95)

附录一　花园幽径句和对照句测试样例

* S51 – The government's plans to raise taxes were defeated. （129；170）

* S52 – The large pins are bright red. （177；208）

S53 – The man came back to his house and was happy. （167；171）

S54 – The man pushed through the door fell. （–10；–18）

* S55 – I told the girl the cat scratched Bill would help her. （36；–9）

* S56 – The man returned to his house was happy. （–64；–5）

S57 – The man who was returned to his house was happy. （125；96）

* S58 – The man whistling tunes pianos. （–33；56）

* S59 – The man who hunts ducks out on weekends. （–17；36）

S60 – The man who is whistling melodies plays pianos. （165；182）

* S61 – The man who whistles all the time tunes pianos for a living. （125；190）

* S62 – The man, who hunts animals, ducks out on weekends. （149；203）

* S63 – The map pins are bright red. （133；190）

S64 – The map pins onto the wall. （54；24）

* S65 – The men run through the arches and screamed. （153；190）

S66 – The men run through the arches screamed. （–1；–37）

* S67 – The old dog follows the footsteps of the young. （156；206）

S68 – The old dog the footsteps of the young. （–173；–150）

S69 – The prime number few. （–151；–161）

S70 – The prime number is forty. （213；228）

* S71 – The prime people number few. （–129；–75）

S72 – The raft floated down the river sank. （34；–4）

S73 – The raft that was floated down the river sank. （101；116）

S74 – The sentry stands are green. （115；103）

S75 – The sentry stands on guard. （179；196）

*S76 – The shotgun pins were rusty from the rain. (121; 183)

S77 – The sign pins onto the wall. (71; 50)

*S78 – The sniper guards the victim in the woods. (91; 172)

S79 – The sniper pins the victim in the woods. (87; 89)

*S80 – The sniper pins were rusty from the rain. (102; 165)

*S81 – The sour drink from the ocean. (−67; −135)

*S82 – The statue stands in the park are rusty. (68; −2)

S83 – The statue stands in the park. (196; 211)

*S84 – The stone rocks during the earthquake. (65; 146)

S85 – The stone rocks were by the seashore. (−4; 10)

S86 – The stopper blocks the sink. (101; 107)

*S87 – The table rocks during the earthquake. (124; 166)

*S88 – The teacher told the children the ghost story had frightened that it wasn't true. (16; −92)

*S89 – The teacher told the children the ghost story that she knew would frighten them. (125; 174)

*S90 – The tomcat curled itself up on the cushion and seemed friendly. (90; 149)

S91 – The tomcat curled up on the cushion seemed friendly. (100; 103)

S92 – The tomcat that was curled up on the cushion seemed friendly. (169; 188)

S93 – The toy rocks near the child are pink. (119; 114)

S94 – The toy rocks near the child quietly. (25; 55)

S95 – The tycoon sold the offshore oil tracts for a lot of money wanted to kill JR. (−25; −65)

*S96 – The tycoon, who was sold the offshore oil tracts for a lot of money, wanted to kill JR. (147; 202)

S97 – The whistling man tunes pianos. (126; 150)

* S98 – Until the police arrest the drug dealers control the street. (-95; -151)

* S99 – Until the police make the arrest, the drug dealers control the street. (111, 152)

S100 – When Fred eats food gets thrown. (-124; -128)

附录二

阅读时间与效果的非独立 t 值测试

被试 N = 126；组 1 和组 2 阅读间隔分别为 5 秒和 10 秒；.05 水平下双侧临界值为 1.96。

NO.	ΣD	ΣD^2	$(\Sigma D)^2$	$N\Sigma D^2$	$N\Sigma D^2 - (\Sigma D)^2$	$[N\Sigma D^2 - (\Sigma D)^2]/(N-1)$	SQRT	t
S1	80	512	6400.00	64512.00	58112.00	464.90	21.56	3.71
S2	-117	401	13689.00	50526.00	36837.00	294.70	17.17	-6.82
S3	62	524	3844.00	66024.00	62180.00	497.44	22.30	2.78
S4	-3	515	9.00	64890.00	64881.00	519.05	22.78	-0.13
S5	26	584	676.00	73584.00	72908.00	583.26	24.15	1.08
S6	-92	446	8464.00	56196.00	47732.00	381.86	19.54	-4.71
S7	-63	485	3969.00	61110.00	57141.00	457.13	21.38	-2.95
S8	-59	469	3481.00	59094.00	55613.00	444.90	21.09	-2.80
S9	-1	561	1.00	70686.00	70685.00	565.48	23.78	-0.04
S10	93	649	8649.00	81774.00	73125.00	585.00	24.19	3.85
S11	4	432	16.00	54432.00	54416.00	435.33	20.86	0.19
S12	26	348	676.00	43848.00	43172.00	345.38	18.58	1.40
S13	120	590	14400.00	74340.00	59940.00	479.52	21.90	5.48
S14	43	489	1849.00	61614.00	59765.00	478.12	21.87	1.97
S15	-48	420	2304.00	52920.00	50616.00	404.93	20.12	-2.39
S16	5	419	25.00	52794.00	52769.00	422.15	20.55	0.24
S17	-14	562	196.00	70812.00	70616.00	564.93	23.77	-0.59

附录二 阅读时间与效果的非独立 t 值测试

续表

NO.	ΣD	ΣD^2	$(\Sigma D)^2$	$N\Sigma D^2$	$N\Sigma D^2 - (\Sigma D)^2$	$[N\Sigma D^2 - (\Sigma D)^2]/(N-1)$	SQRT	t
S18	-63	439	3969.00	55314.00	51345.00	410.76	20.27	-3.11
S19	-66	358	4356.00	45108.00	40752.00	326.02	18.06	-3.66
S20	-28	278	784.00	35028.00	34244.00	273.95	16.55	-1.69
S21	21	455	441.00	57330.00	56889.00	455.11	21.33	0.98
S22	10	612	100.00	77112.00	77012.00	616.10	24.82	0.40
S23	21	523	441.00	65898.00	65457.00	523.66	22.88	0.92
S24	-19	443	361.00	55818.00	55457.00	443.66	21.06	-0.90
S25	-5	217	25.00	27342.00	27317.00	218.54	14.78	-0.34
S26	56	490	3136.00	61740.00	58604.00	468.83	21.65	2.59
S27	45	367	2025.00	46242.00	44217.00	353.74	18.81	2.39
S28	96	548	9216.00	69048.00	59832.00	478.66	21.88	4.39
S29	-70	464	4900.00	58464.00	53564.00	428.51	20.70	-3.38
S30	-5	317	25.00	39942.00	39917.00	319.34	17.87	-0.28
S31	-29	269	841.00	33894.00	33053.00	264.42	16.26	-1.78
S32	16	412	256.00	51912.00	51656.00	413.25	20.33	0.79
S33	88	624	7744.00	78624.00	70880.00	567.04	23.81	3.70
S34	27	481	729.00	60606.00	59877.00	479.02	21.89	1.23
S35	-8	232	64.00	29232.00	29168.00	233.34	15.28	-0.52
S36	8	664	64.00	83664.00	83600.00	668.80	25.86	0.31
S37	26	592	676.00	74592.00	73916.00	591.33	24.32	1.07
S38	-70	658	4900.00	82908.00	78008.00	624.06	24.98	-2.80
S39	-77	543	5929.00	68418.00	62489.00	499.91	22.36	-3.44
S40	-49	197	2401.00	24822.00	22421.00	179.37	13.39	-3.66
S41	-63	263	3969.00	33138.00	29169.00	233.35	15.28	-4.12
S42	-54	402	2916.00	50652.00	47736.00	381.89	19.54	-2.76
S43	-62	434	3844.00	54684.00	50840.00	406.72	20.17	-3.07
S44	-5	475	25.00	59850.00	59825.00	478.60	21.88	-0.23
S45	-78	612	6084.00	77112.00	71028.00	568.22	23.84	-3.27
S46	-35	235	1225.00	29610.00	28385.00	227.08	15.07	-2.32

续表

NO.	$\sum D$	$\sum D^2$	$(\sum D)^2$	$N\sum D^2$	$N\sum D^2-(\sum D)^2$	$[N\sum D^2-(\sum D)^2]/(N-1)$	SQRT	t
S47	-4	410	16.00	51660.00	51644.00	413.15	20.33	-0.20
S48	-47	305	2209.00	38430.00	36221.00	289.77	17.02	-2.76
S49	36	346	1296.00	43596.00	42300.00	338.40	18.40	1.96
S50	57	511	3249.00	64386.00	61137.00	489.10	22.12	2.58
S51	-41	405	1681.00	51030.00	49349.00	394.79	19.87	-2.06
S52	-31	153	961.00	19278.00	18317.00	146.54	12.11	-2.56
S53	-4	242	16.00	30492.00	30476.00	243.81	15.61	-0.26
S54	8	406	64.00	51156.00	51092.00	408.74	20.22	0.40
S55	45	507	2025.00	63882.00	61857.00	494.86	22.25	2.02
S56	-59	475	3481.00	59850.00	56369.00	450.95	21.24	-2.78
S57	29	525	841.00	66150.00	65309.00	522.47	22.86	1.27
S58	-89	641	7921.00	80766.00	72845.00	582.76	24.14	-3.69
S59	-53	503	2809.00	63378.00	60569.00	484.55	22.01	-2.41
S60	-17	245	289.00	30870.00	30581.00	244.65	15.64	-1.09
S61	-65	281	4225.00	35406.00	31181.00	249.45	15.79	-4.12
S62	-54	250	2916.00	31500.00	28584.00	228.67	15.12	-3.57
S63	-57	325	3249.00	40950.00	37701.00	301.61	17.37	-3.28
S64	30	502	900.00	63252.00	62352.00	498.82	22.33	1.34
S65	-37	253	1369.00	31878.00	30509.00	244.07	15.62	-2.37
S66	36	416	1296.00	52416.00	51120.00	408.96	20.22	1.78
S67	-50	288	2500.00	36288.00	33788.00	270.30	16.44	-3.04
S68	-23	243	529.00	30618.00	30089.00	240.71	15.51	-1.48
S69	10	282	100.00	35532.00	35432.00	283.46	16.84	0.59
S70	-15	95	225.00	11970.00	11745.00	93.96	9.69	-1.55
S71	-54	518	2916.00	65268.00	62352.00	498.82	22.33	-2.42
S72	38	588	1444.00	74088.00	72644.00	581.15	24.11	1.58
S73	-15	489	225.00	61614.00	61389.00	491.11	22.16	-0.68
S74	12	406	144.00	51156.00	51012.00	408.10	20.20	0.59
S75	-17	199	289.00	25074.00	24785.00	198.28	14.08	-1.21

附录二 阅读时间与效果的非独立 t 值测试

续表

NO.	$\sum D$	$\sum D^2$	$(\sum D)^2$	$N\sum D^2$	$N\sum D^2 - (\sum D)^2$	$[N\sum D^2 - (\sum D)^2]/(N-1)$	SQRT	t
S76	−62	234	3844.00	29484.00	25640.00	205.12	14.32	−4.33
S77	21	593	441.00	74718.00	74277.00	594.22	24.38	0.86
S78	−81	345	6561.00	43470.00	36909.00	295.27	17.18	−4.71
S79	−2	414	4.00	52164.00	52160.00	417.28	20.43	−0.10
S80	−63	327	3969.00	41202.00	37233.00	297.86	17.26	−3.65
S81	68	414	4624.00	52164.00	47540.00	380.32	19.50	3.49
S82	70	560	4900.00	70560.00	65660.00	525.28	22.92	3.05
S83	−15	171	225.00	21546.00	21321.00	170.57	13.06	−1.15
S84	−81	491	6561.00	61866.00	55305.00	442.44	21.03	−3.85
S85	−14	526	196.00	66276.00	66080.00	528.64	22.99	−0.61
S86	−6	338	36.00	42588.00	42552.00	340.42	18.45	−0.33
S87	−42	340	1764.00	42840.00	41076.00	328.61	18.13	−2.32
S88	108	548	11664.00	69048.00	57384.00	459.07	21.43	5.04
S89	−49	305	2401.00	38430.00	36029.00	288.23	16.98	−2.89
S90	−59	255	3481.00	32130.00	28649.00	229.19	15.14	−3.90
S91	−3	537	9.00	67662.00	67653.00	541.22	23.26	−0.13
S92	−19	259	361.00	32634.00	32273.00	258.18	16.07	−1.18
S93	5	359	25.00	45234.00	45209.00	361.67	19.02	0.26
S94	−30	554	900.00	69804.00	68904.00	551.23	23.48	−1.28
S95	40	522	1600.00	65772.00	64172.00	513.38	22.66	1.77
S96	−55	337	3025.00	42462.00	39437.00	315.50	17.76	−3.10
S97	−24	368	576.00	46368.00	45792.00	366.34	19.14	−1.25
S98	56	372	3136.00	46872.00	43736.00	349.89	18.71	2.99
S99	−41	377	1681.00	47502.00	45821.00	366.57	19.15	−2.14
S100	4	322	16.00	40572.00	40556.00	324.45	18.01	0.22

附录三

时间因素与测试结果的方差分析

分组规模 k = 3（5秒 - 7秒 - 10秒）；组间自由度 k - 1 = 2；样本规模 N = 126；组内自由度 N - k = 123；在 .05 水平下，分子自由度为 2，分母为无穷大（>100），方差临界值为 3.0。

编号	组间平方和	组间自由度	组间均方	组内平方和	组内自由度	组内均方	F
S1	50.59	2	25.30	875.32	123	7.12	3.55
S2	75.66	2	37.83	377.95	123	3.07	12.31
S3	15.34	2	7.67	848.45	123	6.90	1.11
S4	24.14	2	12.07	977.48	123	7.95	1.52
S5	8.1	2	4.05	1057.41	123	8.60	0.47
S6	36.39	2	18.20	498.49	123	4.05	4.49
S7	20.67	2	10.34	781.76	123	6.36	1.63
S8	14.29	2	7.15	688.83	123	5.60	1.28
S9	7.85	2	3.93	841.37	123	6.84	0.57
S10	59.88	2	29.94	899.89	123	7.32	4.09
S11	0.83	2	0.42	693.01	123	5.63	0.07
S12	4.59	2	2.30	782.28	123	6.36	0.36
S13	80.89	2	40.45	790.65	123	6.43	6.29
S14	24.23	2	12.12	779.76	123	6.34	1.91
S15	11.05	2	5.53	717.82	123	5.84	0.95
S16	0.13	2	0.07	1155.69	123	9.40	0.01

附录三 时间因素与测试结果的方差分析

续表

编号	组间平方和	组间自由度	组间均方	组内平方和	组内自由度	组内均方	F
S17	4.35	2	2.18	891.38	123	7.25	0.30
S18	19.75	2	9.88	632.01	123	5.14	1.92
S19	20.59	2	10.30	553.01	123	4.50	2.29
S20	3.3	2	1.65	549.67	123	4.47	0.37
S21	2.86	2	1.43	950.23	123	7.73	0.19
S22	6.88	2	3.44	861.83	123	7.01	0.49
S23	2.13	2	1.07	1147.25	123	9.33	0.11
S24	1.44	2	0.72	1065.06	123	8.66	0.08
S25	0.13	2	0.07	324.37	123	2.64	0.02
S26	18.56	2	9.28	982.29	123	7.99	1.16
S27	8.42	2	4.21	827.47	123	6.73	0.63
S28	37	2	18.50	843.98	123	6.86	2.70
S29	22.01	2	11.01	693.7	123	5.64	1.95
S30	0.13	2	0.07	684.64	123	5.57	0.01
S31	4.16	2	2.08	483.44	123	3.93	0.53
S32	1.78	2	0.89	910.63	123	7.40	0.12
S33	30.86	2	15.43	1241.41	123	10.09	1.53
S34	3.48	2	1.74	810.36	123	6.59	0.26
S35	0.89	2	0.45	359.82	123	2.93	0.15
S36	22.61	2	11.31	1085.44	123	8.82	1.28
S37	7.77	2	3.89	1006.79	123	8.19	0.47
S38	19.97	2	9.99	1051.19	123	8.55	1.17
S39	25.34	2	12.67	918.84	123	7.47	1.70
S40	9.83	2	4.92	335.51	123	2.73	1.80
S41	18.93	2	9.47	346.96	123	2.82	3.36
S42	27.58	2	13.79	1127.52	123	9.17	1.50
S43	17.59	2	8.80	926.53	123	7.53	1.17
S44	7.15	2	3.58	1001.34	123	8.14	0.44
S45	28.9	2	14.45	999.5	123	8.13	1.78

续表

编号	组间平方和	组间自由度	组间均方	组内平方和	组内自由度	组内均方	F
S46	8.58	2	4.29	521.21	123	4.24	1.01
S47	5.48	2	2.74	1014.57	123	8.25	0.33
S48	12.77	2	6.39	505.73	123	4.11	1.55
S49	5.23	2	2.62	672.29	123	5.47	0.48
S50	17.19	2	8.60	1025.29	123	8.34	1.03
S51	10.11	2	5.06	695.51	123	5.65	0.89
S52	4.64	2	2.32	302.46	123	2.46	0.94
S53	0.07	2	0.04	548.59	123	4.46	0.01
S54	0.51	2	0.26	994.13	123	8.08	0.03
S55	8.74	2	4.37	948.04	123	7.71	0.57
S56	13.81	2	6.91	1107.57	123	9.00	0.77
S57	46.35	2	23.18	977.7	123	7.95	2.92
S58	31.73	2	15.87	873.34	123	7.10	2.23
S59	11.21	2	5.61	1054.13	123	8.57	0.65
S60	1.16	2	0.58	499.98	123	4.06	0.14
S61	17.24	2	8.62	512.24	123	4.16	2.07
S62	12	2	6.00	468.12	123	3.81	1.58
S63	15.57	2	7.79	547.4	123	4.45	1.75
S64	8.33	2	4.17	1032.64	123	8.40	0.50
S65	7.24	2	3.62	559.92	123	4.55	0.80
S66	7.26	2	3.63	1000.06	123	8.13	0.45
S67	14.37	2	7.19	410.06	123	3.33	2.16
S68	4.54	2	2.27	618.11	123	5.03	0.45
S69	0.93	2	0.47	614.62	123	5.00	0.09
S70	1.37	2	0.69	260.02	123	2.11	0.32
S71	12.93	2	6.47	878.59	123	7.14	0.91
S72	5.86	2	2.93	1005.52	123	8.17	0.36
S73	1.59	2	0.80	917.57	123	7.46	0.11
S74	1.61	2	0.81	838.21	123	6.81	0.12

续表

编号	组间平方和	组间自由度	组间均方	组内平方和	组内自由度	组内均方	F
S75	1.73	2	0.87	372.67	123	3.03	0.29
S76	15.68	2	7.84	425.29	123	3.46	2.27
S77	2.71	2	1.36	945.69	123	7.69	0.18
S78	26.04	2	13.02	612.2	123	4.98	2.62
S79	0.91	2	0.46	699.1	123	5.68	0.08
S80	15.91	2	7.96	618.33	123	5.03	1.58
S81	19.54	2	9.77	920.94	123	7.49	1.30
S82	20.8	2	10.40	1165.21	123	9.47	1.10
S83	1.86	2	0.93	330.05	123	2.68	0.35
S84	26.51	2	13.26	960.33	123	7.81	1.70
S85	8.42	2	4.21	1044.36	123	8.49	0.50
S86	0.57	2	0.29	727.55	123	5.92	0.05
S87	8.53	2	4.27	692.98	123	5.63	0.76
S88	49.86	2	24.93	912.29	123	7.42	3.36
S89	10.01	2	5.01	495.06	123	4.02	1.24
S90	173.81	2	86.91	784.23	123	6.38	13.63
S91	0.74	2	0.37	833.1	123	6.77	0.05
S92	2.4	2	1.20	500.75	123	4.07	0.29
S93	0.58	2	0.29	859.6	123	6.99	0.04
S94	4.21	2	2.11	1069.36	123	8.69	0.24
S95	9.66	2	4.83	778.62	123	6.33	0.76
S96	13.12	2	6.56	528.45	123	4.30	1.53
S97	3.18	2	1.59	621.47	123	5.05	0.31
S98	16.02	2	8.01	616.21	123	5.01	1.60
S99	8.48	2	4.24	715.28	123	5.82	0.73
S100	0.96	2	0.48	677.6	123	5.51	0.09

附录四（一）

高考英语成绩与英语专业四级成绩相关系数统计

N	X	X^2	Y	Y^2	XY
1	95	9025	46	2116	4370
2	127	16129	47	2209	5969
3	109	11881	47	2209	5123
4	81	6561	48	2304	3888
5	102	10404	49	2401	4998
6	107	11449	50	2500	5350
7	92	8464	50	2500	4600
8	130	16900	50	2500	6500
9	118	13924	51	2601	6018
10	123	15129	51	2601	6273
11	105	11025	51	2601	5355
12	99	9801	52	2704	5148
13	121	14641	52	2704	6292
14	95	9025	52	2704	4940
15	93	8649	53	2809	4929
16	128	16384	54	2916	6912
17	84	7056	54	2916	4536
18	112	12544	54	2916	6048
19	119	14161	55	3025	6545
20	119	14161	56	3136	6664

附录四（一） 高考英语成绩与英语专业四级成绩相关系数统计

续表

N	X	X²	Y	Y²	XY
21	100	10000	56	3136	5600
22	124	15376	56	3136	6944
23	122	14884	56	3136	6832
24	120	14400	56	3136	6720
25	129	16641	56	3136	7224
26	117	13689	56	3136	6552
27	131	17161	56	3136	7336
28	123	15129	56	3136	6888
29	94	8836	57	3249	5358
30	132	17424	57	3249	7524
31	118	13924	58	3364	6844
32	128	16384	58	3364	7424
33	124	15376	58	3364	7192
34	91	8281	58	3364	5278
35	124	15376	60	3600	7440
36	129	16641	60	3600	7740
37	130	16900	60	3600	7800
38	138	19044	60	3600	8280
39	124	15376	60	3600	7440
40	131	17161	60	3600	7860
41	137	18769	60	3600	8220
42	116	13456	60	3600	6960
43	125	15625	60	3600	7500
44	124	15376	60	3600	7440
45	129	16641	60	3600	7740
46	107	11449	60	3600	6420
47	124	15376	60	3600	7440
48	123	15129	60	3600	7380
49	137	18769	60	3600	8220
50	120	14400	61	3721	7320

续表

N	X	X^2	Y	Y^2	XY
51	129	16641	61	3721	7869
52	121	14641	61	3721	7381
53	94	8836	61	3721	5734
54	124	15376	62	3844	7688
55	128	16384	62	3844	7936
56	122	14884	62	3844	7564
57	135	18225	62	3844	8370
58	116	13456	62	3844	7192
59	127	16129	62	3844	7874
60	127	16129	62	3844	7874
61	125	15625	62	3844	7750
62	129	16641	63	3969	8127
63	130	16900	63	3969	8190
64	135	18225	63	3969	8505
65	131	17161	64	4096	8384
66	122	14884	64	4096	7808
67	117	13689	64	4096	7488
68	135	18225	64	4096	8640
69	123	15129	64	4096	7872
70	125	15625	64	4096	8000
71	126	15876	64	4096	8064
72	130	16900	64	4096	8320
73	125	15625	64	4096	8000
74	131	17161	64	4096	8384
75	124	15376	64	4096	7936
76	132	17424	65	4225	8580
77	130	16900	65	4225	8450
78	131	17161	65	4225	8515
79	132	17424	65	4225	8580
80	123	15129	66	4356	8118

附录四（一） 高考英语成绩与英语专业四级成绩相关系数统计

续表

N	X	X²	Y	Y²	XY
81	135	18225	66	4356	8910
82	142	20164	67	4489	9514
83	131	17161	67	4489	8777
84	129	16641	67	4489	8643
85	127	16129	68	4624	8636
86	126	15876	68	4624	8568
87	135	18225	68	4624	9180
88	121	14641	68	4624	8228
89	128	16384	68	4624	8704
90	126	15876	68	4624	8568
91	132	17424	68	4624	8976
92	132	17424	68	4624	8976
93	136	18496	69	4761	9384
94	135	18225	69	4761	9315
95	132	17424	69	4761	9108
96	124	15376	69	4761	8556
97	138	19044	70	4900	9660
98	118	13924	70	4900	8260
99	120	14400	70	4900	8400
100	132	17424	70	4900	9240
101	125	15625	70	4900	8750
102	120	14400	70	4900	8400
103	127	16129	71	5041	9017
104	135	18225	71	5041	9585
105	122	14884	71	5041	8662
106	139	19321	71	5041	9869
107	127	16129	72	5184	9144
108	130	16900	72	5184	9360
109	125	15625	72	5184	9000
110	135	18225	73	5329	9855

续表

N	X	X²	Y	Y²	XY
111	134	17956	73	5329	9782
112	135	18225	73	5329	9855
113	134	17956	74	5476	9916
114	133	17689	74	5476	9842
115	130	16900	74	5476	9620
116	132	17424	74	5476	9768
117	121	14641	74	5476	8954
118	128	16384	75	5625	9600
119	139	19321	76	5776	10564
120	126	15876	76	5776	9576
121	124	15376	77	5929	9548
122	134	17956	77	5929	10318
123	134	17956	78	6084	10452
124	137	18769	79	6241	10823
125	132	17424	79	6241	10428
126	133	17689	81	6561	10773

附录四（二）

高考英语成绩与英语专业四级成绩相关系数分析

n	$\sum X$	$\sum X^2$	$\sum Y$	$\sum Y^2$
126	15599	1949575	7969	511773
$n\sum XY$	$\sum X \sum Y$	$n\sum XY - \sum X \sum Y$	$n\sum Y^2$	$(\sum Y)^2$
125197506	124308431	889075	64483398	63504961
$n\sum X^2$	$(\sum X)^2$	$n\sum X^2 - (\sum X)^2$	$n\sum Y^2 - (\sum Y)^2$	$\sum XY$
245646450	243328801	2317649	978437	993631
\[$n\sum X^2 - (\sum X)^2$\]\[$n\sum Y^2 - (\sum Y)^2$\]			$r_{126-2} = .59$	
2.26767E+12			$p < .05$	

备注：在.05风险水平下，自由度无穷大（df>100）时双侧临界值为.1946

结论：高考英语成绩与英语专业四级英语成绩具有强相关性

附录五（一）

高考总成绩与英语专业四级成绩相关系数统计

N	X	X^2	Y	Y^2	XY
1	400	160000	46	2116	18400
2	605	366025	47	2209	28435
3	490	240100	47	2209	23030
4	421	177241	48	2304	20208
5	479	229441	49	2401	23471
6	591	349281	50	2500	29550
7	408	166464	50	2500	20400
8	605	366025	50	2500	30250
9	518	268324	51	2601	26418
10	577	332929	51	2601	29427
11	485	235225	51	2601	24735
12	516	266256	52	2704	26832
13	540	291600	52	2704	28080
14	441	194481	52	2704	22932
15	469	219961	53	2809	24857
16	570	324900	54	2916	30780
17	409	167281	54	2916	22086
18	563	316969	54	2916	30402
19	597	356409	55	3025	32835
20	570	324900	56	3136	31920

附录五（一）　高考总成绩与英语专业四级成绩相关系数统计

续表

N	X	X^2	Y	Y^2	XY
21	412	169744	56	3136	23072
22	602	362404	56	3136	33712
23	513	263169	56	3136	28728
24	563	316969	56	3136	31528
25	601	361201	56	3136	33656
26	563	316969	56	3136	31528
27	599	358801	56	3136	33544
28	502	252004	56	3136	28112
29	410	168100	57	3249	23370
30	558	311364	57	3249	31806
31	532	283024	58	3364	30856
32	598	357604	58	3364	34684
33	566	320356	58	3364	32828
34	322	103684	58	3364	18676
35	597	356409	60	3600	35820
36	599	358801	60	3600	35940
37	604	364816	60	3600	36240
38	559	312481	60	3600	33540
39	548	300304	60	3600	32880
40	565	319225	60	3600	33900
41	537	288369	60	3600	32220
42	519	269361	60	3600	31140
43	586	343396	60	3600	35160
44	600	360000	60	3600	36000
45	603	363609	60	3600	36180
46	568.8	323533.44	60	3600	34128
47	453	205209	60	3600	27180
48	591	349281	60	3600	35460
49	597	356409	60	3600	35820
50	591	349281	61	3721	36051

· 275 ·

续表

N	X	X^2	Y	Y^2	XY
51	571	326041	61	3721	34831
52	563	316969	61	3721	34343
53	475	225625	61	3721	28975
54	598	357604	62	3844	37076
55	575	330625	62	3844	35650
56	560	313600	62	3844	34720
57	562	315844	62	3844	34844
58	480	230400	62	3844	29760
59	601	361201	62	3844	37262
60	597	356409	62	3844	37014
61	580	336400	62	3844	35960
62	517	267289	63	3969	32571
63	559	312481	63	3969	35217
64	588	345744	63	3969	37044
65	591	349281	64	4096	37824
66	563	316969	64	4096	36032
67	563	316969	64	4096	36032
68	601	361201	64	4096	38464
69	591	349281	64	4096	37824
70	566	320356	64	4096	36224
71	597	356409	64	4096	38208
72	537	288369	64	4096	34368
73	598	357604	64	4096	38272
74	551	303601	64	4096	35264
75	490	240100	64	4096	31360
76	577	332929	65	4225	37505
77	570	324900	65	4225	37050
78	556	309136	65	4225	36140
79	601	361201	65	4225	39065
80	566	320356	66	4356	37356

附录五（一）　高考总成绩与英语专业四级成绩相关系数统计

续表

N	X	X^2	Y	Y^2	XY
81	565	319225	66	4356	37290
82	575	330625	67	4489	38525
83	577	332929	67	4489	38659
84	570	324900	67	4489	38190
85	601	361201	68	4624	40868
86	597	356409	68	4624	40596
87	596	355216	68	4624	40528
88	566	320356	68	4624	38488
89	578	334084	68	4624	39304
90	598	357604	68	4624	40664
91	570	324900	68	4624	38760
92	556	309136	68	4624	37808
93	605	366025	69	4761	41745
94	597	356409	69	4761	41193
95	594	352836	69	4761	40986
96	504	254016	69	4761	34776
97	596	355216	70	4900	41720
98	570	324900	70	4900	39900
99	568.7	323419.69	70	4900	39809
100	599	358801	70	4900	41930
101	555	308025	70	4900	38850
102	496.6	246611.56	70	4900	34762
103	598	357604	71	5041	42458
104	596	355216	71	5041	42316
105	591	349281	71	5041	41961
106	601	361201	71	5041	42671
107	605	366025	72	5184	43560
108	599	358801	72	5184	43128
109	474	224676	72	5184	34128
110	575	330625	73	5329	41975

续表

N	X	X^2	Y	Y^2	XY
111	605	366025	73	5329	44165
112	562	315844	73	5329	41026
113	597	356409	74	5476	44178
114	599	358801	74	5476	44326
115	578	334084	74	5476	42772
116	605	366025	74	5476	44770
117	565	319225	74	5476	41810
118	586	343396	75	5625	43950
119	557	310249	76	5776	42332
120	553	305809	76	5776	42028
121	547	299209	77	5929	42119
122	599	358801	77	5929	46123
123	578	334084	78	6084	45084
124	601	361201	79	6241	47479
125	589	346921	79	6241	46531
126	567	321489	81	6561	45927

附录五（二）

高考总成绩与英语专业四级成绩相关系数分析

n	ΣX	ΣX^2	ΣY	ΣY^2
126	70218.1	39498428.69	7969	511773
$n\Sigma XY$	$\Sigma X \Sigma Y$	$n\Sigma XY - \Sigma X\Sigma Y$	$n\Sigma Y^2$	$(\Sigma Y)^2$
562366980	559568038.9	2798941.1	64483398	63504961
$n\Sigma X^2$	$(\Sigma X)^2$	$n\Sigma X^2 - (\Sigma X)^2$	$n\Sigma Y^2 - (\Sigma Y)^2$	ΣXY
4976802015	4930581568	46220447.33	978437	4463230
$[n\Sigma X^2 - (\Sigma X)^2][n\Sigma Y^2 - (\Sigma Y)^2]$			$r_{126-2} = .42$	
4.52238E+13			$p < .05$	

备注：在.05风险水平下，自由度无穷大（df>100）时双侧临界值为.1946

结论：高考总成绩与英语专业四级英语成绩具有中度相关性

附录六(一)

英语专业四级成绩分组的卡方检验

Category	<60	60-64	65-69	≥70
O	34.00	41.00	21.00	30.00
E	32.25	32.25	32.25	32.25
O-E	1.75	8.75	-11.25	-2.25
$(O-E)^2$	3.06	76.56	126.56	5.06
$(O-E)^2/E$	0.09	2.37	3.92	0.16
X^2	\multicolumn{4}{c}{6.55 (p<.05)}			

备注:在.05水平下,df=3,临界值为7.82
结论:被试按照以上TEM分数划分的组别不具有显著差异

附录六（二）

英语专业四级不同成绩组测试结果的方差分析

分组规模 k = 4（＜60；60—64；65—69；≥70）；组间自由度 k - 1 = 3；样本规模 N = 126；组内自由度 N - k = 122；在 .05 水平下，分子自由度为 3，分母为无穷大（＞100）方差临界值为 2.61。

编号	组间平方和	组间自由度	组间均方	组内平方和	组内自由度	组内均方	F
S1	7.05	3.00	2.35	293.10	122.00	2.40	0.98
S2	3.24	3.00	1.08	103.46	122.00	0.85	1.27
S3	22.17	3.00	7.39	294.54	122.00	2.41	3.06
S4	17.84	3.00	5.95	282.49	122.00	2.32	2.57
S5	9.71	3.00	3.24	381.78	122.00	3.13	1.03
S6	6.93	3.00	2.31	144.5	122.00	1.18	1.95
S7	4.19	3.00	1.40	255.47	122.00	2.09	0.67
S8	8.62	3.00	2.87	239.35	122.00	1.96	1.46
S9	5.28	3.00	1.76	247.58	122.00	2.03	0.87
S10	31.88	3.00	10.63	278.48	122.00	2.28	4.66
S11	0.67	3.00	0.22	228.32	122.00	1.87	0.12
S12	7.62	3.00	2.54	309.59	122.00	2.54	1.00
S13	11.1	3.00	3.70	237.76	122.00	1.95	1.90
S14	7.61	3.00	2.54	217.38	122.00	1.78	1.42
S15	24.31	3.00	8.10	208.91	122.00	1.71	4.73

续表

编号	组间平方和	组间自由度	组间均方	组内平方和	组内自由度	组内均方	F
S16	10.86	3.00	3.62	384.25	122.00	3.15	1.15
S17	6.58	3.00	2.19	301.87	122.00	2.47	0.89
S18	4.94	3.00	1.65	197.91	122.00	1.62	1.02
S19	14.52	3.00	4.84	165.83	122.00	1.36	3.56
S20	7.13	3.00	2.38	172.24	122.00	1.41	1.68
S21	8.05	3.00	2.68	323.26	122.00	2.65	1.01
S22	5.91	3.00	1.97	275.46	122.00	2.26	0.87
S23	7.46	3.00	2.49	380.87	122.00	3.12	0.80
S24	8.47	3.00	2.82	340.35	122.00	2.79	1.01
S25	5.86	3.00	1.95	98.46	122.00	0.81	2.42
S26	9.59	3.00	3.20	331.71	122.00	2.72	1.18
S27	3.7	3.00	1.23	286.84	122.00	2.35	0.52
S28	8.79	3.00	2.93	284.01	122.00	2.33	1.26
S29	1.34	3.00	0.45	242.54	122.00	1.99	0.22
S30	6.99	3.00	2.33	231.65	122.00	1.90	1.23
S31	2.48	3.00	0.83	112.74	122.00	0.92	0.89
S32	10.1	3.00	3.37	274.83	122.00	2.25	1.49
S33	6.11	3.00	2.04	434.04	122.00	3.56	0.57
S34	6.29	3.00	2.10	296.25	122.00	2.43	0.86
S35	0.24	3.00	0.08	101.23	122.00	0.83	0.10
S36	16.03	3.00	5.34	352.1	122.00	2.89	1.85
S37	10.48	3.00	3.49	346.13	122.00	2.84	1.23
S38	8.31	3.00	2.77	363.47	122.00	2.98	0.93
S39	28.92	3.00	9.64	308.54	122.00	2.53	3.81
S40	3.81	3.00	1.27	112.55	122.00	0.92	1.38
S41	7.44	3.00	2.48	71.42	122.00	0.59	4.24
S42	6.15	3.00	2.05	209.56	122.00	1.72	1.19
S43	24.92	3.00	8.31	316.46	122.00	2.59	3.20
S44	21.46	3.00	7.15	315.08	122.00	2.58	2.77

附录六(二) 英语专业四级不同成绩组测试结果的方差分析

续表

编号	组间平方和	组间自由度	组间均方	组内平方和	组内自由度	组内均方	F
S45	19.71	3.00	6.57	335.29	122.00	2.75	2.39
S46	0.08	3.00	0.03	143.03	122.00	1.17	0.02
S47	12.88	3.00	4.29	300.32	122.00	2.46	1.74
S48	1.63	3.00	0.54	135.3	122.00	1.11	0.49
S49	6.04	3.00	2.01	231.83	122.00	1.90	1.06
S50	37.48	3.00	12.49	287.89	122.00	2.36	5.29
S51	8.37	3.00	2.79	191.58	122.00	1.57	1.78
S52	5.05	3.00	1.68	80.42	122.00	0.66	2.55
S53	13.7	3.00	4.57	174.3	122.00	1.43	3.20
S54	12.28	3.00	4.09	327.22	122.00	2.68	1.53
S55	3.18	3.00	1.06	308.79	122.00	2.53	0.42
S56	9.74	3.00	3.25	369.54	122.00	3.03	1.07
S57	3.86	3.00	1.29	366.18	122.00	3.00	0.43
S58	4.64	3.00	1.55	301.24	122.00	2.47	0.63
S59	25.06	3.00	8.35	326.65	122.00	2.68	3.12
S60	1.9	3.00	0.63	166.04	122.00	1.36	0.47
S61	6.96	3.00	2.32	152.7	122.00	1.25	1.85
S62	6.13	3.00	2.04	145.25	122.00	1.19	1.72
S63	3.54	3.00	1.18	153.77	122.00	1.26	0.94
S64	9.75	3.00	3.25	354.6	122.00	2.91	1.12
S65	4.31	3.00	1.44	228.91	122.00	1.88	0.77
S66	3.83	3.00	1.28	323.1	122.00	2.65	0.48
S67	5.56	3.00	1.85	90.44	122.00	0.74	2.50
S68	10.79	3.00	3.60	180.43	122.00	1.48	2.43
S69	4.38	3.00	1.46	194.92	122.00	1.60	0.91
S70	9.4	3.00	3.13	108.26	122.00	0.89	3.53
S71	19.27	3.00	6.42	282.03	122.00	2.31	2.78
S72	7.76	3.00	2.59	339.06	122.00	2.78	0.93
S73	17.75	3.00	5.92	286.58	122.00	2.35	2.52

续表

编号	组间平方和	组间自由度	组间均方	组内平方和	组内自由度	组内均方	F
S74	2.82	3.00	0.94	280.56	122.00	2.30	0.41
S75	0.68	3.00	0.23	108.18	122.00	0.89	0.26
S76	6.86	3.00	2.29	134.42	122.00	1.10	2.08
S77	2.18	3.00	0.73	296.36	122.00	2.43	0.30
S78	24.87	3.00	8.29	220.84	122.00	1.81	4.58
S79	1.34	3.00	0.45	238.7	122.00	1.96	0.23
S80	13.8	3.00	4.60	194.17	122.00	1.59	2.89
S81	19.51	3.00	6.50	295.7	122.00	2.42	2.68
S82	30.32	3.00	10.11	361.62	122.00	2.96	3.41
S83	6.41	3.00	2.14	68.86	122.00	0.56	3.79
S84	16.08	3.00	5.36	309.96	122.00	2.54	2.11
S85	4.92	3.00	1.64	352.36	122.00	2.89	0.57
S86	3.49	3.00	1.16	233.89	122.00	1.92	0.61
S87	1.62	3.00	0.54	212.09	122.00	1.74	0.31
S88	23.91	3.00	7.97	295.59	122.00	2.42	3.29
S89	5.42	3.00	1.81	166.94	122.00	1.37	1.32
S90	7.05	3.00	2.35	293.1	122.00	2.40	0.98
S91	1.74	3.00	0.58	267.92	122.00	2.20	0.26
S92	6.66	3.00	2.22	180.27	122.00	1.48	1.50
S93	5.54	3.00	1.85	284.6	122.00	2.33	0.79
S94	14.84	3.00	4.95	323.49	122.00	2.65	1.87
S95	9.3	3.00	3.10	231.81	122.00	1.90	1.63
S96	7.24	3.00	2.41	179.59	122.00	1.47	1.64
S97	2.93	3.00	0.98	205.11	122.00	1.68	0.58
S98	1.79	3.00	0.60	187.01	122.00	1.53	0.39
S99	1.11	3.00	0.37	234.31	122.00	1.92	0.19
S100	2.88	3.00	0.96	210.78	122.00	1.73	0.56

附录七

The Penn Treebank 词类标记集*

1. CC   Coordinating conjunction 连词
2. CD   Cardinal number 基数词
3. DT   Determiner 限定词
4. EX   Existential there 存在句
5. FW   Foreign word 外来词
6. IN   Preposition/subordinating conjunction 介词或从属连词
7. JJ   Adjective 形容词
8. JJR   Adjective, comparative 形容词比较级
9. JJS   Adjective, superlative 形容词最高级
10. LS   List item marker 列表标识
11. MD   Modal 情态助动词
12. NN   Noun, singular or mass 个体或集体并列名词
13. NNS   Noun, plural 复数名词
14. NNP   Proper noun, singular 单数专有名词
15. NNPS   Proper noun, plural 复数专有名词
16. PDT   Predeterminer 前位限定词
17. POS   Possessive ending 所有格标记
18. PRP   Personal pronoun 人称代词

---

* http://www.ldc.upenn.edu/acl/J/J93/J93-2004.pdf.

19. PP$ Possessive pronoun 所有格代词
20. RB Adverb 副词
21. RBR Adverb, comparative 副词比较级
22. RBS Adverb, superlative 副词最高级
23. RP Particle 小品词
24. SYM Symbol (mathematical or scientific) 数学或科学符号
25. TO to 单词 to
26. UH Interjection 插入语
27. VB Verb, base form 动词基本形式
28. VBD Verb, past tense 动词过去式
29. VBG Verb, gerund/present participle 动词现在分词
30. VBN Verb, past participle 动词过去分词
31. VBP Verb, non-3rd ps. sing. present 动词非三单现在时
32. VBZ Verb, 3rd ps. sing. Present 动词三单现在时
33. WD Twh-determiner wh 限定词
34. WP wh-pronoun wh 代词
35. WP$ Possessive wh-pronoun wh 所有格代词
36. WRB wh-adverb wh 副词
37. # Pound sign
38. $ Dollar sign
39. . Sentence-final punctuation
40. , Comma
41. : Colon, semi-colon
42. (Left bracket character
43.) Right bracket character
44. " Straight double quote
45. ' Left open single quote
46. " Left open double quote
47. ' Right close single quote

48. "   Right close double quote

（Marcus et al.，1993）

部分补充更新代码：

Marcus et al.，1994，The Penn Treebank：Annotating Predicate Argument Structure［J］from http：//www.ldc.upenn.edu/Catalog/desc/addenda/LDC1999T42/

1.	*	"Understood" subject of infinitive or imperative
2.	*EXP*	expletive
3.	*ICH*	interpret constituent here
4.	*PPA*	permanent predictable ambiguity
5.	*RNR*	right node raising
6.	0	Zero variant of that in subordinate clauses
7.	ADJP	Adjective phrase
8.	ADV	clausal and NP adverbials
9.	ADVP	Adverb phrase
10.	CLF	true clefts
11.	CLR	closely related
12.	DIR	direction & trajectory
13.	ETC	the second conjunct after UCP
14.	FRAG	pieces of text
15.	HLN	headlines and datelines
16.	IMP	clauses with empty subjects
17.	INTJ	interjection
18.	LGS	logical subjects in passives
19.	LOC	location
20.	LST	list markers
21.	MNR	manner
22.	NBAR	phrasal nodes
23.	NIL	Marks position where preposition is interpreted in pied-

		piping contexts
24.	NOM	non NPs that function as NPs
25.	NP	Noun phrase
26.	PP	Prepositional phrase
27.	PRD	non VP predicates
28.	PRP	purpose and reason
29.	S	Simple declarative clause
30.	SBAR	Clause introduced by subordinating conjunction or 0, top level labelling apart from S, usually for complete structure
31.	SBARQ	Direct question introduced by wh-word or wh-phrase, WH-questions, top level labelling apart from S, usually for complete structure
32.	SBJ	surface subject
33.	SINV	Declarative sentence with subject-aux inversion, top level labelling apart from S, usually for complete structure
34.	SQ	Subconstituent of SBARQ excluding wh-word or wh-phrase, auxiliary inverted structures, top level labelling apart from S, usually for complete structure
35.	T	Trace-marks position where moved wh-constituent is interpreted
36.	TMP	temporal phrases
37.	TRC	topicalized and fronted constituents
38.	TTL	titles
39.	UCP	unlike conjoined phrase
40.	UNF	unfinished constituents
41.	VOC	vocatives
42.	VP	Verb phrase
43.	WHADVP	wh-adverb phrase

44. WHNP   wh-noun phrase
45. WHPP   wh-prepositional phrase
46. X   Constituent of unknown or uncertain category

附录八

Stanford parser 的依存关系代码与解析[*]

Stanford parser 依存关系指统领成分（governor, regent or head）和依附成分（dependent）两者间关系。下面的代码按照字母顺序排列。定义采用 Penn Treebank 词类和短语标签。

关系代码：

abbrev -	abbreviation modifier
acomp -	adjectival complement
advcl -	adverbial clause modifier
advmod -	adverbial modifier
agent -	agent
amod -	adjectival modifier
appos -	appositional modifier
arg -	argument
attr -	attributive
aux -	auxiliary
auxpass -	passive auxiliary
cc -	coordination

---

[*] 英文部分源自 Marie-Catherine de Marneffe and Christopher D. Manning 2008 年编写的 *Stanford typed dependencies manual*，http://nlp.stanford.edu/downloads/dependencies_manual.pdf。中文翻译参考了 http://dict.cnki.net/和http://translate.google.com.hk 的术语翻译。

ccomp -	clausal complement with internal subject
comp -	complement
complm -	complementizer
conj -	conjunct
cop -	copula
csubj -	clausal subject
csubjpass -	passive clausal subject
dep -	dependent
det -	determiner
dobj -	direct object
expl -	expletive (expletive "there")
infmod -	infinitival modifier
iobj -	indirect object
mark -	marker (word introducing an advcl)
mod -	modifier
mwe -	multi-word expression modifier
neg -	negation modifier
nn -	noun compound modifier
npadvmod-	noun phrase adverbial modifier
nsubj -	nominal subject
nsubjpass -	passive nominal subject
num -	numeric modifier
number -	element of compound number
obj -	object
parataxis -	parataxis
partmod -	participial modifier
pcomp	prepositional complement
pobj -	object of preposition
poss -	possession modifier

possessive-	possessive modifier ('s)
preconj -	preconjunct
predet -	predeterminer
prep -	prepositional modifier
prepc	prepositional clausal modifier
prt -	phrasal verb particle
punct -	punctuation
purpcl -	purpose clause modifier
quantmod-	quantifier modifier
rcmod -	relative clause modifier
ref -	referent
rel -	relative (word introducing a rcmod)
root -	root
subj -	subject
tmod -	temporal modifier
xcomp -	clausal complement with external subject
xsubj -	controlling subject

关系代码解析：

abbrev：abbreviation modifier 缩略语修饰关系。名词短语的缩略形式通过将名词添加圆括号的方式来表示，如"The Australian Broadcasting Corporation（ABC）"表示为 abbrev（Corporation，ABC）。

acomp：adjectival complement 动词的形容化补语关系。动词的形容化补语形式是指具有补语功能的形容性动词。如"She looks very beautiful"表示为 acomp（looks，beautiful）。

advcl：adverbial clause modifier 副词性从句修饰关系。动词短语或句子的副词性修饰成分是指用来修饰动词的附属成分，包括条件从句、时间从句等。如"The accident happened as the night was falling"可表示为 advcl（happened，falling），"If you know who did it, you should tell the teacher"可表示为 advcl（tell, know）。

advmod：adverbial modifier 副词性修饰关系。词的副词性修饰成分是指用来修饰单个词的副词或副词词组。如"Genetically modified food"可表示为 advmod（modified, genetically），"less often"可表示为 advmod（often, less）。

agent：施事关系。动作的发出者，常出现在表被动的介词 by 的后面。如"The man has been killed by the police"可表示为 agent（killed, police），"Effects caused by the protein are important"可表示为 agent（caused, protein）。

amod：adjectival modifier 形容词性修饰关系。词的形容词性修饰成分是指用来修饰名词及短语的形容词。如"Sam eats red meat"可表示为 amod（meat, red）。

appos：appositional modifier 同位语修饰关系。具有相同指称的同位语成分，如"Sam, my brother"可表示为 appos（Sam, brother），"Bill（John's cousin）"可表示为 appos（Bill, cousin）。

attr：attributive 系动词补语关系。常出现在"to be""to seem""to appear"等句式中作为补语出现，如"What is that?"可表示为 attr（is, What）。

aux：auxiliary 助动关系。在句中起到助动词作用，如"Reagan has died"可表示为 aux（died, has），"He should leave"可表示为 aux（leave, should）。

auxpass：passive auxiliary 被动性助动关系。在句中包含了助动词的被动信息，如"Kennedy has been killed"可表示为 auxpass（killed, been）和 aux（killed, has），"Kennedy was/got killed"可表示为 auxpass（killed, was/got）。

cc：coordination 并列关系。具有并列功能，通常把连词前第一个成分作为统领成分，如"Bill is big and honest"可表示为 cc（big, and），"They either ski or snowboard"可表示为 cc（ski, or）。

ccomp：clausal complement 从句性补语关系。动词、形容词等的从句性补语成分是指从句中具有内在主谓关系，整个从句充当补语，通常被修饰的词是"fact""report"等，如"He says that you like to swim"可表示为ccomp（says，like），"I am certain that he did it"可表示为ccomp（certain，did），"I admire the fact that you are honest"可表示为ccomp（fact，honest）。

complm：complementizer 标句关系。其在从句性补语关系（ccomp）中存在，通常包括从属连词"that""whether"，如"He says that you like to swim"可表示为complm（like，that）。

conj：conjunct 合取式关系。通过并列连词"and""or"等连接的关系，通常把连词前第一个成分作为统领成分，其他部分为附属，如"Bill is big and honest"可表示为conj（big，honest），"They either ski or snowboard"可表示为conj（ski，snowboard）。

cop：copula 系词关系。系词关系是指系动词与表语成分之间的关系，通常把表语成分作为统领，如"Bill is big"可表示为cop（big，is），"Bill is an honest man"可表示为cop（man，is）。

csubj：clausal subject 从句性主语关系。主语由从句充当，当主句动词是实意动词时，实意动词为统领成分。当主句动词是系动词时，后面的表语成分作为统领。如"What she said makes sense"可表示为csubj（makes，said），"What she said is not true"可表示为csubj（true，said）。

csubjpass：passive clausal subject 从句式被动主语关系。从句在被动主句中充当主语，如"That she lied was suspected by everyone"可表示为csubjpass（suspected，lied）。

dep：dependent 依附关系。依附关系是指当系统由于各种原因无法在两词间判定它们清晰的依存关系时采用的标注关系。如"Then, as if to show that he could, …"可表示为dep（show，if）。

det：determiner 限定词关系。通常出现在名词前，如"The man is here"可表示为det（man，the），"Which book do you prefer?"可表示为det（book，which）。

dobj：direct object 直接宾语关系。如"She gave me a raise"可表

示为 dobj（gave，raise），"They win the lottery"可表示为 dobj（win，lottery）。

expl：expletive 存在补足关系。通常出现在表存在的"there be"句式中，动词作为统领成分，如"There is a ghost in the room"可表示为 expl（is，There）。

infmod：infinitival modifier 名词性不定式关系。用来修饰名词的不定式关系，如"Points to establish are…"可表示为 infmod（points，establish），"I don't have anything to say"可表示为 infmod（anything，say）。

iobj：indirect object 间接宾语关系。如"She gave me a raise"可表示为 iobj（gave，me）。

mark：marker 标记关系。存在于副词性从句修饰关系（advcl）中，通常指"because""when""although"等具有引领功能的从属连词，但不包括"that""whether"等，如"Forces engaged in fighting after insurgents attacked"可表示为 mark（attacked，after）。

mwe：multi-word expression 多词表达关系。多个词构成独立整体统一使用时出现的关系，包括 rather than, as well as, instead of, such as, because of, instead of, in addition to, all but, such as, because of, instead of, due to 等。如"I like dogs as well as cats"mwe（well，as）可表示为 mwe（well，as），"He cried because of you"可表示为 mwe（of，because）。

neg：negation modifier 否定性关系。否定词和被否定成分间的关系，如"Bill is not a scientist"可表示为 neg（scientist，not），"Bill doesn't drive"可表示为 neg（drive，n't）。

nn：noun compound modifier 复合名词关系。多名词组合后共同修饰某一名词时形成的关系，通常最右侧名词作为统领成分，如"Oil price futures"可表示为 nn（futures，oil），nn（futures，price）。

npadvmod：noun phrase as adverbial modifier 名词词组作为副词修饰关系。当名词词组在句中具有副词功用时形成的关系，包括：（i）测量类词组，用来表示形容词词组（ADJP）/副词词组（ADVP）/介词词组（PP）中心词与测量词之间的关系；（ii）当名词词组出现在动

· 295 ·

词词组中却又不充当宾语时；(iii) 经济类建构词，通常出现在副词或类似介词的名词词组中，如 "＄5 a share"，"per share"；(iv) 浮动性反身代词；(v) 其他固有名词表达方式。如 "The director is 65 years old" 可表示为 npadvmod (old, years)，"6 feet long" 可表示为 npadvmod (long, feet)，"Shares eased a fraction" 可表示为 npadvmod (eased, fraction)，"IBM earned ＄5 a share" 可表示为 npadvmod (＄, share)，"The silence is itself significant" 可表示为 npadvmod (significant, itself)，"90% of Australians like him, the most of any country" 可表示为 npadvmod (like, most)。

　　nsubj：nominal subject 名词主语关系。如 "Clinton defeated Dole" 可表示为 nsubj (defeated, Clinton)，"The baby is cute" 可表示为 nsubj (cute, baby)。

　　nsubjpass：passive nominal subject 被动性名词主语关系，如 "Dole was defeated by Clinton" 可表示为 nsubjpass (defeated, Dole)。

　　num：numeric modifier 数词关系。数词关系是用来指数词与其修饰名词间所形成的关系。如 "Sam eats 3 sheep" 可表示为 num (sheep, 3)。

　　number：element of compound number 复合数词成分关系。在构成复合数词时形成的部分与整体的关系。如 "I lost ＄3.2 billion" 可表示为 number (＄, billion)。

　　parataxis：parataxis 意合关系。源自希腊文中 "place side by side"，意指两个成分关系非常亲密，一般同时出现，包括括号关系，句子成分与分号或冒号间形成的关系等。如 "The guy, John said, left early in the morning" 可表示为 parataxis (left, said)。

　　partmod：participial modifier 分词关系。用来修饰名词或句子时所形成的分词关系，如 "Truffles picked during the spring are tasty" 可表示为 partmod (truffles, picked)，"Bill tried to shoot demonstrating his incompetence" 可表示为 partmod (shoot, demonstrating)。

　　pcomp：prepositional complement 介词补语关系。介词补语关系是

附录八　Stanford parser 的依存关系代码与解析

指当介词的补语成分是从句或是介词词组（偶尔也会是副词词组）时形成的关系，如"We have no information on whether users are at risk"可表示为 pcomp（on，are），"They heard about you missing classes"可表示为 pcomp（about，missing）。

pobj：object of a preposition 介词宾语成分。如"I sat on the chair"可表示为 pobj（on，chair）。

poss：possession modifier 所有权关系。如"their offices"可表示为 poss（offices，their），"Bill's clothes"可表示为 poss（clothes，Bill）。

possessive：possessive modifier 所有格关系。如"Bill's clothes"可表示为 possessive（Bill，'s）。

preconj：preconjunct 前合关系。通常出现在名词前，作为连词组合体的一个前奏成分出现，具有强调功能，包括"either""both""neither"等。如"Both the boys and the girls are here"可表示为 preconj（boys，both）。

predet：predeterminer 前限定关系。在对限定词修饰时形成的关系，如"All the boys are here"可表示为 predet（boys，all）。

prep：prepositional modifier 介词性修饰关系。动词、形容词或名词的介词性修饰关系是指它们与修饰它们的介词词组间形成的关系，如"I saw a cat in a hat"可表示为 prep（cat，in），"I saw a cat with a telescope"可表示为 prep（saw，with），"He is responsible for meals"可表示为 prep（responsible，for）。

prepc：prepositional clausal modifier 介词从句性修饰关系。动词、形容词或名词的介词从句性修饰关系是指它们与修饰它们的介词从句间形成的关系，如"He purchased it without paying a premium"可表示为 prepc without（purchased，paying）。

prt：phrasal verb particle 词组性动助词关系。动词词组中动词与它的附属成分间形成的关系，如"They shut down the station"可表示为 prt（shut，down）。

punct：punctuation 标点关系。如"Go home!"可表示为 punct

· 297 ·

(Go, !)。

purpcl: purpose clause modifier 目的性从句修饰关系。动词的目的性从句修饰关系是指动词与表示目的的带有"in order to"或"to"的词之间形成的关系。如"He talked to him in order to secure the account"可表示为 purpcl (talked, secure)。

quantmod: quantifier phrase modifier 量词组修饰关系。通常修饰数词时形成的关系,如"About 200 people came to the party"可表示为 quantmod (200, About)。

rcmod: relative clause modifier 相关从句修饰关系。名词的相关从句修饰关系是修饰性从句与被修饰的名词组之间的关系,"I saw the man you love"可表示为 rcmod (man, love),"I saw the book which you bought"可表示为 rcmod (book, bought)。

ref: referent 所指关系。指示词与被指词间形成的关系,如"I saw the book which you bought"可表示为 ref (book, which)。

rel: relative 相关性关系。关系从句中的相关性关系通常由 WH-phrase 引领,而且关系词不充当从句主语,如"I saw the man whose wife you love"可表示为 rel (love, wife)。

root: root 根源关系。根源关系是指句子的主根关系,通常用"ROOT"来做统领成分。如"I love French fries."可表示为 root (ROOT, love),"Bill is an honest man"可表示为 root (ROOT, man)。

tmod: temporal modifier 时间修饰关系。如"Last night, I swam in the pool"可表示为 tmod (swam, night)。

xcomp: open clausal complement 开放性从句补充关系。动词或者形容词的开放性从句补充关系是附属句自身没有主语但却被外在主语所限制的一种关系。如"He says that you like to swim"可表示为 xcomp (like, swim),"I am ready to leave"可表示为 xcomp (ready, leave)。

xsubj: controlling subject 控制性主语关系。控制性主语关系是指出现在开放性从句补充关系(xcomp)中统领成分与外在主语间的关系。如"Tom likes to eat fish"可表示为 xsubj (eat, Tom)。

附录九

中英文姓名对照表

A

Allen K 艾伦
Altmann G 奥尔特曼
Andreu L 安德鲁
Arai M 阿拉里

B

Baddeley A D 巴德利
Bader M 巴德
Bailey K G D 贝利
Ball T 鲍尔
Barss A 巴斯
Bever T G 贝弗
Blozis S A 布洛兹斯
Bock J K 博克
Boland J E 博兰
Bornkessel I 博恩克思尔
Bornkessel-Schlesewsky I 博恩克思尔－施莱苏斯基

Bos L S 博斯
Boston M F 博斯顿
Botvinick M 博特威尼克
Branigan H P 布兰尼根
Breen M 布林
Brennan J 布伦南
Bresnan J W 布鲁斯南
Brouwer H 布劳威尔
Brown C 布朗
Burgess C 伯吉斯

C

Cantor J 坎托
Caplan D 卡普兰
Carlson G 卡尔森
Carlson M 卡尔森
Carpenter P A 卡彭特
Carullo J J 卡鲁罗
Chang F R 钱格
Christensen K R 克里斯滕森

Christiansen M H 克里斯蒂安森
Christianson K 克里斯琴森
Clifton C 克利夫顿
Clifton Jr C 克利夫顿
Connine C 康尼恩
Crain S 克雷恩
Crocker M W 克罗克
Cupples L 卡皮尔斯

D

Daneman M 达内门
Darowski E S 达罗斯基
Daugherty K G 多尔蒂
Davis M H 戴维斯
Dean Fodor J 迪安福多尔
DeDe G 戴德
Dennis Y 丹尼斯
Desmet T 德斯米特
Dragoy O 德拉戈尔
Druey M D 德鲁伊
Duffy J H 达菲

E

Eastwick E C 伊斯特威克
Elman J L 埃尔曼
Engle R W 恩格尔
Ericsson K A 埃里克森

F

Farmer T A 法默
Federmeier K D 费德米尔
Ferraro V 费拉罗
Ferreira F 费雷拉
Fine A B 法恩
Fitz H 菲茨
Fitzroy A B 菲茨罗伊
Florian Jaeger T 弗洛里安·耶格
Fodor J A 福多尔
Fodor J D 福多尔
Ford M 福特
Forster K I 福斯特
Frazier L 弗雷泽
Friederici A D 弗里德里西
Frisson S 弗里森

G

Garnham A 加纳姆
Garnsey S M 加恩西
Garrett M 加勒特
George M S 乔治
Gibson E 吉布森
Gibson E A F 吉布森
Gilliom L A 吉利奥姆
Gompel R P G 冯冈普尔

Gordon P C 戈登
Gorrell 戈雷尔
Grain S 格兰
Griffith T 格里菲思
Grodner D 格罗德内尔
Groothusen J 格鲁苏珊
Grosz B J 格罗斯

H

Hagoort P 哈古尔特
Hale J T 黑尔
Halliwell J F 哈利韦尔
Hambrick D Z 汉布里克
Hare M 黑尔
Hartsuiker R J 哈特苏克尔
Hayes D P 海斯
Henderson J M 亨德森
Hendrick R 亨德里克
Herschensohn J 赫申松
Hickok G 希科克
Hillyard S A 希利亚德
Hinton G E 欣顿
Hitch G 希契
Hoeks J 霍克斯
Hoeksema J 霍克斯玛
Hoffinan J E 霍夫南
Holcomb P J 霍尔库姆
Hollbach S C 霍尔拜

Hollingworth A 霍林沃思
Holmes V M 霍尔摩斯
Hopf J M 霍普夫
Husband E M 赫斯本德
Hussey E 赫西

I

Inoue A 英尔
Intelligence A 英特里真斯

J

Jaeger T F 耶格
Jansma B M 詹斯玛
Jasper H H 贾斯珀
Jesse S 杰西
Johnson M 约翰逊
Jung H 荣格
Just M A 贾斯特

K

Kaan E 卡恩
Kaplan R M 卡普兰
Keller F 凯勒
Keller T A 凯勒
Kello C 凯罗
Kelly L A 凯利

Kempen G 肯彭
Kemper S 肯珀
Kemtes K A 凯姆特斯
Kennedy A 肯尼迪
Kidd E 基德
Kielar A 基拉
Kim A 金
Kim G 金
Kimball J 金博尔
King J 金
Kintsch W 金特斯
Kizach J 凯泽斯
Knoeferle P 诺夫勒
Koelsch S 凯尔奇
Kondo H 康德
Kotz S A 科茨
Kurtzman H 库兹曼
Kutas M 库塔斯

L

Luke S G 卢克

M

MacDonald M C 麦克唐纳
Mak W M 马克
Malsburg T 马尔斯伯格
Mannes S 曼内斯

Marcinkiewicz M A 马尔钦凯维奇
Marcus M P 马库斯
Mazuka R 马佐卡
McClelland J 麦克莱兰
McClelland J L 麦克莱兰
McConnell K 麦康奈尔
McElree B 麦克尔里
Mclaughlin J 麦克劳克林
McLean J F 麦克莱恩
McRae K 麦克雷
Mecklinger A 梅克林格
Meltzer-Asscher A 梅尔策阿斯切
Meng M 孟
Milne R W 米尔恩
Mitchell D C 米切尔
Miyake A 米亚科
Molfese D L 莫尔费斯
Molfese V J 莫尔费斯
Moon N 穆恩
Morgan-Short K 摩根肖特
Morris R K 莫里斯
Mulac A 穆拉克
Murray W S 默里
Myers E 迈尔斯

N

Neville H 内维尔
Ni W 倪

Nicol J L 尼科尔
Nitschke S 聂赤克
Novick J M 诺维克
Nyvad A M 尼瓦德

O

Oberauer K 奥伯罗尔
Olmos J G 奥尔莫斯
Opitz B 奥皮茨
O'Regan J K 奥里根
Osaka M 奥萨卡
Osaka N 奥萨卡
Osterhout L 奥斯特豪特
Ouden den D B 乌登

P

Patson N D 帕特森
Pearlmutter N J 帕尔玛特
Pearson J 皮尔逊
Peelle J E 皮尔
Pereira F 佩雷拉
Phillips C 菲利普斯
Pickering M J 皮克林
Pollatsek A 波拉德思克
Pritchett B L 普里切特
Pylkkänen L 派尔凯内

R

Race D S 雷斯
Rayner K 雷纳
Roehm D 勒默
Rumelhart D E 拉梅尔哈特

S

Salamoura A 萨勒穆拉
Sammler D 萨蒙拉
Sanders L D 桑德斯
Santorini B 桑托里尼
Sanz C 桑斯
Sanz-Torrent M 桑斯托伦特
Schlesewsky M 施莱修斯基
Schriefers H 施里弗斯
Sedivy J C 塞迪维
Seely R E 西利
Seidenberg M S 塞登伯格
Serratrice L 塞拉瑞斯
Severens E 塞弗恩斯
Simon H A 西蒙
Snedeker J 斯内德克
Snider N E 斯奈德
Souza A S 苏泽
Spivey M J 斯皮维
Spivey-Knowlton M 斯皮维－诺尔顿

Staub A 斯托布
Steedman M 斯蒂德曼
Steedman N 斯蒂德曼
Steinhauer K 斯坦豪尔
Stowe K 斯托
Stowe L A 斯托
Sturt P 斯特尔特
Susan M 苏珊
Swaab T Y 斯瓦柏
Swets B 斯威茨

T

Tanenhaus M 塔嫩豪斯
Tanenhaus M K 塔嫩豪斯
Tanner D 坦纳
Taraban R 塔拉班
Teubner-Rhodes S 托伊布纳-罗兹
Thompson C 汤普森
Thompson S A 汤普森
Thothathiri M 索萨瑞里
Tooley K M 图利
Traxler M J 特拉克斯勒
Trueswell J C 特鲁斯威尔
Tunstall S 滕斯托尔

V

Vasishth S 瓦什斯特
Von Cramon D Y 冯克拉蒙
Vonk W 冯科
Vos S H 沃斯
Vuong L C 武昂

W

Warren T 沃伦
Waters G S 沃特斯
Weber A 韦伯
Wells J B 韦尔斯
Williams J N 威廉斯
Williams R S 威廉斯
Witzel J 威策尔

Y

Yurchenko A 尤尔琴科

Z

Zechner K 泽克内尔
Zervakis J 泽瓦克斯

后 记

  明天，我即将登上 388 客机离开雅典，离开这座留下我一年美好记忆的雅典娜之都。作为国家留学基金委公派雅典大学的访问学者，我有幸在雅典大学从事了一年的科学研究。虽然这段美好的经历即将成为难忘的往事，但人生驿站中的甘美仍值得慢慢啜饮、细细品味。

  希腊是我国"一带一路"经济倡议南线的欧洲桥头堡。2016 年 4 月，中国政府与希腊政府就希腊最大的比雷埃夫斯港（Piraeus port）的私有化达成了正式协议。中国远洋集团首先以 2.805 亿欧元购得比雷埃夫斯港 51% 股权，然后五年内投资该港 3.5 亿欧元，投资完成后可以 8800 万欧元再收购 16% 股权，实现对比雷埃夫斯港 67% 的控股。

  站在比雷埃夫斯港码头，看着地中海蓝蓝的天空，感受着爱琴海徐徐的海风，领略着大型渡轮进出海港的繁忙景象，心中无比自豪。国家强盛，旅居国外的游子才有可能挺直腰杆，对此深有感触。

  港口码头对岸是希腊内政部的签证中心，负责对在希腊长居的外国人发放居留证。比雷埃夫斯港协议签署时间不久，我到内政部办理个人的居留证。当我把国家留基委政府担保的英文函和雅典大学的希腊文邀请函等材料递交给签证官时，受到了热情的接待。在一一检查过我的材料后，签证官员遗憾地说我的保险单没有提供希腊文译件，恐怕不能通过审查。得到这个遗憾的答复时我有几分落寞：一则，异国他乡要找到能将保险单翻译成希腊文的合法译员实属不易，而且即使找得到人翻译文件也需时日，短期无法完成，那也就意味着居留证近期无望；再则，从我的住所 Zografou 到 Piraeus，需要横穿整个雅典，往返也需要不少时间，我甚至不知道需要跑几趟才能把居留证办下来。看来只能下次再来了。

　　拿了材料，谢过签证官，我从签证室出来。屋外候着的申请人各行各业，五花八门，各色人等。临别时，签证官并没有常规性地招下一个申请人入内，而是在用希腊文打电话汇报的样子，并在即时贴上飞快地写着什么。当我刚走出大厅，签证官在后面叫我，微笑着递给我一张即时贴说，上面有外交部翻译中心的详细地址和电话，为便于我打车和问路，她已经把希腊文地址翻译成了英语，我可以到该中心进行预约和翻译；另外，如果我能够保证将翻译后的保险单及时送回内政部签证中心的话，她获准可以为我先行办理居留证。

　　太好了！我忙不迭地点头称谢作保证。等我再次从内政部出来时，手里多了一张方方正正的希腊文居留证和一张委托外交部翻译中心为我翻译保险单的函。我庆幸自己享受了一次超国民待遇。签证官正是通过这种方式表达了对中希两国深入合作的美好祝愿。

　　希腊的居留证类似于其他国家的"绿卡"，具有长居和工作许可的功能。从获准居留的时刻开始，我便成了美丽雅典的长居客。

　　初到雅典，蓝白相间的色调让人难忘。雅典位于欧洲南部，自然环境优越，是欧洲的文明发源地。这里阳光充沛，海水湛蓝，遍地都是白色的大理石。有人称希腊是"3S"国度，分别代表阳光（sun）、大海（sea）和砂石（sand）。希腊的国旗也是蓝白相间的。这种蓝与白的和谐让人震撼。

　　雅典人的自律让人敬佩。我到雅典时恰逢圣诞前夕。街道两旁，结满了金色的橘子。绿色的橘子树，挂满了累累硕果，一派祥和喜庆。有的临街店铺就把圣诞彩灯挂在门口的橘子树上，一闪一闪，非常漂亮。虽然受到经济危机影响，希腊生活水准降低了很多，但欧洲人骨子里的自尊让他们细心呵护着自己的城市。无论是老叟还是顽童，没有一个人伸手去摘路边的金橘，任由这些金色果实点缀着城

后　记

市。如有零星点点的金橘掉落下来，也很快被临街店铺或居民清理干净。如果说雅典市容市貌的整洁优美是雅典人自律所形成的静态亮丽风景的话，那么整座城市繁忙交通系统的井然有序则是雅典人自律所形成的动态唯美画面。

雅典视时间为金钱，交通工具的付费采用限时方式。在中国，我们采用的是路线制，即坐什么车付什么费。公交车、地铁、城轨各自计算各自的票价，各交通工具间一般不联通，通常以乘坐的距离作为付费的标准。雅典的计费方式是时间，票价随乘车时间不同而不同。最普通的90分钟交通工具的通票是1.4欧元。在这个时间段内，任何城市交通工具都是联通的，可以任意上下转换。雅典几乎没有人查票（一年中我只遇到过一回），大家都很自觉地在机器上打卡缴费。所有的交通工具都采用无障碍模式，没有闸门和门禁，已经缴费的乘客可以快速通过，没有缴费的乘客则在通过缴费器时打卡，车票遂启动90分钟有效模式。由于雅典的缴费系统是建立在相互信任的基础之上的，所以，很少有查票的工作人员出现，每个人都恪守着自己的道德底线。这种自律让整个雅典即使在高峰时间也能快速分流人群，很少出现人流汹涌等待缴费过闸口的拥堵局面。

一座城市，给人震撼之感的不是大而是有内涵。雅典则是这样一座历史悠久但生机盎然的城市。

雅典的名胜古迹众多。走在街上，不时会看到一个个立着的古迹标识，通常是希腊文和英文的双语对照。这种把古迹保护和城市建设巧妙组合在一起的模式让人耳目一新，穿梭其间，颇有画中行的意味。在所有的古迹中，最著名的当属卫城和新古典主义建筑三部曲了。

卫城是希腊古典建筑的代表作，风格优雅和谐。建于卫城之上的山门雄伟壮观，雅典娜胜利女神庙（Temple of Athena Nike）独具风格，帕特农（Parthenon）神庙庄严肃穆，依瑞克提翁神殿（Erechtheion）少女石柱悠闲自得。古今中外文人墨士对卫城古迹群迤逦风光描写得汁味醇厚，对其千姿百态的大理石人物浮雕描写得惟妙惟肖。其代表性的建筑多立克柱式和爱奥尼亚柱式成为古希腊建筑之美的源泉。

除了卫城，新古典主义三部曲的建筑也值得一看。在雅典市中心宪法广场（Syntagma）西北，有一条大学街，即 Panepistimiou 大街，这里就是雅典大学古色古香的老校门。分列校门两边的是国家图书馆和柏拉图的雅典学院遗址。这三个古建筑被称为希腊著名的新古典主义建筑三部曲。刚到雅典时，我就住在大学街南面的 Arethusa 酒店。

非常感谢 Booking 和 Arethusa 酒店的服务人员。我在预定 12 月 10 日到 12 月 12 日的酒店住宿时，算错了时差（雅典比广州晚 6 个小时），忘记了 10 日我还在飞往雅典的航班上。等我坦诚地承认是自己的错误导致出现了预定问题并请求顺延时，网站和酒店客服人员提供了很好的服务，同意免费让我顺延一天。这个小小的意外，让我感受到了雅典的友好。

雅典的旅游业已经很成熟，客服人员的整体素质超乎我们的想象。当我们在克里特岛 Chania 的 Kalamaki 进行调研时，入住了 Corinna Mare 酒店。酒店经理 Costa 曾随父母在广州和北京旅居过，所以，对来自中国的我们相当友好。不仅非常热心地提示我们怎样从 Souda 港抵达酒店，而且为我们的入住提供了相当好的服务。临别时，Costa 竟驱车从 Kalamaki 赶到 Souda 港，给前期到达港口候船准备返回雅典的我们送来了克里特岛山上采酿的农家蜂蜜，让我们一行很感动。希望有机会再回到雅典，回到克里特，再次有机会见到 Costa。

希腊是欧洲文明的起源，雅典是希腊文明的明珠，而雅典大学则是这颗明珠上最璀璨的部分。

雅典大学是希腊最古老和最著名的大学。这里最崇尚的是民主。就像希腊的国旗所表达的那样："不自由毋宁死。"学生们上课通常采用讨论式，气氛比较热烈。在我给大学生们做有关中国语言和文化的讲座时，学生们积极发言，甚至有两个同学站起来用汉语向我提问题。随着中国远洋集团开始控股比雷埃夫斯港，我相信越来越多的普通雅典居民会更多地了解并亲近中国。除了思想上的自由，大学校园

后　记

建设也处处可见自由的影子。走在大学校园里，看不到摄像头，就像在雅典街头看不到摄像头一样。雅典人不允许窥视别人，即使是摄像头也被认为是对他们自由的侵犯。

与个人的民主自由相对，希腊的官方文件对申请人的出身却有着强烈的探究性。在申请税号和居留证时，工作人员除了确认我的名和姓（欧洲习惯是名在前，姓在后；中国人的习惯则相反）之外，还需要我提供父母亲的姓名。在国内，除了出生证上需要了解父母信息外，一般情况只需要提供个人的信息就可以了。这个习惯或许是为了凸显家族继承性，亦或许是为了方便官方借助父母的姓名区分申请人，减少由于姓名相同带来的纳税困扰。

自由之下更需要慎独。在国外，没有人告诉你该干什么、该怎么做。社会是完全开放的，网络是完全开放的，甚至，性，也是完全开放的。每个人必须为自己的行为负责，负完全的责任。在这里，连父母也对成年孩子完全放开。有种大浪淘沙的感觉。如果你是杂质，慢慢就在这种完全的自由中被淘汰了。买东西自己付费、坐地铁自己刷卡、乘公交车自己缴费、迷路时希腊美女也会毫无顾忌地领你走好远为你指路。整个社会对你都是开放的、包容的。它默认你会恪守社会道德。希腊保留了古欧罗巴人的优良传统。宽松的社会环境所形成的这种相互信任的传统需要每个个体的呵护，以使其延续下去。对个体而言，也只有慎独才会真正融入这个社会中，享受人与人之间的彼此尊重并消除不同肤色人种之间的隔阂。

人生是分阶段的：读万卷书、行万里路，最后才是人生感悟。如果只读书不行路，很容易陷入死读书的阶段。不登高山，不知天之高也；不临深溪，不知地之厚也。这也是为什么很多文人志士都需要云游四方，大概就是进入行万里路的阶段了吧。操千曲而后晓声，观千剑而后识器。深刻的人生感悟想必是万卷书与万里路的终极感悟吧。蜂采百花酿甜蜜，多有经历的人生通常也更有芬芳。留学一年，无法忘怀的是国内外师长和专家曾给予的热情而真挚的帮助。

感谢原希腊驻加拿大大使 Alexandris 先生及夫人。他们除了盛情邀请我在其府上欢度圣诞外，还亲自带我登上雅典之巅的 Lycabettus 山欣赏整个雅典的美景。让我们全家难以忘怀的是：大使亲自开着奔驰车载我们全家到马拉松湖游览，并在马拉松大坝风景地邀请我们与其共进烛光晚餐。临回国前，大使及夫人又邀请我参观雅典大学古建筑并设宴为我饯行。大使及夫人的谈话风趣幽默，让人印象深刻。其府上悬挂的巨幅中国凤凰图和摆放的中国太师椅让人感受到大使一家与中国文化源远流长的渊源。

感谢希腊驻广州总领事馆的副领事 Anna Aslanidou 女士。据说我是广州地区第一个到希腊进行访学的学者，由于希腊政府没有单独针对访问学者的签证，而旅游签或工作签又与访学目的有出入，所以，在签证发放过程中 Anna 女士尽其所能为我提供了签证建议，使我能顺利完成在雅典大学的访学。

感谢雅典大学 Christina 副教授。在雅典生活学习的一年时间，Christina 为我提供了良好的访学环境。此外，她还与先生 Evan 一起领我考察了雅典的多处古迹，包括马拉松小镇古迹、波塞冬神庙，希腊的第二大岛埃维亚岛（Evia）西部的哈尔基斯（Chalcis）旋桥，以及多个古东正教堂遗址。在科研合作方面，Christina 为我在雅典大学进行语言实验提供了条件，让我能够按期保质完成科学实验。

感谢中国驻希腊大使馆的邹肖力大使及夫人。2016 年春节前夜，邹大使及夫人安排文化处老师通知我到使馆参加联欢并聚餐，让我们这些留学人员感受到了祖国的温暖。而且，大使馆还让我在 2016 年国庆期间，以留学生代表的身份接受了到访国家领导人的接见，并非常有幸地与国家领导人和同行的众部长们合影留念，这个经历让我终生难忘。

感谢中国驻希腊大使馆文化处的张展老师和沈蕾老师。希腊因经济危机实行资本管制，每周只能取现 420 欧。国家留基委发放的奖学金如果不能按时足额发放，我将无法统筹安排生活费的使用。张老师和沈老师多方协调使我的奖学金得以顺利拨付。

感谢国家留基委的陆国静老师。在签证问题和奖学金发放的过程

后　记

中，陆老师多次通过邮件和电话与我沟通，为我妥善解决了签证中的棘手问题，并为奖学金的发放提供了很多便利。

感谢北京外国语大学的王曼老师。王老师有着聪敏的雅典生活智慧，她与我分享了很多留学经验。在签证延期和银行开户等诸多方面，王老师无私地给予了指导和帮助。

感谢留学生余琛瑱同学。当我为了签证延期焦头烂额不知如何办理的时候，余同学发来了移民局的相关信息，并很细心地把英语翻译成了希腊文，为我后期打车时减少与司机的语言交流障碍提供了条件。

感谢上海外国语大学的白帆同学。为了交流的方便，我需要学习一些基本的希腊问候语和致谢词等。白帆同学一遍遍地发来语音以便我模仿。还好，我这个老学生的发音赢来了雅典居民的大拇指。这都是白帆老师的功劳。

留学一年，除了中外友好人士的帮助外，来自亲戚朋友的默默支持也让我感动，尤其在父母相继住院的情况下。2016年6月25日凌晨，母亲脑干梗塞病危。在母亲失去意识的重症监护期间，众多的老师和朋友伸出了至关重要的援手。有了他们的关心和爱护，母亲才奇迹般康复。如果没有他们的鼎力相助，我恐怕再也没有机会可以喊声"妈妈"了。

感谢山东烟台山医院的王振海主任。王主任接到父亲关于母亲跌倒并失去意识的求助电话后，第一时间提供了医疗担保，并开通了绿色通道，为母亲的无障碍治疗提供了有利保证。而且，在母亲出院后，父亲又由于操劳过度住进医院的情况下，即将出国考察的王主任妥善安排了父亲住院治疗的相关事项，使父亲得到了有效治疗。

感谢山东烟台山医院的阎志慧医生。阎医生带领团队积极调整治疗方案，为母亲恢复意识和康复出院做出了最大的努力。

感谢南京大学的魏向清教授，广东省人民医院的雷黎明副教授，中山大学附属医院的林浩铭副教授，北京第二外国语大学的李伟娜副教授，烟台毓璜顶医院的李春香教授以及鲁东大学的孙世利副教授。

他们以最快的速度联系到自己的医生朋友，并提供了各地医院对脑干梗塞治疗的最有效方案，为医疗组选定最佳方案奠定了基础。

感谢所有为母亲康复和父亲治疗做出贡献的人，包括我的家人。感谢哥哥杜家涛、嫂子邱福君，姐姐杜凌波、姐夫彭明，侄女杜乾以及外甥彭嵩。他们轮流照看失去意识的母亲直到其康复出院。他们的辛苦尽孝换来了我留学的硕果。感谢妻子于屏方，女儿杜声悦和儿子杜声誉。他们在辗转知道母亲病危后，替我行孝，飞赴家乡探望母亲。

在母亲病危失去意识的这段时间里，作为整个家族的家长，父亲沉着应对，妥善安排抢救和护理，起到了定海神针的作用。曾戎马大半生的八旬老人为了不耽误我们夫妻在外地的工作学习，坚持不给雅典的我和广州的妻子发病危通知。老人在医院有效组织看护并安排接待收到病危通知来探望的亲友。从他的从容淡定的处事风格仍然可以看到四十六年前指挥中国战机打下美军侦察机的指挥官的风采。

父亲告诉我：自古忠孝难两全。奶奶病危过世时，父亲因战备需要远驻海防，没有机会回家送自己的母亲一程。虽为人生憾事，但对得起部队和国家。父亲一再强调：作为国家外派留学人员，我已经不再属于家庭个体，而是属于国家，没有国家的安排，不可以回国。父亲这种识大体顾大局的自觉意识深深地打动着我。这种源自于骨子里的信仰会由父亲及我一直传承下去的。

人生是传记，每一页都密密麻麻地记载着我们的喜怒哀乐。雅典留学生活的点点滴滴以及这一年发生的所有故事都将载入我自己的史册。作为雅典的过客，我感悟到：美丽人生，不光在于能知，还在于能行，知行合一方能发挥自己的最大潜能。源洁则流清，形端则影直。为善则预，为恶则去，这或许是知行的最高境界吧。

杜家利　雅典 Zografou Iroon 58
2016 年 12 月 6 日